Companies Are People, Too

Discover, Develop, and Grow Your Organization's True Personality

Sandra Fekete

With LeeAnna Keith

WILEY

John Wiley & Sons, Inc.

Published by John Wiley & Sons, Inc., Hoboken, New Jersey.
Published simultaneously in Canada.

For general information on our other products and services, please contact our Customer Care Department within the U.S. at (800) 762-2974, outside the United States at (317) 572-3993, or fax (317) 572-4002.

Wiley also publishes its books in a variety of electronic formats. Some content that appears in print may not be available in electronic books. For more information about Wiley products, visit our web site at www.Wiley.com.

Library of Congress Cataloging-in-Publication Data:

Fekete, Sandra.
    Companies are people, too : discover, develop, and grow your organization's true personality / Sandra Fekete with LeeAnna Keith.
        p. cm.
Published simultaneously in Canada.
Includes bibliographical references and index.
    ISBN 0-471-23610-1 (cloth : alk. paper)
1. Organizational behavior.   2. Corporate culture.   I. Keith, LeeAnna.
II. Title.
    HD58.7 .F43 2003
    658-dc21   2002153129

Printed in the United States of America
10 9 8 7 6 5 4 3 2 1

Contents

⑯   Sizing Up the Competition, Partners,
         and Clients   210
⑰   What If You Don't Like Who You Are?   227
⑱   Being Yourself on Purpose   234

      Appendix: Validating CAP2   241
      Notes   245
      Index   249

Preface

Great companies and organizations project a strong sense of themselves that everyone can recognize: Disney's imagination, Nike's drive, IBM's methodical dependability, or Nordstrom's service. These companies know who they are, and they behave that way consistently, day in and day out. Successful, enduring companies have at their core a personality that we connect with and understand. In fact, all companies have a personality—because companies are people, too.

While there are some interesting points of comparison between the personalities of corporations versus human individuals, the real significance of the title of this book pertains to the relationship between an organization and the people who get the work done. At its core is an 84-item questionnaire that will assess the innate strengths, growth opportunities, character, and values of your company. The idea is to get business leaders to recognize the personality of the company they serve and to use this information to take performance to a higher level.

This book will help you discover, articulate, and live your company's personality. It is written for leaders who want their companies to thrive over the long term, regardless of who is at the helm. It is for inquisitive leaders who know there is something special deep within their companies that people need to understand and connect with. It is for involved leaders who jump in the trenches and work these concepts into every fiber of the company. Finally, this book is for leaders who are willing to check their egos at the door and set aside their own personal preferences in favor of leading the company according to its own set of values and preferences.

You can use the information you will learn about your company to strengthen your brand, know what to change and what to keep, and attract and keep employees and customers who share your values. Use it to differentiate yourself from your competition and to gain consistency in behavior and decisions from your staff. On a personal level, use it to see what kind of leader you really are — whether you're leading the company from your own biases and preferences or are acting as its steward, building on the qualities and characteristics that have brought it this far and will carry it through the future.

You can trust the information you read because it's based on research. Companies Are People, Too® (CAP2) is used at more than 100 organizations, each of which has validated the accuracy of its profile. The instrument is subjected to an ongoing scientific validation process for reliability and continuous improvement. This work has been greatly encouraged and influenced by the research platforms and findings of Jim Collins and Jerry Porras, reported in their book *Built to Last*,[1] and of Arie DeGeus for his book *The Living Company*.[2] Their work proved that organizations that were in touch with who they are and what they stand for, and that live it every day, are more successful and long-lived than those that don't. Collins's latest research, published in his book *Good to Great*,[3] reinforces that great leaders lead to their companies' strengths and values, which means setting aside their personal preferences.

BACKGROUND AND ACKNOWLEDGMENTS

As the owner of a marketing communications firm, Fekete + Company, which I founded in 1983, I've seen and learned a lot— both from running my own business and from being involved in my clients' businesses. The major lesson has been that *our companies are not us.*

Years of listening to CEOs telling me what made their companies great so that we could create marketing campaigns for them led me to disbelieve most of what I heard. More often than not, there was a disconnect between what they perceived the company's strengths to be and the reality of what their customers and staff experienced. (Our research shows that 8 of 10 CEOs perceive their companies' personalities differently than do the other people who work there.) I followed my instincts on the path to developing a tool that would enable my firm to help our clients discover who their companies really were so that we could develop truthful marketing messages and our clients could deliver on their promises to their customers.

The journey has been collaborative all the way. A group of experts have been attracted to the idea one by one, and each has helped make CAP2 great. Karen Twinem, a trusted associate and friend, was the first to intuitively grasp the idea that a company's personality is *not* based on the sum of the individual personalities of the people who work there. She intensely researched and wrote the initial questionnaire and profiles, and interpreted the results of the first companies who took the questionnaire.

Today, CAP2 is used by companies in the United States and abroad. We have diligently gathered and analyzed data from each of those organizations in a rigorous validation process led by Gerald Macdaid, former chief executive of the Center for Applications of Psychological Type. Jerry's work separates CAP2 as the only scientifically validated assessment device in the field of organizational personality.

You will learn from examples of companies that have participated in Companies Are People, Too discovery sessions led by myself and qualified consultants, particularly organizational coach Roy Shafer. Roy's work with children's museums and science and technology centers around the world has created a number of success stories in an industry that was jolted out of its nonprofit mind-set by competition from the profit-minded entertainment industry. That these institutions have emerged intact, many with elaborate new (and expensive) facilities, is a testimony to the power of initiating change with CAP2 as the foundation. Roy is to be credited with the development and integration of the CAP2 Decision Making Framework in his work with nonprofits, higher education, and for-profit companies. His application makes CAP2 truly systemic to an organization, providing far-reaching results for sustainable success.

To help you understand how your personal leadership style might positively or negatively impact your company's personality and how it gets work done, Henry (Dick) L. Thompson, Ph.D., president and CEO of High Performing Systems, Inc., has written leadership profiles specifically for this book in Chapter 8. An early proponent of CAP2, Dick has also developed training programs to qualify consultants to work with the instrument to guide companies as they discover, articulate, and live their personalities.

How an idea becomes a book was uncharted territory for me. Guiding me through the process, including securing John Wiley & Sons as our publisher, was Vicki Lenz—author, speaker, and now a qualified CAP2 consultant and trainer.

LeeAnna Keith deserves all the credit for pulling everything together in prose that is instructional and compelling. Her intellect enabled her to quickly grasp and even become an expert at organizational personality. Her inquisitive nature led her to thoroughly research and present the cases of some well-known companies that illustrate how personality can be used (or not used) to alter a company's fate.

LET'S BEGIN

Companies Are People, Too is a beginning, not an end. It is a diagnostic tool that will give you insightful information about your company and about yourself. CAP2 alone can't make a sick company healthy any more than an x-ray can cure a broken bone or a spot on a lung. I've seen impressive results, like double-digit growth five years in a row, when CEOs embrace and work CAP2. I've also witnessed fun-time sessions that produce meager results when managers fail to follow up on the work or where no one takes responsibility for acting on what they've learned. As for the latter example, when we ask participants to cite their concerns about doing the program, we frequently hear, "Nothing will really change." That kind of skepticism is usually very truthful and founded on their experience with your company. It's up to you as leader to make it different this time—to set new expectations and see the work through until things *do* change.

One of the benefits CAP2 offers is the opportunity to build consensus. You can discover what everyone believes, add it up, and interpret it without taking a lot of anyone's time or energy. This is not a business solution produced in a vacuum. That's why we recommend that you share the insights of this book with other members of your organization, especially decision makers, opinion leaders, and influencers. Get them to answer the questionnaire and participate in the exercises from the subsequent chapters. As you begin to experience the power of personality, consider bringing in a facilitator to help you dig deeper and make what you've learned systemic to your organization.

There's work to be done, and we show you how to do it. We offer explanation and application in three sections entitled "Discover," "Articulate," and "Live." First, in the "Discover" section, we introduce you to the theories behind CAP2 and allow you to answer the questions for your company, using the abbreviated version in the book or the full questionnaire online. You'll discover your company's strengths and growth opportunities, communication style, work environment, values, ideal clients, and more. In learning how to lead with personality, you'll have an opportunity to discover your own leadership style and to compare your personal preferences to those of your company.

In the next section, "Articulate," we guide you through the process of bringing your company to life by creating its persona and defining its core vision, mission, and values. You'll learn how to develop marketing messages and orientation programs that say who you really are.

Wrapping it up is the "Live" section, which provides plenty of examples and ideas to help you do and be what your company is and stands for. In all of our work with companies, the hang-up is not usually on *what* needs to be done, but on *how* to get it done. Companies Are People, Too is a doing model more than a planning model. If you concentrate on leading the company according to its values and preferences, and allow the company to be itself on purpose, you will achieve clarity, consistency, and alignment in your business operations. That's the CAP2 promise. The result? You will be irresistibly attractive to your ideal customers, investors, corporate partners, and employees.

Companies Are People, Too

INTRODUCTION

① Every Company Has a Personality

Do you know what makes your company tick?

People answer that question in different ways. Most talk in terms of products produced, services provided, numbers of employees, locations of offices, or annual revenues. Others attempt to describe the organization's culture. But what is it really? What is it about your company that people intuitively sense and feel? And why is it so difficult to articulate who you are as an organization?

Prepare to open your mind to a new way of understanding your company, department, or nonprofit institution. The key is personality—a familiar concept when applied to human beings, adapted here to serve as a tool for business management.

The purpose of this book is twofold. First, we'll give you the means to discover, understand, and articulate what makes your organization or company tick. Second, we'll show you how to put this new self-awareness to work. *Companies Are People, Too* provides useful insights for strategic planning, branding, human relations, and change management. More important, we'll show you how to use the information you gain as an in-the-moment decision-making framework appropriate for employees at every level in your organization.

You will see that once a company knows who it really is, the answers to questions such as, "Where are we going?" and "How do we get there?" become clearer and the path to success is more easily navigated.

The Companies Are People, Too concept helps you:

- Define and live according to your core values
- Develop and implement business strategy
- Make informed, proactive decisions
- Align marketing with company values and strengths

3

- Serve as a catalyst for change
- Differentiate your organization from competitors'
- Set performance standards for increased productivity and efficiency

It gives you:

- A strong sense of identity
- A common language for communication purposes
- Continuity in messages and behavior
- Ability to consistently deliver on expectations
- Ability to identify and retain ideal customers and staff
- A framework for decision making
- Consistency, clarity, and alignment

Can the contents of this book change your mind about what makes your company tick? Absolutely, if your mind is open to change.

YOUR COMPANY HAS PERSONALITY, TOO

Mention the statement, "Every company has personality," and many people intuitively nod in agreement. Why? Is it because, as human beings, we recognize the human characteristics of an intimate environment? All of us have an idea of what personality is and of the sometimes profound differences among individuals. This awareness provides a ready frame of reference about people that we can adapt for organizations.

For individuals, personality shapes values, behavior, daily routines, likes, and dislikes. The same is true for companies. Just like

From the Fekete Files

Sometimes the truth is hard to face. The CEO of a successful gourmet food manufacturing company wasn't prepared to hear that the strengths of his company were quality, delivery, and customer satisfaction. He wanted innovation to be what made his company tick. His wife was dismayed to learn that the company was very bottom line–oriented in making decisions about the family-owned business—she wanted to be more focused on the happiness of the people who worked there. We recommended that the CEO allow his management team to focus on making the most of the company's personality (i.e., as a reliable, high-quality company) while he worked on setting up a think tank, "borrowing" employees and using consultants to form rotating innovation teams.

people, companies have definite preferences for taking in information, processing it, making decisions, and getting things done. Just as awareness of personality preferences might help you predict the way you or a friend will react under certain circumstances, you can use your understanding of your company's personality to plan, guide, or make business decisions. And just as understanding personality helps you understand yourself, your family, and your friends, the concepts developed in this book help you develop a new level of familiarity with your company.

What influences a company's personality? The founding principles, the founders' preferences and values, the industry, the company's or institution's maturity, and the unpredictable results all seem to play a part. There are no hard-and-fast rules. Just as we can't explain why siblings (even twins) have different personalities despite similarities of environment and heredity, we can't pinpoint reasons why company personalities can be so distinct. But we believe that, for companies and human beings alike, diversity can be a source of strength. We are also convinced beyond the shadow of a doubt that every personality has a power, purpose, and place of its own.

When you discover and embrace your company's personality using the techniques described in this book, you can tap into the power of its hidden dimensions. The best part is that you already have everything you need to realize the full promise of that personality.

ORGANIZATIONS ARE ALIVE

A company is more than the sum of its assets. Organizations have *soul*—a vibrant, dynamic energy that transcends the material reality. Yes, organizations are made up of individuals, inventories, infrastructures, products, and markets. These physical components combine to form a pattern of aspiration and achievement that stretches back to the past (in all but the most fledgling start-ups) and reaches for the future. Businesses have a reason for being. We can recognize the extent to which they exercise an independent will. They are certainly vulnerable to hurt, and while all institutions have a life span, very few survive as long as the people who create them. Companies that exploit their inherent strengths, though, live for decades or centuries.

An important business book published recently asks its readers to conceive of companies as living beings with the will and the potential to survive. The Dutch scholar and analyst Arie de Geus based his observations of the life of corporations on the oldest and most successful companies in the world, including 100-year-old Royal Dutch Shell, where de Geus made his distinguished career. de Geus observed that the corporations most likely to thrive and grow old were the ones that nurtured their awareness of the company as a living entity. Among the four characteristics of long-lived companies—sensitivity to the environment, a strong sense of identity, tolerance for experimentation, and conservative financing—readers of de Geus's book may have recognized a handful of traits typical of successful human individuals.[1] Living companies and their leaders kept the long-term viability of the enterprise close to the heart and first on the list of priorities. This sense of participation in something larger than themselves cultivated the capacities of managers for stewardship and vision.

Another recent study of long-lived businesses, *Built to Last—Successful Habits of Visionary Companies,* emphasizes the importance of knowing how and why the living company exists. Authors James Collins and Jerry Porras found that leaders of the most successful companies could summarize the core ideology and purpose of their business in very few words.[2] The ideas were so familiar—so close to the surface of daily operations—that employees at every level could articulate them. Understanding personality provides a means for identifying the purpose and values that are most important to your organization. What's more, the values associated with your company's personality are easy to convey to employees, customers, investors, and business partners.

Companies Are People, Too offers a comprehensive guide to focusing your company's energy on what's important. Self-awareness can be the wellspring of success in defining mission and values, energizing the staff, articulating brand identity, and planning and executing business strategy. With the insights developed in this book, you can achieve clarity, consistency, and alignment in your company's operations. Equipped with a sense of who it is, you can proceed to care for your living organization and to help it achieve the full potential of its personality.

THE IDEA OF PERSONALITY TYPE

Many of the insights of business management are derived from the study of the human psyche. Human psychology and the science of business management emerged as academic disciplines and therapeutic methods at roughly the same time, early in the twentieth century. Like psychology, theories of business management encompass a broad range of convictions, practices, and (sometimes contending) schools of thought.

For almost 100 years, business managers and professional management consultants have adapted psychological concepts to the demands of the workplace. Some strategies have focused on businesses as assemblies of human beings, emphasizing the psychology of individual behavior. Other psychological approaches to businesses and institutions, including the one developed in this book, have explored the psychology of the organization as a whole, attributing the characteristics of human beings to the collective enterprises of corporations.

Companies Are People, Too draws on the school of thought established by the Swiss psychologist Carl Gustav Jung in the 1940s and 1950s and refined by the mother-daughter team of Katherine Cook Briggs and Isabel Briggs Myers. Carl Jung's observations have provided the foundation for a wide variety of theories of personality type. The best-known school of thought is associated with the mother-daughter team of Katherine Cook Briggs and Isabel Briggs Myers, who applied Jungian psychology to their profiles of bank employees, schoolchildren, and medical students in their local community during and after World War II. Briggs and Myers developed a diagnostic tool, the Myers-Briggs Type Indicator (MBTI®), to help individuals assess their personality preferences. In addition to Jung's scales for measuring sensation versus intuition, thinking versus feeling, and extraversion versus introversion, Myers and Briggs evaluated tendencies in a fourth category, the preferred way of dealing with the outside world. An individual's external expression, in Jungian fashion, reflects either a tendency to judge, structure, and formalize routines or a tendency toward perception, flexibility, and spontaneity. The dynamic interaction of the four categories of preference generates yet more complexity, and thus the 16 MBTI personality types can claim to represent the full range of human diversity. CAP2 is based on the conclusion that companies, like people, have preferred ways of focusing energy, gathering information, making decisions, and structuring work. Within each of the four dimensions there are two preferences. Every person favors either one of the two preferences in each dimension. Sixteen possible personality types result from combinations of the dimensions and preferences. (See Figure 1.1.)

Focusing Energy

Extroverted: Energized by the outer world of people and things

Introverted: Turns to the inner world of ideas and images for energy

Gathering Information

Sensing: Trusts information that comes in through the five senses (tangibles)

Intuitive: Gives more weight to information received by way of insight and imagination

Making Decisions

Thinking: Bases decisions on objective principles and facts

Feeling: Weighs decisions against people issues and concerns

Structuring Work

Judging: Prefers a structured, decided life where things get done in an organized fashion

Perceiving: Prefers a flexible and adaptable lifestyle and open-ended deadlines

FIGURE 1.1   Personality indicators.

In CAP2 workshops, we illustrate the impact of preferences on productivity with a simple exercise, which we invite you to try. (See Figure 1.2.)

Few people are truly ambidextrous; however, most of us can complete this exercise. Signing our names with our nonpreferred hand takes more energy. It's less productive. But we can do it. Imagine being asked to work outside of your natural preferences day in and day out (i.e., doing all your writing with your nonpreferred hand). You could do it, but you wouldn't be very efficient, and you would be very miserable. Are the people in your company expected to perform within guidelines that don't honor their natural preferences? How much productivity are you losing? Is your company being asked to operate outside of its inborn preferences? How is that impacting its success and longevity?

Many businesses and MBA programs administer personality type indicators to applicants, employees, and students. Perhaps you are already familiar with your own personality profile. If so,

Sign your name as you normally do: _____

Now sign with your nonpreferred hand: _____

FIGURE 1.2   Preferences exercise.

From the Fekete Files

To develop CAP2, we first imagined our company, Fekete + Company, as a person. We answered a personality type questionnaire as we each thought the "person" Fekete + Company would. We were then able to substitute business and organizational language for human descriptions. The resulting profile described our company—what it was like to work with us, what we loved to do, and what we didn't—to a tee. Yet, none of us shared the personality preferences of Fekete + Company. It truly had its own way of being.

you know that many programs give you a four-letter code to serve as shorthand for your personality type. A person for whom Myers-Briggs Type Indicator (MBTI) results indicate a tendency to be extroverted, sensing, thinking, and judging might call him- or herself an ESTJ, while somebody with opposite preferences would be an INFP—introverted, intuitive, feeling, perceiving. Taking into account the dynamic interaction of the four dimensions, this shorthand designation suggests a wide range of habits and tastes to people familiar with the idea of personality type. The titles of CAP2 leadership profiles (described in more detail in Chapter 8) are designed to take some of the mystery and memorization out of the idea of type by assigning memorable names to the different personalities. Rather than a four-letter code, the CAP2 self-study helps you identify a leadership persona that matches your personality preferences at work.

② Companies Are People, Too: The Concept and Promise

Companies Are People, Too adapts theories of personality type developed for human beings to organizations. Like programs in personality type analysis designed for individuals, CAP2 relies on a diagnostic tool made up of 84 multiple choice (A or B) questions that reveal personality preferences for companies. A brief version of the questionnaire appears in Chapter 3, and readers are also invited to participate online at www.companiesarepeopletoo.com/booktrial. Before submitting to formal analysis, however, we urge you to read more about the fundamental concepts of personality in organizations. Equipped with information about type, you may find yourself identifying your organization's personality preferences on your own.

The idea that organizations share some of the characteristics of individuals is easy to grasp. Most of us have encountered companies with strong, recognizable personalities: the upright local manufacturing plant, the friendly neighborhood bake shop, the respected family law firm going gray around the temples. Other organizations project personality in their brand identity: Saturn is "different," Disney is "magical," and Apple Computers are designed for freethinkers.

Distinctive on the surface (in some cases), company personality preferences are even more significant for determining the hidden infrastructure of the organization. Is honesty always the best policy? Will charts and tables help you make your case before the board? How firm are deadlines? Personality type analysis affords a measure of insight into a company's priorities, routines, and mannerisms—its little victories and vices, its secret dreams. Understanding personality can yield practical, useful information for managers, employees, partners, investors, and clients.

CAP2 adapts the Jungian psychological model to the peculiar

life form of the corporation. Like human beings, companies and institutions occupy a particular time and place, with identifiable birth dates, growth rates, names, and addresses. Both individuals and corporations (which include public institutions such as non-profits as well as business enterprises) are recognized by govern-ments as legal entities with the power to act, make contracts, and appear before the courts. In fact, the term *corporation,* which derives from the Latin word for *body,* denotes the official recogni-tion by the state that the enterprise has assumed a living, physical form. Like human beings, corporations take in information, make decisions, and engage with the outside world. Their collective preferences regarding these essential acts provide the basic com-ponents of company personality. Let's discuss these four dimen-sions from an organizational viewpoint.

FOCUSING ENERGY

Just as individuals can be either extroverted or introverted, organ-izations are divided into two main groups. (See Figure 2.1.) Some derive their organizational focus from external factors, including markets, competitors, partners, and corporate sponsors. Compa-nies in a second, somewhat smaller group have an introverted sensibility focused on inventions; technologies; values; or oppor-tunities for growth, employment, and wealth creation. Organiza-tional focus seems to reflect the aspirations and perspiration of the company founders. Unless other factors change, a company mod-eled on a rival firm tends to preserve its extroverted character, while a business that purports to be unique can hope to remain introverted as long as it stays true to its distinctive culture. Other conditions affecting organizational focus include company size and age, geographical scope, lawsuits, market conditions, and continuity in management. The expiration of a patent, for exam-ple, might require an introverted company to pay closer attention to the competition. Over time, this shift could result in the devel-opment of a new, extroverted orientation.

Organizational focus shapes a company's preferences for com-munications, community building, and action. Extroverted or-ganizations are talkers: They consult with experts, collaborate among departments, communicate in face-to-face meetings, and promise the moon in sales presentations. Introverted organiza-tions like to make sure they put their money where their mouth is, developing ideas in well-researched, carefully considered

Extroverted	Introverted
• Learns by doing	• Conducts research before taking action
• Prefers less intense work with many customers	• Prefers in-depth work with fewer customers
• Presents ideas in conceptual form for discussion	• Presents ideas in complete, well-thought-out form, such as a presentation or formal memo
• Frequent brainstorming and planning sessions	
• Employees assist each other with work	• Rare brainstorming and planning sessions
• Internal communication by talking in person or on the phone	• Employees tend to work alone
• May overdo sales efforts	• Internal communication by memos and e-mail
	• May undersell in sales presentations

FIGURE 2.1   Organizational focus preferences.

memoranda, safeguarding procedures, and encouraging employees to reflect and imagine. The two kinds of orientation are equally well adapted to the needs and outlooks of corporations, though certain industries tend to favor one camp or the other. Extroverted organizations can be found in businesses with a strong public relations component, in competitive industries, or where collaboration and outsourcing provide a competitive advantage. Introverted companies emerge primarily on the cutting edge of new technology, in specialized consumer markets, and wherever creativity and genius hold sway.

GATHERING INFORMATION

An organization's preferences for information gathering exert a strong influence on behavior. Like individuals, corporations tend to favor different (but equal) information-gathering techniques. (See Figure 2.2.) Sensing organizations use corporate approximations of the five physical sensations to gauge market conditions or the quality and fit of products and services. Carefully observing real and current surroundings, they value specificity, measurement, and breadth of research. Companies that rely on their senses listen carefully to their clients and customers and monitor minute variations of supply and demand in their given industry.

Sensing	Intuitive
• First asks for details about each situation	• First asks, "What does this mean? What might happen?"
• Tends to do work in traditional ways	• Tries to find new ways to do work
• Provides specific, detailed, step-by-step directions	• Gives the general direction in which work should progress
• "If it's not broke, don't fix it"	• "Everything can and should be improved"
• Sets straightforward, attainable goals	• Sets inspiring, difficult-to-attain goals
• More concerned about exactly what the customer said	• More concerned about what the customer meant
• Sales presentations with substantial array of detailed facts	• Sales presentations that enthusiastically present possibilities

FIGURE 2.2   Information-gathering preferences.

Groups that favor intuition tend to step back from market data and concentrate on the bigger picture. Intuitive organizations excel at making connections—recognizing unheralded relationships and emerging trends. Preoccupied by the future, intuitive groups embrace a vision of what could be rather than a commitment to understanding the world as it is. Information-gathering preferences shape an organization's goal orientation, its divisional structure, and the rhythms of work. While sensing companies pursue incremental adaptations, market research, and efficient routines, intuitive types seek out challenges, unmarked territory, and new methodologies. Employees of sensing organizations earn points for being thorough and reliable, while their counterparts in the intuitive groups are rewarded for insight and their willingness to take risks.

MAKING DECISIONS

Decision-making preferences influence the way an organization understands and acts on information. While information gathering is a form of perception, decision making engages an organization's powers of judgment. In Jungian psychology and MBTI type analysis, the terms *thinking* and *feeling* are used to describe the opposing poles of decision-making preferences. (See Figure 2.3.) Many business organizations, however, tend to cast a doubtful eye

Thinking	Feeling
• Impersonal, "get down to business" office environment	• Warm office environment with emphasis on group harmony
• Rules are rules	• Willing to bend rules under some circumstances
• Finds it easier to criticize than to express appreciation	• Finds it easier to express appreciation than to criticize
• Telling the unvarnished truth is more important than being tactful	• Being tactful is as important as telling the truth
• Logical, detached, and analytical approach to problems	• Seeks solutions based on company values, with impact on people taken into account
• Getting the best quality is more important than brand or customer loyalty	• Brand or customer loyalty is more important than getting the best quality
• Little time spent on team building or coaching staff	• Energized by team building and coaching staff

FIGURE 2.3   Decision-making preferences.

on the intrusion of feeling or emotion into the workplace, even when they endorse the overarching values and practices associated with the feeling preference.

Decision making in thinking organizations is guided by objective principles, while feeling organizations rely on values. To understand the distinction, it is helpful to note that principles have a universal effect, applying equally to all people in all situations, while values take into account individual interests, consequences, and worth. A company with a thinking preference asserts the importance of logic and relies on the objective critique as the best way to reach conclusions. A company with a feeling preference, in contrast, endorses harmony as a goal and tends to see criticism as a form of confrontation. Decision-making preferences exert the most direct impact on personnel matters, but also shape a company's self-image, its response to its competition, and its marketing strategy. Thinking organizations embrace rules and regulations that affect each employee equally, while feeling groups evaluate personnel matters on a case-by-case basis. A feeling organization can be extraordinarily, emotionally committed to displacing or even destroying any firm—competitor, client, or vendor—that steps on its values. In thinking organizations, the tendency to be blunt sometimes spills over into public relations. While both sets of preferences have limitations and blind spots, each provides a comprehensible context for effective decision making.

Information gathering and decision making are relatively insensitive to external factors such as industry or market conditions. Representatives of each of the types can be found in companies of all sizes, in all industries, among extroverted and introverted companies alike.

STRUCTURING WORK

Preferences regarding work style, the final category in our analysis, govern the way an organization deals with and presents itself to the world outside. Work style preferences influence scheduling, procedures, and sensitivity to changes in the environment. (See Figure 2.4.) Judging companies are geared toward decision making and tend to endorse strategies that guarantee results on a predictable schedule. Perceiving groups rely primarily on the information-gathering dimension, adjusting their methods to opportunities or hazards in the environment. The judging tendency is found in organizations that favor planning, deadlines, and follow-through. Perceiving preferences tend toward flexibility, spontaneity, and individual initiative. Preferences in work style show some sensitivity to industries and market conditions. Companies that integrate goods and services from a variety of vendors or divisions (such as construction firms or media conglomerates) can benefit from the judging tendency to adopt schedules and tactical planning. Companies that depend on market conditions and the vagaries of competition (such as venture capital firms or design houses) may do better when they tailor their actions in keeping their options open.

The dynamic interaction of the four dimensions—organizational focus, information gathering, decision making, and work style—produces the distinctive characteristics of personality. In combination, one dimension exerts its influence on another with sometimes subtle and other times dramatic effects. The personality profiles developed in Companies Are People, Too take these relationships into account, with special attention to the impact of preference combinations on communications, dealing with change, and relationships with clients. In lieu of the four-letter MBTI types and psychological terminology, CAP2 profiles assign memorable names and specific behaviors to personality types. We believe you will recognize your organization among the personality profiles in the "Discover" section.

Judging	Perceiving
• Long-term planning in place	• Uncomfortable with long-term planning, preferring to keep options open
• Avoids deadline crunch through rigid scheduling	• Energized by deadline-prompted pressure
• Makes and follows meeting agendas	• Sets a meeting purpose, but is flexible about topics discussed
• Stressed when the unexpected occurs	• Energized by the unexpected
• Tends to make quick decisions and resist changing, even if new data emerges	• Tends to delay decisions until enough data is gathered, and is willing to change the decisions
• Tends to regulate and control employees' system of organization	• Employees use their own system of organization
• Punctuality demanded at meetings	• Employees can be late to meetings if more important matters occur

FIGURE 2.4   Work style preferences.

THE CAP2 PROMISE

Using the idea of personality type can mean tangible benefits for leaders of organizations. The analytical method described in the pages that follow is a tool for aligning your company's short-term operations with its long-term aspirations and values. (See Figure 2.5.) CAP2 is about being yourself on purpose—that is, making informed choices about personnel and behavior in order to achieve internal consistency. It's about establishing an in-the-moment decision-making framework. CAP2 can help you show up more like yourself every day and project your unity and self-confidence to the world outside. We believe that when you're true to yourself, you become irresistibly attractive to your ideal customers and prospective employees.

Understanding your company's personality allows you to:
• Be yourself on purpose
• Establish an in-the-moment decision-making framework
• Show up more like yourself every day
• Become irresistibly attractive to your ideal customers and employees

---

FIGURE 2.5   The CAP2 promise.

DISCOVER

In this section, you will discover the Companies Are People, Too take on your organization's personality. Plus we've thrown in a brief questionnaire about your own personality preferences and our thoughts on your leadership style. This is the heart of the Companies Are People, Too method: a precision-tooled diagnostic designed to assess your organization's fundamental characteristics. We've tried to outline the ideal conditions and instructions for completing the questionnaire, which is reprinted in a short version on pages 22 through 25.

We strongly encourage you to go online to take the complete diagnostic questionnaire. Just visit www.companiesarepeopletoo .com/booktrial and follow the instructions.

Once you have completed the questionnaire and calculated the results, consult the CAP2 profile for your company. Here you'll discover a wealth of information about your company's personality and preferences. We've also included a sample profile for each personality type based on a well-known company or organization. You can find out what your company may have in common with powerhouses such as Nike and Ford Motor Company, or breakthrough achievers such as Xerox, Atari, and Mary Kay Cosmetics. We think it's important for you to know that the companies profiled in our case studies have not completed the CAP2 diagnostic. Instead, we've used public information about their behavior, systems, and company history to identify their personality preferences and then cross-checked our results with the CAP2 profile. In Chapter 16, we've described this technique in greater detail in order to help you make a thumbnail sketch of personality preferences for companies that are important to your business.

The leadership exercises introduce personality type for individuals. Most readers who complete this separate questionnaire will discover differences—and in some cases polar oppositions—between their own preferences and the organization's. That's OK. In fact, we hope you'll reflect on what's different in order to better familiarize yourself with concrete examples about personality preferences. When you know your own style, you're more likely to recognize the personality in your company. And where differences prevail, we urge you to lead with the company's preferences rather than your own. By adapting your priorities and work style to suit the needs of the company, you achieve greater harmony and efficiency.

For both the CAP2 and the leadership diagnostics, however, the exercises in the Discover section are merely the beginning of healthy relationships at work. In subsequent chapters we'll explore how to articulate your company's needs and aspirations, and how best to live in harmony with the character of the organization. First things being first, we'll want to start with introductions. If you turn the page, you'll find some very important people we'd like you to meet.

③ Discover Your Company's Personality

The business world is accustomed to numerical indicators of performance. Stock prices measure market value. Accounting procedures and environmental audits indicate how a company meets projections, standards, or regulations. Statistical figures describe markets, commitments, and trends. We have confidence in numbers because quantitative measurements give us a frame of reference suitable for a broad range of business activities. Some quantitative measures are very precise, while others are subjective or estimated. But numbers from respected sources carry substantial authority throughout the business world.

Companies Are People, Too is a kind of qualitative assessment of business information. Here, we recognize that numbers and percentages are only part of the story for understanding the nature of your work. What some would call the soft side of business management explores aspects of your organization that numbers cannot fully convey. That being said, we want to emphasize that the CAP2 program, as part of the mainstream business culture, relies on quantitative measurements and techniques to assess the soft side of your business. The two questionnaires that follow assign a numerical value to your choices about factors that pertain to personality preferences. We admit that it's not rocket science! If you identify the formula at work in the abbreviated diagnostic exercises in this chapter, you'll quickly see that it's little more than counting and common sense. The trick is in the psychological insights revealed by your answer to each question. The CAP2 diagnostic reflects years of scholarly and applied research on the subject of personality in organizations. It's also worth repeating that, unlike some quantitative measures, categories of personality preference are fundamentally nonjudgmental. While we urge you to strive to live and work in harmony with your company's personality, our profiles address matters of motivation and typical behaviors too complex to be described as good or bad, sufficient or insufficient. The basic elements of your company's personality (and your own) open the doors to a world of possibilities. What you make of it is up to you.

The diagnostic is designed to reveal the preferences at the heart of your company's operations and character. When you answer accurately and without prejudices, you illuminate things about your company that you might not even know. After all, understanding the influence of the unconscious dimension is part of the promise of Jungian psychology and the CAP2 method. We have used the results to fashion the case study narratives of the 16 company personalities in this chapter as well as the more in-depth profiles found in Chapters 4, 5, 6, and 7. The personality profiles are CAP2's most valuable assets, and you'll be surprised by how compelling their descriptions of company personality can be.

Each profile has a name, which is designed to be memorable and appropriate. The profile begins with a snapshot of your company's personality preferences, which correspond to the letter categories of personality preferences used in the Myers-Briggs Type Indicator.[1] Each snapshot conveys the literal meaning of your organization's preferences in each dimension, listed in order of its most dominant function. You can use the snapshot to remind yourself of your company's preferences in the four dimensions—organizational focus, information gathering, decision making, and work style—when we discuss the implications of preferences later in the book. The first part of the profile offers a detailed description of the type. After the description, you will find bulleted lists of your company's characteristic strengths and weaknesses, work environment, values, and communication style. Each profile also provides lists of typical sources of energy, signs of stress, behavior during conflict, and approaches to managing change. As a bonus, we have included our best estimate of the characteristic traits of your ideal clients.

The CAP2 company profiles are rich with information about your organization. In fact, we'll devote most of this book to explaining and providing examples for the information compressed in these pages. You can use your profile to address a wide range of challenges and opportunities in your business, and we urge you to keep it handy for regular reference. Learning more about your company is the first step to leading it toward being itself on purpose and making it irresistibly attractive to its ideal customers, associates, and partners.

WHO SHOULD PARTICIPATE

Anyone familiar with the values and routines of your company can accurately assess its personality. Since our data shows that 85 percent of the time, the CEO perceives the company differently than does the rest of the staff, we strongly suggest that you include others in this exercise. For CAP2 workshops, we recommend that decision makers, opinion leaders, and influencers participate. Most organizations sign up their entire management team. Many companies elect to have their entire staff take the questionnaire. Some even include board members and customers in order to measure outsider perspectives against inside perceptions.

HOW TO TAKE THE QUESTIONNAIRE

On the next pages you will find the short form of the CAP2 diagnostic tool for organizations (see Figure 3.1). For the most accurate results, we urge you to supplement the exercise provided here with a visit to www.companiesarepeopletoo.com/booktrial, where you can complete the more comprehensive online assessment that evaluates your company's preferences in greater detail. As the owner of this book, you are entitled to a free, one-time use of the online assessment. Most people can complete the 84-question online version in 15 minutes or less. The online version will tally your scores for you and provide you with the resulting profile. Two pointers for achieving the most reliable results:

- Choose the answer that best describes your company, not yourself or your boss.
- Choose the answer that usually describes your company as it is now, not the way you or the management wish it to be.

SCORESHEET FOR MULTIPLE USERS

For the most accurate results, include as many of your management team members and/or decision makers, opinion leaders, and influencers as possible. Have each person answer the questions, then use the scoresheet in Figure 3.2 to tally multiple-user scores for the short form. Be sure to make extra copies to accommodate all of your participants.

Write in the total number of As and Bs selected by each participant next to each person's name. Add up the As and the Bs in each column and write the total at the bottom. Translate the totals

Circle A or B

Organizational Focus

This organization tends to feel the most energized about:
A. working directly with customers and other people
B. developing ideas, products, and services in-house

This organization tends to react to change:
A. quickly
B. after giving it some thought

Employees are:
A. encouraged to get to know each other socially
B. simply expected to work well together

This organization tends to communicate internally by:
A. in-person conversations and phone calls
B. notes, memos, letters, and e-mail

At this organization, people are encouraged to:
A. talk things through as they're working them out
B. think things through before talking about them

Select the word that best describes this organization:
A. sociable
B. independent

Select the word that best describes this organization:
A. intense
B. low-key

Total number of As circled: _____
Total number of Bs circled: _____

If As are the highest number, record #1 in the blank below.
If Bs are the highest number, record #2 in the blank below.

Organizational focus: _____ (#1 or #2)

Circle A or B

Information Gathering

This organization values:
A. common sense more than imagination
B. imagination more than common sense

When developing a plan, the most important thing to discuss is:
A. the practical details of the plan implementation
B. the vision behind the plan

This organization's new products and services tend to be:
A. cost-effective, practical extensions of successful products or services
B. innovative ideas, often different from the current product line

This organization is more likely to:
A. make changes one step at a time
B. make many changes at once

FIGURE 3.1 Organizational Questionnaire (Short Form)

Select the word that best describes this organization:
A. practical
B. innovative

Select the word that best describes this organization:
A. traditional
B. imaginative

Select the word that best describes this organization:
A. down-to-earth
B. visionary

Total number of As circled: _____
Total number of Bs circled: _____

If As are the highest number, write #3 below.
If Bs are the highest number, write #4 below.

Information gathering: _____ (#3 or #4)

Circle A or B

Decision Making

The potential impact of a decision on employees and others is:
A. rarely considered
B. usually considered as a factor in the decision

This organization believes that it is more important to be:
A. fair and absolutely impartial
B. reasonable, but compassionate

This organization tends to believe:
A. people don't have to like each other to work together well
B. group harmony is important to get jobs done well

Decision making in this organization is:
A. primarily based on a logical, detached, and analytical approach
B. primarily based on values, taking into account the impact on people

This organization expects workers to:
A. leave their personal problems at home
B. be supportive and caring when coworkers have problems

Select the word that best describes this organization:
A. critical
B. encouraging

Select the word that best describes this organization:
A. impersonal
B. personal

Total number of As circled: _____
Total number of Bs circled: _____

(continued)

If As are the highest number, write #5 below.
If Bs are the highest number, write #6 below.

Decision making: _____ (#5 or #6)

Circle A or B

Work Style

This organization encourages workers to:
A. develop a step-by-step plan for a project at its beginning
B. keep options open, allowing the project to evolve

Meetings tend to:
A. follow a set, often written, agenda
B. have a general purpose, but remain open to discussion on other topics

After decisions are made, this organization is more likely to:
A. develop follow-up plans, assign responsibility, and set a schedule
B. leave the option open for changing the decision later

This organization:
A. tends to regulate individual employees' organizational systems
B. allows employees to develop their own systems

This organization is weaker at:
A. gathering information
B. making decisions

Select the word that best describes this organization:
A. punctual
B. relaxed

Select the phrase that best describes this organization:
A. decisive and regimented
B. reasonably organized chaos

Total number of As circled: _____
Total number of Bs circled: _____

If As are the highest number, write #7 below.
If Bs are the highest number, write #8 below.

Work style: _____ (#7 or #8)

Determine the Results

From each of the four preceding sections, record your chosen number from the bottom of the column. Then, turn to page 26 to translate the four digits to your organization's personality type.

_____	_____	_____	_____
Organizational focus (1 or 2)	Information gathering (3 or 4)	Decision making (5 or 6)	Work style (7 or 8)

Name	Organizational Focus		Information Gathering		Decision Making		Work Style	
	A	B	A	B	A	B	A	B
Totals								

Organizational focus:
If As are the highest number, record #1 in the space below.
If Bs are the highest number, record #2 in the space below.

Information gathering:
If As are the highest number, record #3 in the space below.
If Bs are the highest number, record #4 in the space below.

Decision making:
If As are the highest number, record #5 in the space below.
If Bs are the highest number, record #6 in the space below.

Work style:
If As are the highest number, record #7 in the space below.
If Bs are the highest number, record #8 in the space below.

Organizational focus (1 or 2)	Information gathering (3 or 4)	Decision making (5 or 6)	Work style (7 or 8)

FIGURE 3.2 Multiple-user scoresheet.

to the corresponding number in the space provided below the chart, then compare the final four-digit number to the profile list. Now match the resulting four-digit number with your company personality profile.

1357 = "Playing by the Rules" (p. 40)
1358 = "Thriving on Risky Business" (p. 58)
1367 = "Doing the Right Thing" (p. 44)
1368 = "We Aim to Please" (p. 63)
1457 = "Driven to Lead" (p. 101)
1458 = "If We Can't Do It, No One Can" (p. 97)
1467 = "Seeing the Big Picture in Human Terms" (p. 82)
1468 = "It's Fun to Do Good Work" (p. 78)
2357 = "Solid as a Rock" (p. 30)
2358 = "Action, Action—We Want Action!" (p. 49)
2367 = "You Can Count on Us" (p. 35)
2368 = "Working to Make a Difference" (p. 54)
2458 = "In Pursuit of Intellectual Solutions" (p. 92)
2459 = "Going All Out for Greatness" (p. 87)
2467 = "Vision Driven by Values" (p. 68)
2468 = "Quest for Meaningful Work" (p. 73)

You can find your company's personality name with the corresponding profile and case study narratives in Chapters 4 through 7.

Important note: For consistency, all profiles will be listed in the order that they appear in Figure 3.3 (left to right, top to bottom). For those readers who are interested in the corresponding type letters, we have provided them beneath the titles in this figure only.

Self-validating the results is extremely important if you intend to put Companies Are People, Too to work in your company. Rarely does a single person's viewpoint stand up to the accuracy test. If you or a small group from the management team announce to the staff that the company's personality profile resulting from your score(s) is "the way it is," prepare for some resistance from the troops.

Since this is a consensus-building device, we encourage you to include several people in this exercise and use the multiple-user scoresheet. In CAP2 workshops, we prepare a worksheet for characteristic strengths and one for characteristic weaknesses. We then divide the users into small groups to discuss the results. If the profile is accurate, the groups should be able to list two or three examples of how each strength and weakness comes to life in the company.

"Solid as a Rock" (ISTJ)	"You Can Count on Us" (ISFJ)	"Vision Driven by Values" (INFJ)	"Going All Out for Greatness" (INTJ)
"Action, Action —We Want Action" (ISTP)	"Working to Make a Difference" (ISFP)	"Quest for Meaningful Work" (INFP)	"In Pursuit of Intellectual Solutions" (INTP)
"Thriving on Risky Business" (ESTP)	"We Aim to Please" (ESFP)	"It's Fun to Do Good Work" (ENFP)	"If We Can't Do It, No One Can" (ENTP)
"Playing by the Rules" (ESTJ)	"Doing the Right Thing" (ESFJ)	"Seeing the Big Picture in Human Terms" (ENFJ)	"Driven to Lead" (ENTJ)

FIGURE 3.3   Profile titles sorted by name and corresponding type letters.

For example, a paint retailer that profiled as a "Thriving on Risky Business" personality has as a strength: "A solution-oriented organization that is excellent at responding to situations as they emerge, resulting in a firefighter or gunslinger mentality. Values action more than ideas." The workshop group listed examples that supported that this is, in fact, a strength of the company, such as, "When a complaint is received, we go straight to the job site to solve the problem. We are empowered to make decisions on the spot to correct the situation. Our action-oriented response has done a lot to help us get repeat business." On the other hand, a weakness on the profile indicated that this was "an organization that tends to neither understand nor care about what makes people tick. Its emphasis on action can create an impatient, demanding environment." The group noted that there was no formal review system in place, morale was low, and staff turnover was higher than industry norms.

Figure 3.4 shows a sample strengths worksheet for a community college that profiled as "Action, Action—We Want Action!"

Figure 3.5 shows a sample weaknesses worksheet for the same "Action, Action—We Want Action!" community college.

Education Is an Adventure

Strengths Worksheet

1. An exciting, even adventurous, organization with a firm commitment to excellence, a love of risk taking, and a tendency to follow its impulses.

Examples: _____
_____
_____

2. Tends to be composed of a group of smaller, self-directed departments or teams, performing with significant independence under a management umbrella.

Examples: _____
_____
_____

3. Often presents its course offerings in an entertaining and aesthetically pleasing manner. It may offer an unusual number of hands-on learning opportunities and action experiences. It also may use film and video extensively.

Examples: _____
_____
_____

4. A fearless organization that can be counted on to do the unexpected. Tends to see its work as an art or a performance, seeking quality for its visual appeal as well as its educational impact.

Examples: _____
_____
_____

5. Thrives on "impossible" challenges. Succeeds where others fail because it readily uses unorthodox approaches and enjoys adapting to changes.

Examples: _____
_____
_____

6. Seeks to be a master in its own field of specialty rather than to do all things well.

Examples: _____
_____
_____

FIGURE 3.4 Sample strengths worksheet for an "Action, Action—We Want Action!" community college.

Education Is an Adventure

Growth Opportunities Worksheet

1. Tends to have minimal concern about communication, particularly verbal communication between organizational elements, which can damage cooperative efforts.

Examples: _____
_____
_____

2. May be insensitive to the feelings of its staff.

Examples: _____
_____
_____

3. Needs an especially high-quality staff for long-term survival, because the organization does not focus energy on long-term planning, resource development, or strategic marketing. It behaves like a start-up company.

Examples: _____
_____
_____

4. If the organization does create strategic plans, it tends to abandon them regularly, preferring the freedom to react to situations as they develop.

Examples: _____
_____
_____

FIGURE 3.5   Sample weaknesses worksheet.

In the next four chapters we will focus on organizational profiles and case studies, giving you an in-depth look at the strengths and weaknesses of the different personalities. We also connect each personality with a real life company.

④ Profiles of Practicality

We look at four personalities in this chapter, all of which are, by nature, practical, realistic, and dependable. There is a stabilizing force in companies with this temperament, so much so, that change is difficult to champion. These companies are rooted in a foundation of strong systems, plans, and defined procedures. They "feel" institutional, and tend to value hierarchy and organization.

"Solid as a Rock" companies appreciate order and logic, while "You Can Count on Us" companies believe in moral reasoning. "Playing by the Rules" organizations attempt to establish order and consistency for their customers and employees, and "Doing the Right Thing" companies strive to create a family-like atmosphere that engenders trust.

"SOLID AS A ROCK"

Snapshot

- Focuses on information that is factual, real, and current
- Makes decisions using logic, analysis, and cause-and-effect reasoning
- Is energized by the inner world of ideas and experiences
- Prefers a structured, organized, and planned environment

For many people, this type of organization personifies corporate America. Stable, reliable, and sensible, the organization takes its work very seriously, and it expects everyone else to do the same.

To the outside world, the organization appears to be right on target almost all the time. Outsiders don't get to see all the inner workings of this rather closed organization. Decisions are made internally, relying on the organization's own inside experts, and it keeps its policies and procedures to itself. There may be an air of mystery even within the organization itself, since decisions are made quietly and without much collaboration.

Customers and clients of the organization can count on receiving focused service. This efficient workhorse will provide products and services on time and as promised, within established guidelines.

Innovative and totally new ideas are not this organization's strong suit. It might provide new ideas that would affect certain aspects of a product or service, but it's unlikely to stick its neck way out for something totally new and different. The only thing that motivates this organization to make changes is its strong sense of right and wrong. If the organization decides that it needs to make a change to make something right in its mind, then it will make the changes in a deliberate, step-by-step manner.

Employees can count on being dealt with in a fair, logical, impartial (but also impersonal) manner. Procedures, standards, and guidelines exist to let employees know exactly what is expected of them. These are expected to be followed with few or no exceptions. Principle will guide decisions, not the personal feelings that might be involved.

Rituals and traditions are the most important way that this organization stays connected with its employees. It is likely to have many traditions that outsiders may not understand, and employees are expected to participate out of a sense of loyalty.

Characteristic Strengths

Prototypical coolly efficient company
Developing, maintaining, and enforcing high standards
Organized for success
Efficient
Master of data and logical analysis
Decisive; able to make quick decisions
Delivers what it promises
Constantly improves and strengthens its offering
Avoids unforced errors by thinking before acting
Focused on the moment

Characteristic Weaknesses

Occasionally assumes too many responsibilities (e.g., excessively high standards), overburdening its resources
Occasionally too rigid to respond to changing situations and opportunities

Can become perplexed or limit opportunities by avoiding solutions requiring innovation, new theories, or dealing with ambiguity

Not uncommon to ignore people management issues and individual needs

Frequently unable to appreciate the value or necessity of change

High standards may turn into unjustified righteousness

Occasionally ignores or distrusts instincts

May ignore the future for the present

Can miss opportunities by overthinking and failing to act

May overly rely on historical data and logical thinking to the exclusion of external, and often qualitative, information about the outside world of markets, trends, and competition

May not appreciate the benefits of process, teamwork, and collaboration

Can decide too quickly, ignoring potentially critical data

Work Environment

Decisions may be made quietly and without much collaboration

Maintains a high work ethic; the company is always very busy

Serious, with little room for chitchat

Traditions are prominent; corporate culture is celebrated

Maintains a discreet, low-key, and conservative public image

Maintains control through standards, rules, and procedures

Runs efficient meetings

Structured, analytical, and observant: predictable

Fair but private, contained, impersonal

Probing, scrutinizing, critical

Sees the world in black and white

Values

Excellence
Hard work
Tradition
Achievement
Customers
Efficiency
Control
Responsibility

Communication Style

Centers on logic and links with the past

Language is functional and will often refer to tasks and duties

Prefers to give directives and structure rather than information

Fair, impartial, impersonal

In meetings, seeks connection with the task first

Begins presentations with details first
Brief and concise, dealing with concrete issues on a realistic level
Prefers writing and e-mail to meetings

Sources of Energy

Serving customers efficiently
Achieving excellence
Improving productivity
Traditions
Sense of control through mastery

Signs of Stress

Loses its grounding in common sense
Becomes excessively pessimistic, especially about the future
Becomes mired in details and unimportant facts
Decision-making capabilities erode

Behavior during Conflict

Not afraid to confront rule breakers
Will examine its system to ensure that it can handle conflict rationally
Will defend its position vigorously, using logic as a weapon

Approaches to Managing Change

Prefers continuity and stability
Will consult internal data sources (databases, experience, and vision)
to determine what part of the company should be preserved and
what part may change
Sufficient time will be allowed to reflect, analyze, and relate to histor-
ical frameworks
If change is acceptable, will quickly implement it
If the change is not acceptable, will become inflexible

Ideal Clients

Need infrastructure, stability, and discipline
Require reliable, long-term service with predictable quality
Seek to associate with the company's conservative image and tradi-
tional values
Value the peace of mind that comes from dealing with a rock-solid
company that has its act together
Need the development, maintenance, and/or logical analysis of huge
databases
Value the high quality that comes from hard work

Case Study

We'll look at the Ford Motor Company for an illustration of "Solid as a Rock" tendencies.

Ford Motor Company is an introverted organization; that is, it takes its energy from its own ideas and experiences and relies on a largely internal frame of reference. It's a preference that traces its roots to the irascible Henry Ford. Ford stamped his likeness on the organization and jealously guarded his prerogatives throughout the first 50 years of the company's existence. The Ford family tradition of leadership has kept this inward-looking preference alive and has tried to keep Ford's far-reaching operations in line with the founder's original vision: to get more people driving cars, and to make money on volume of sales rather than on profit margins. The company's ability to stay true to this vision illustrates the importance of tradition among "Solid as a Rock" organizations.

For all of Henry Ford's genius as an inventor and an entrepreneur, the success of the Ford can be found in its attention to factual, real, and current information. For example, Ford conceived of the world's first factory assembly line on the basis of extensive and intensive studies of the efficiency of movement in assembling cars. Statistical measurement and time-and-motion studies became important indices of every dimension of production and distribution. In using sensory information to create and refine its methods, Ford epitomized two of the chief strengths of the Solid profile: the mastery of data management and logical analysis, and the commitment to constantly improve and strengthen services and products.

Ford's commitment to principles (and discomfort with individualism) has also lent itself to unusual and sometimes unique human relations management. In the 1920s, at the prompting of Henry Ford, the company doubled the wage rate to reflect what Ford saw as an appropriate living wage. At the same time, the company went to great lengths to ensure that workers conformed to the standard of loyalty that Solid organizations demand, and also to monitor employees' behaviors off the job in a wide range of other categories. Today's Ford no longer tries to replicate the model worker, but its relationships are regulated by close cooperation with auto workers' unions and other contractual obligations. Individualized consideration—characteristic of the opposite end of the spectrum of personality preferences—has little role in day-to-day personnel management.

Ford has also helped to set the standard for the regulated, structured work environment. The company's tendency toward planning and systems is a hallmark of the "Solid as a Rock" persona. For illustration of the influence of the judging tendency at Ford, we can look at the importance of statistical data management to Ford's manufacturing, distribution, and marketing. Beginning in the 1950s, a group of number-crunching "Whiz Kids" brought a comprehensive business methodology to Ford that linked almost all business decisions to statistical measurement and meticulous accounting procedures, deemphasizing the human element in favor of systems. While this statistical method has become less influential over time, Ford continues to rely on the management of careful budgets and schedules to coordinate activities across its sprawling divisions.

Like other "Solid as a Rock" institutions, Ford periodically absorbs its share of complaints from those who see its deliberate, procedural management style as oppressive and old fashioned. But the Solid company's ability to consistently deliver good service and fair profits testifies in its defense. It may sometimes fall behind the pace of innovation or become entrenched in unproductive habits, but this type of organization is capable of recognizing its mistakes and reorganizing with great energy. Once a "Solid as a Rock" organization decides to make something right in its mind, it will make whatever changes it finds necessary in a deliberate, step-by-step plan of action.

"YOU CAN COUNT ON US"

Snapshot

- Focuses on information that is factual, real, and current
- Makes decisions based on values and their impact on people
- Is energized by the inner world of ideas and experiences
- Prefers a structured, organized, and planned environment

This type of organization feels a strong sense of responsibility for its work, its clients, and its employees. It is at its best when doing something where its hard work and responsibility are valued. Bedrock loyalty and attention to detail combine to produce a stream of top-quality work for its clients.

Decisions in this pragmatic atmosphere are made based on a clear sense of right and wrong and concern for the common welfare. This people orientation is tempered with a down-to-earth, commonsense approach that takes into account lessons learned along the way. Details from hands-on experience are meticulously filed away (both mentally and physically) and used as a reference going forward.

Traditional and solid, this is unlikely to be a cutting-edge organization. While products and services are usually not state of the art, they are reliable, and the organization stands behind them. Knowledge, ideas, and theories are highly valued in this intellectual environment, but ideas will always be tested against facts.

History and tradition are an important part of the organization. Rituals, mottoes, and procedures (even if they seem odd to outsiders) are treasured and used to help bring newcomers into the loop. There is a strong sense of belonging in this organization, and it makes people feel welcome, as long as they accept its traditions and protocol.

Structured and reliable, this organization will have and religiously use handbooks and procedures. It will provide sensible answers to employees' and clients' questions about any issue that arises. Meetings take place to discuss policies and to preserve traditional rites, but not often to brainstorm or discuss new directions or ideas.

There is a definite hierarchy in place at this organization, and decisions may be made privately and not shared with others. If the employees, who are supposed to trust their superiors, lose this sense of trust and belonging, it could lead to trouble. The group may start reminiscing about the past and how "perfect" things used to be, or may assume that the whole organization is falling apart.

Characteristic Strengths

Maintains a strong reputation for consistently reliable, top-quality work
Forges and maintains productive, long-term relationships
Establishes and preserves the procedures and traditions necessary for long-term success
Churchillian determination—will never quit
An inner sense of what people want and need
A harmonious workplace that draws the best from people
Avoids unforced errors by thinking before acting
Accurately anticipates needs and problems and schedules accordingly

Characteristic Weaknesses

Inherent skepticism toward unproved ideas may translate to lowered expectations, leading to lowered performance
Occasionally assumes too many responsibilities (e.g., excessively high standards), overburdening its resources

Frequently unable to appreciate the value or necessity of change

Can become perplexed or limit opportunities by avoiding solutions requiring innovation, new theories, or dealing with ambiguity

Not uncommon to ignore business issues for people issues

May ignore the future for the present

Occasionally too rigid to respond to changing situations and opportunities

Can decide too quickly, ignoring potentially critical data

Work Environment

Harmony achieved by people caring and being cared for in a low-key environment

Common sense and practicality

Decisions made quietly and without much collaboration

Exhibits a high work ethic; the company is always very busy

Traditions and corporate culture are prominent and celebrated

Maintains control through standards, rules, systems, hierarchies, and procedures

Individual responsibility has high visibility

Committed to causes

Action oriented

Values

Customer
Responsibility
Tradition
Loyalty
Quality
Harmony
Control
Family

Communication Style

Centers on people in a way that addresses relationships and the past

Language is functional and will often refer to tasks and duties

Prefers to give information rather than directives

Fair, impartial, impersonal

Prefers face-to-face interaction

Concrete, step-by-step, sequential, and highly detailed

In meetings, seeks connection with people first

Begins presentations with details first

Contained, thoughtful, and reflective

Sources of Energy

Sense of belonging and family
Satisfying the customer
Serving the needs of people
Being in control

Signs of Stress

Becomes emotional
Decision-making capabilities erode
Becomes excessively pessimistic, especially about the future
Becomes mired in details and unimportant facts

Behavior during Conflict

Prefers to ignore or avoid conflict at all cost
Will determine if the company is meeting people's needs
Will react viciously if a value has been trampled

Approaches to Managing Change

Prefers continuity and stability, maintaining what is
Will consult internal data sources (databases, experience, and vision) to determine what part of the company should be preserved and what part may change
Sufficient time will be allowed to reflect, analyze, and relate to historical frameworks
Will ask if the change is practical, has worked before, and is socially acceptable
If the change is consistent with the values of the company, will move quickly to implement it
Change will be in the form of incremental, small steps (more like adapting)
If change is not consistent with the integrity of the company, will become inflexible

Ideal Clients

Produce products or services that benefit people in some tangible way
Value loyalty and seek a long-term relationship
Require attention to detail in long-term projects
Respect the high quality that comes from hard work
Value a tradition of loyalty and reliability
Enjoy being part of the corporate "family"
Relish the peace of mind that comes from being in total control of the situation

Case Study

The "You Can Count on Us" profile is especially well suited to organizations that provide human services, such as the Metropolitan Life Insurance Company.[1] MetLife shares the four basic elements of the Count on Us type: It's energized by the inner world of ideas and experiences, focused on information that is factual, real, and current, committed to values and their impact on people, and comfortable in a structured, organized, and planned environment. MetLife's introverted character is revealed in its serious, traditional, and insulated sense of itself. Established in 1868, the company has occupied a landmark building in midtown Manhattan for generations. Its paneled boardroom has been the scene of MetLife's most important discussions for more than 100 years.[2]

Despite its comfortable preoccupation with tradition, the company has proven itself to be a keen observer of market conditions. The "You Can Count on Us" gift for precise measurement has served as MetLife's mainstay in the most important task of any insurance firm: actuarial calculations of statistics about profit and risk. Within this industry, sensory information-gathering preferences provide a concrete advantage. Today, MetLife uses the same basic observation techniques for evaluating the appeal of new products and markets—assembling statistical data on income levels and asking what the company can do to meet the needs of middle-class earners.[3]

MetLife is in the business of caring. Among policyholders, the company's commitment to productive, long-term relationships is the sine qua non of the MetLife brand. For employees of an industry giant, however, the Count on Us inclination to promote harmony and trust at all costs has proven more problematic. During its 100-plus years as a mutual society, Metropolitan Life Insurance employed a staff of managers, accountants, and sales agents who gradually came to see themselves as something of a privileged caste. The Count on Us commitment to values and their impact on people reached an unsustainably extreme level of influence, with unlimited sick days and lax standards for performance. Under the leadership of Robert Benmosche, the insurance giant has sharply reined in its workforce, executing large-scale layoffs and imposing more stringent performance and compensation standards. But MetLife remains a place where "You Can Count on Us" feelings rule the day. Because its business is dependent on enduring and unique relationships between customers and agents, MetLife will always consider the individual impact of every decision.

The insurance industry is all about planning and schedules, so it's natural for companies like MetLife to embrace a judging work style preference. Being able to envision the long term and project feasible financial outcomes requires MetLife to hold closely to a narrow equilibrium between outlays and income. That means the company relies on comprehensive structures and mechanisms even when it deals with unexpectedly favorable news, such as variations in the capital markets that increase its cash assets. In fact, MetLife and similar institutions are so functionally tied to schedules that they have difficulty making changes even when they recognize the necessity (as seen in the scandal and lawsuit arising from rate differentials for black and white policyholders—obsolete since the 1940s, but so difficult to rectify that the company ended up paying $150 million in damages). This tendency toward rigidity, typical of the Count on Us type, is the downside of having consistently reliable procedures.

Clients and investors will embrace a company that they can count on. Within eight months of the MetLife IPO, shares in the venerable insurer were the most widely held stock in the United States. Its success underscores the winning combination of the Count on Us profile: an inner sense of what people want and need, combined with a determination to provide the best quality of service.

"PLAYING BY THE RULES"

Snapshot

- Makes decisions using logic, analysis, and cause-and-effect reasoning
- Focuses on information that is factual, real, and current
- Is energized by the outer world of people and activity
- Prefers a structured, organized, and planned environment

In this organization, rules are made to be followed, not broken. It thrives on order, continuity, and consistency. Details are important, and the bottom line means everything.

This action-oriented organization is always ready and eager to take charge, run things, and run them very well. This company has high expectations for itself and its employees, delivering work efficiently and on time.

Dependable and consistent, it takes a solid, businesslike approach to work that allows it to establish things and keep them going. The organization values and works to achieve maximum benefit from its resources, feeling that time is money.

Not a trendsetter, this company usually doesn't develop innovative new products or services. Instead, with its careful planning and strategizing, the organization delivers good work that clients can count on.

It has a tendency to avoid risk, testing and retesting new ideas and products to ensure quality and accuracy. The only scenario where an organization of this type might undertake risk is one where all the key employees think something is a good idea; then, it might forge ahead.

Friendly in an impersonal way, this organization approaches human interaction through rituals and traditions. It tends to think that everyone should accept its opinions as facts, so those with other ideas may be viewed as dissenters or troublemakers. It also tends to hire and keep only the "right" kind of people—those who agree with and adhere to its ideas and policies.

This organization can become rigid and inflexible, losing out on the creativity and opportunities that other ideas have to offer. It finds it hard to accept the fact that tried and trusted ways may not always be the best solution.

Characteristic Strengths

Establishes and preserves the procedures and traditions necessary for long-term success

Highly skilled at planning, strategy, and logistics

Efficient

Results-oriented and decisive

Makes the best of a given situation; maximizes the status quo

Constantly improving and strengthening

Prepared to act on opportunities

Tightly focused and in touch with reality

Dependable and consistent

Characteristic Weaknesses

May miss great opportunities because of an aversion to risk

Occasionally assumes too many responsibilities (e.g., excessively high standards), overburdening its resources

Frequently unable to see the value or necessity of change

May ignore people management issues and individual needs

Can miss opportunities by avoiding solutions requiring innovation, new theories, or dealing with ambiguity

May ignore the future for the present

Occasionally follows procedures so intently that it may lose sight of the larger picture

Can be so focused on efficiency it ignores effectiveness

May decide too quickly

Often too rigid to respond to changing situations

Work Environment

High work ethic; the company is always very busy

Traditions are prominent; corporate culture is important

Predictable, stable, orderly

Task oriented

Scheduled and efficiently run

Serious, with little room for chitchat

Harmony achieved through teamwork

Work is done with a steady energy

Values

Logic

Efficiency

Tradition

Achievement

Accuracy

Caution

Predictability

Communication Style

Language is functional and will often refer to tasks and duties

Prefers to give directives and structure rather than information

Concrete, specific, and brief

Logical, with cause-and-effect reasoning

Begins presentations with details first

Prefers writing and e-mail

Sources of Energy

Sense of belonging, tradition

Achievement

When things work well and according to plan

Signs of Stress

Becomes excessively pessimistic, especially about the future
Becomes mired in details and unimportant facts
Loses objectivity
Becomes explosively emotional
Decision-making capabilities erode

Behavior during Conflict

Confronts rule breakers
Will examine its systems to ensure that it can handle conflict
Will defend its position vigorously, using logic as a weapon

Approaches to Managing Change

Prefers continuity and stability, maintaining what is
Will engage in critical questioning, using internal values or logic
Change must be practical and proven
Change will come from getting things to run more efficiently
If questions are adequately answered, will move quickly to plan,
  organize, and implement change

Ideal Clients

Need highly detailed work done
Insist on dependability and consistency
Value a conservative and traditional company
Want to act immediately on developing opportunities that fit a prede-
  termined plan
Appreciate a logical, analytical, and practical assessment of complex
  or sensitive issues
Need problems solved immediately and with existing resources

Case Study

The "Playing by the Rules" organization is the embodiment of faith
in common sense, order, and professionalism. Examples include
classic big bureaucracies such as IBM and Eastman Kodak, as well
as many manufacturing firms and other organizations that rely on
systems management, scheduling, and contract fulfillment.

Interaction with clients and the public provides the "Playing by
the Rules" organization with its reason for being. The origins of
IBM, which developed the rudiments of its mechanical calculator
in response to a U.S. Census Bureau design contest, illustrate the

strong influence of external factors on this type. Because they aim to become the Establishment, smaller organizations with this worldview have a knack for building ties to the community that can endure for generations.

Tradition—habits and beliefs that have been proven effective over time—plays a guiding role at "Playing by the Rules" companies. Uncomfortable with risk, these organizations tend to test and retest new ideas and products to ensure quality and accuracy. The only scenario where an organization of this type might undertake a significant risk is one where all the key employees think something is a good idea. While no stranger to innovation (IBM, after all, is the company that gave us the personal computer, the bar code, and the ATM), this type is committed to rigorous evaluation and market research.

Friendly but formal, "Playing by the Rules" institutions have a clear understanding of their corporate culture and prefer to hire people who agree with and adhere to the values of that culture. These values tend toward conservative routines and personal styles. At IBM, the executive's dark suit and tie has emerged as an enduring popular image. Individual performance is rewarded with special recognition and awards; however, "Playing by the Rules" firms adopt uniform, impersonal standards for pay, promotion, and personnel management. IBM was a pioneer in the creation of standardized benefit packages, paid vacations, and written equal opportunity policies.

While law and order provides much of the strength of the "Playing by the Rules" personality, the rigid structure of this kind of organization sometimes acts as a brake on continued success. Convinced that its methods represent the right way of doing business, these groups may fail to recognize or acknowledge the complaints of clients and employees who are not satisfied with playing by the rules.

"DOING THE RIGHT THING"

Snapshot

- Makes decisions based on values and their impact on people
- Focuses on information that is factual, real, and current
- Is energized by the outer world of people and activity
- Prefers a structured, organized, and planned environment

This type of organization radiates a gracious attitude that attracts a high level of trust. These organizations tend to be polite and friendly, always attempting to do the appropriate thing. They tend to focus outward with a self-confident, if somewhat formal, appearance.

Whether public or private, large or small, this organization tends to have an element of "family" to its culture. It wants the people in the organization to be included and involved, encouraging social connections and support among staff members.

These organizations tend to have a strong emphasis on service to the customer and to the community. They seek to benefit others in a practical way. They also tend to be fiscally conservative.

This type of organization is likely to see itself as a trustee for its values, which tend to be traditional. It may even take a dark view of the outside world as a deteriorating environment.

These companies listen well. They pay close attention to customer needs, adapting services and products as necessary to provide the right results.

This organization tends to avoid conflict for as long as possible. It also tends to do nothing when it feels a stress between a need to take action and the fear of hurting others and/or doing something inappropriate. This is particularly noticeable during efforts to improve operational efficiency.

The strong sense of what is appropriate can limit innovation and produce rather conservative products. Most of these organizations view themselves as institutions with very high standards and a superior level of integrity. They guard their reputations, and they honor their word.

Characteristic Strengths

Excels at customer service
Sensitive to subtle market signals and to customer needs
Highly focused on completing tasks, projects, and initiatives
Preserves traditions
Efficient
Projects a strong traditional and conservative image
Gifted at sales
Creates a harmonious workplace
Capitalizes on new opportunities by moving quickly
Organizes everything

Characteristic Weaknesses

Occasionally assumes too many responsibilities (e.g., responding to too many needs), overburdening its resources

Often too rigid to respond to changing situations and opportunities

Can miss opportunities by avoiding solutions requiring innovation, new theories, or dealing with ambiguity

Can decide too quickly

Not uncommon for feelings to overrule good business sense

May implement change for the sake of change, without sufficient rationale

May become distracted by people problems, forgetting the task at hand

Work Environment

Exhibits a strong work ethic; the company is always very busy

Honors personal and corporate traditions

Maintains control through standards, rules, and procedures

Harmonious: warm and friendly, supportive

Respects hierarchy, norms, and rules

Socializing and corporate events are commonplace

Strong service orientation

Belongs to numerous organizations

Attention given to individual needs

Teamwork and group contribution flourish

Values

Customer

Community

Teamwork

Dependability

Harmony

Family

Fun

Loyalty

Efficiency

Integrity

Tradition

Communication Style

Centers on people

Language is functional and will often refer to tasks and duties

Prefers to give information rather than directives

Language is concrete and specific

Prefers face-to-face interaction

In meetings, seeks connection with people first

Begins presentations with details first

Thinks out loud, and the pace is rapid

Sources of Energy

Developing and realizing human potential
Tradition
Engaging and serving people
Dedication to causes
Personal affirmations

Signs of Stress

Loses ability to connect with employees and clients
Overwhelmed by responsibilities
Distracted by small or irrelevant details
Harmony turns to hypersensitivity
Finds fault instead of solutions

Behavior during Conflict

Prefers to avoid conflict
Will make sure the company is meeting people's needs
Will react viciously if a value has been stepped on

Approaches to Managing Change

Prefers predictability and constancy; change is threatening
Will engage in critical questioning
Will ask if the change is practical, has worked before, and is socially
    acceptable
Will consider the human aspect and whether all will benefit
If internal questions are adequately answered, will move quickly to
    plan, organize, and administer change
Change will come from getting things to run more efficiently

Ideal Clients

Want the best possible customer service
Produce products or services that contribute to the benefit of all
Appreciate meaningful relationships built on ethical standards
Require business results now
Value the company's reputation and integrity
Want to be associated with a blue-chip image
Enjoy being part of the "family" and collaborating as a team
Need to identify and jump on emerging opportunities quickly

Case Study

In a psychological study, William Bridges described the Procter &
Gamble corporation as an example of organizations with "Doing

the Right Thing" preferences (which Bridges identified using the designation ESFJ).[4] This company has a sterling reputation for compassionate management and corporate integrity. At Procter & Gamble, policies designed to improve the experience of workers and satisfy the interests of workers' unions date back to the 1880s.

Procter & Gamble and other "Doing the Right Thing" organizations rely on factual, real, and current information when evaluating the business environment. The sensing preference can be traced in its reliance on polling and market research for planning and assessment. Procter & Gamble was among the first U.S. companies to employ formal market research, establishing an in-house research center in 1924. Companies that share this preference will accept no substitute for hard data that covers the range of significant indicators in their given markets.

"Doing the Right Thing" companies give first priority to values and the impact of decisions on individuals. It's a sensibility that arises naturally in organizations where family relations have predominated, including Procter & Gamble in the early years, when the families of two sisters cast their lot together. This preference for feeling over thinking extends beyond the family unit to the company as a whole. For Procter & Gamble, this commitment is reflected in the company's compassion and pride in its factory workforce. As early as 1919, P&G's articles of incorporation declared that "the interests of the company and its employees are inseparable."

Another characteristic of the "Doing the Right Thing" companies is a judging preference that leads them to act on acts in accordance with their own plans even in the face of changing circumstances. Procter & Gamble has proven itself to be impervious to the most intimidating business environments—its establishment in 1837 coincided with the greatest financial panic in history to that time.

Procter & Gamble lists integrity, trust, and leadership among its core values. These values reflect the desire of this type of company to do the right thing by benefiting others in a practical way. Whether serving their customers' needs or ensuring harmony and fairness in the workplace, this firm provides the model of the "Doing the Right Thing" profile.

⑤ Profiles of Action

The next four personalities thrive on action and are not averse to taking risks. Change is fun, and no problem is insurmountable. An air of immediacy is felt in companies that share this temperament. Planning is not as valued as finding a practical, resourceful solution and immediately putting it to the test— with everyone standing by to come up with another one if the first solution doesn't work.

The "Action, Action—We Want Action" companies push themselves to perform under pressure, and "Working to Make a Difference" companies work as a group towards new innovations. Those with "Thriving on Risky Business" preferences relish new challenges, while "We Aim to Please" organizations go all out to solve customers' problems.

"ACTION, ACTION—WE WANT ACTION!"

Snapshot

- Makes decisions using logic, analysis, and cause-and-effect reasoning
- Focuses on information that is factual, real, and current
- Is energized by the inner world of ideas and experiences
- Prefers a flexible, spontaneous, and changing environment

Life on the edge suits this organization just fine, thank you. Risk taking is routine and motivates the company. An exciting place to be, the organization thrives on difficult challenges, relishing the action and the chance to troubleshoot.

Crisis situations create the organization's finest hours. It will step up, figure out what needs to be done, and then act on its analysis and its impulses to solve the problem. Rules and regulations will not be an obstacle; it will take whatever approach is necessary to get results.

Work is not just work—it's a show, a performance that should be pleasing both visually and aesthetically. It's understood that the work itself should also be excellent. The organization expects to achieve perfect mastery of its craft—nothing more, nothing less. It will not want to do it all; it just wants to do the thing it's good at, to do it very well, and to be recognized for that contribution.

No dreamers here—this organization is extremely realistic, taking a very concrete here-and-now view of things. Skeptical, pragmatic, and analytical, it will approach problems in a hands-on, practical way. Theories and speculation have no place here.

Independence is the name of the game in this organization. Hierarchies and respect for traditional management structures are practically nonexistent. The organization likes to be spontaneous—who needs rules and regulations? Respect is accorded to staff members who are accurate, practical, logical, and of course talented, with little tolerance for philosophers and traditionalists.

Since the environment at the organization is so loose and unstructured, there won't be many formal communications, training opportunities, or policies set in place. The main goal is always the quality of the product or service; the main questions are whether or not the organization is successfully mastering its craft and whether it is successfully presenting that craft to the customer.

In the traditional corporate world, the organization would be considered one of the loners. It's unlikely that the organization is going to be very involved with trade associations or in interactions with others outside the company. Unfortunately, customers may not understand this closed culture, seeing it as almost mysterious and wondering about the lack of communication.

While the organization is cutting edge and has its strengths, it would certainly benefit from having employees who are good at long-term planning and goal setting. In addition, employees with finely tuned communication skills would be helpful when communicating with customers.

Characteristic Strengths

Capable of concentrating attention and resources in the moment for quick and powerful impact

Attains product or service excellence and continual improvement

Adapts opportunistically to changing customer needs

Fearless risk taker, filled with optimism
Efficient
Understands its market through skillful analysis of customers
Keeps its cool in a crisis
Logical, practical realism
Can optimize operations to maximize returns
Able to capitalize on last-minute developments and options

Characteristic Weaknesses

So absorbed in action that it may lose sight of long-term goals
Changes direction and priorities leading to unstability
May overly rely on historical data and logical thinking to the exclusion of external, and often qualitative, information (markets, trends, and competition)
Can become perplexed or limit opportunities by avoiding solutions requiring innovation, new theories, or dealing with ambiguity
Not uncommon to ignore people management issues
May ignore the future for the present
Tendency to misinterpret activity as progress
Often needs help with outside communications
May apply a quick fix when a long-term solution is required
Frequently needs help with follow-through

Work Environment

Seeks perfection through incremental and continuous improvements
The company is a stage, and work is a place to perform and create an impact
Impulsive and spontaneous, with freedom of action
Work is an adventure, frequently involving risk
Largely a closed universe with little contact with the outside world
Prefers personal accomplishments to team accomplishments
Action abounds, hands-on
Little formal communication or training
Welcomes an occasional crisis, troubleshooting is routine
Not structured or regulated
Procedures are not allowed to get in the way of performance
Steady optimism

Values

Excellence
Autonomy
Quality

Efficiency
Logic
Spontaneity
Independence
Risk taking
Integrity
Challenge

Communication Style

Centers on the present in an analytical and logical way
Language is colorful, but most likely concrete and realistic
Prefers to give directives and structure rather than information
Factual, concise, blunt, and contains concrete examples
Prefers writing and e-mail
In meetings, seeks connection with the task first
Begins presentations with details first
Concerned with the moment

Sources of Energy

Opportunity to perform, especially in crises
Achieving excellence
Solving problems, troubleshooting
Crisis situations in general
Improving efficiency

Signs of Stress

Becomes excessively logical, rebellious
Dwells on mistakes of the past and ignores immediate problems
Loses objectivity
Becomes explosively emotional
Becomes excessively pessimistic, especially about the future

Behavior during Conflict

Not comfortable with conflict
Will examine its systems to ensure that it can handle conflict
Will seek to win with logic
Sees no point in trying to understand interpersonal conflict
If challenged, will become defensive

Approaches to Managing Change

Uncomfortable with change not of its own making
Prefers continuity and stability

Will gather information about the change, seeking to determine what part of the company should be preserved and what part may change

Will seek time to reflect, analyze, and relate to historical frameworks

Change will come only to those pieces that are not integral to identity and core values

If change is acceptable, will move forward on its own timetable

Ideal Clients

Desire a cool head to troubleshoot risky projects

Appreciate a problem solver not afraid to bend or break the rules

Need a quick fix based on logical analysis and prior experience

Require a product or service that demands constant refinement

Prefer an action-oriented and hands-on atmosphere requiring little formal communication

Need to be shielded from problems through rapid, competent, and proactive response to developing problems

Require a variety of project work that leverages internal experience and databases

Case Study

Home Depot, the Atlanta-based hardware chain, embodies the grit and drive of the Action organization—introverted, sensing, thinking, and perceiving. Being introverted means that Home Depot is energized by its own ideas and experiences. You can see the tendency in the company's origins, which brought together a talented management team— Bernie Marcus and Arthur Blank—who had recently been fired and were in search of a business opportunity. Believing in their vision of a no-frills do-it-yourself emporium, Marcus and Blank drew on their inner resources of determination and ingenuity to build the country's largest hardware chain. Their refusal to diversify Home Depot offerings (another manifestation of the introverted preference) has created a unique and consistent shopping experience for millions of customers.

As a nationwide chain of warehouses that serve double duty as Home Depot retail space, the company relies on information that is factual and current to manage inventory and distribution. In fact, Home Depot's reliance on sensory data has resulted in the creation of some of the most sophisticated systems of accounting controls in any retail industry. Home Depot also calls on its board members and executives to use their five senses to evaluate operations in franchise outlets, requiring regular in-person visits to stores across the country.

Action companies prefer to make decisions based on logic, analysis, and cause-and-effect reasoning rather than human considerations. That kind of value system means that Home Depot does not hesitate to use powerful incentives to bring employees and (especially) suppliers into line with expectations. In the aftermath of a class-action sex discrimination lawsuit in the 1990s, for example, Home Depot implemented the first major computerized system for hiring and promotion in the United States, thereby endorsing the ultimate expression of faith in logic.

The Home Depot tradition has embraced do-it-yourself as a management style as well as a consumer market. For a network of independently owned franchises, this preference for a flexible, spontaneous, and changing work environment has left a visible imprint. Home Depot franchisees are famous for their autonomy from overarching structures and procedures. This loose organizational ethos gives local outlets the freedom to take advantage of variations in supply and demand in their own sphere of operations. In keeping with the experience of founders Marcus and Blank, who described the process of being fired and building their new business as "being hit in the ass with a golden horseshoe," the company has acted in accordance with its own perception of what was right without regard for oversight or schedules.[1]

"WORKING TO MAKE A DIFFERENCE"

Snapshot

- Makes decisions based on values and their impact on people
- Focuses on information that is factual, real, and current
- Is energized by the inner world of ideas and experiences
- Prefers a flexible, spontaneous, and changing environment

Actions speak louder than words in this type of organization. It prefers hands-on work, especially if it is helping its clients and doing work that is consistent with its own values and beliefs.

These organizations excel at work that requires expertise and grace, such as the fine arts. They pay a great deal of attention to detail and have a unique ability to see and hear the small things that others may miss.

Reserved and somewhat modest, this organization may undersell itself. This reserve may also make it seem like the organization takes a while to warm up to clients and vendors, but its warmth and loyalty become apparent as the relationship develops. Clients and vendors who let the relationship develop will find that this organization deeply values their association.

This organization treats work as play, often turning it into a friendly competition. It likes to win and is willing to take risks to do so.

The organization is also a kind, supportive environment, loyal to its clients, its employees, and its ideals. Harmony and peace are important. To the outside world, it may appear to be a fairly closed organization, since it generates its ideas from within and then expresses them through actions, not words.

Informality is the key to this work environment. Formal communication, long-range planning, and meetings are rare. Instead, the organization expresses itself through actions and the work itself. Systems may be poorly developed and unorganized. This organization will benefit from having employees who will organize formal systems, helping it get and stay organized.

Characteristic Strengths

Maintains a reputation for elegant attention to details
Highly sensitive to subtle market signals
Good insight into its customers' needs and motivations
Capable of concentrating attention and resources for quick and powerful impact
Responds immediately to crises, efficiently mobilizing people
Solves immediate and concrete problems with available resources
Efficient, resourceful and prepared
Risk taker, filled with optimism
Creates a harmonious workplace that draws the best from people

Characteristic Weaknesses

Desire for details and perfection may hinder action
May lose sight of long-range goals
Can favor the means over the ends
Not uncommon for feelings to overrule good business sense
May ignore the future for the present
Can become perplexed or limit opportunities by avoiding solutions requiring innovation
On occasion, mistakes current optimism for long-term health
May apply a quick fix when a long-term solution is required

Work Environment

The company is a stage and work is a place to perform
Work is play or friendly competition
Impulsive and spontaneous
Optimistic, cheerful, friendly
Focused in the moment, creating an impact
Exudes the creative element
Harmony achieved through mutual respect
Physically attractive and comfortable
Minimum of structure, rules, routines, politics, traditions

Values

Excellence
Action
Harmony
Personal dignity
Hard work
Cooperation

Communication Style

Centers on the present and on people
Language is concrete and specific and may be colorful
Prefers to speak through its actions and results
Factual, direct, friendly, and contains personal examples
Prefers face-to-face interaction
Structured
In meetings, seeks connection with people first
Begins presentations with details first
Contained, thoughtful, and reflective
Comments have already been carefully thought through
Formal meetings and communications are rare

Sources of Energy

Opportunity to perform, especially in crises
Fixing problems
Breaking new ground, challenging the status quo, breaking the rules
Pleasing others

Signs of Stress

Becomes emotional
Becomes excessively pessimistic, especially about the future

Loses its ability to connect with employees and clients
Harmony turns to hypersensitivity

Behavior during Conflict

Prefers to avoid conflict
Will determine if the company is meeting people's needs
Will react viciously if a value has been trampled

Approaches to Managing Change

Prefers continuity and stability
Uncomfortable with change that does not come from within
Will gather information about the change, seeking to determine what
    part of the company should be preserved and what part may
    change
Will seek time to analyze and relate to historical frameworks
Will ask if the change is practical and is socially acceptable
If the change is acceptable, will move forward on its own timetable in
    a series of small, incremental changes

Ideal Clients

Provide an important product or service to people
Require attention to the smallest detail
Appreciate flair and style
Interface effectively with its informal systems and structure
Value long-term relationships
Need to have a major impact in a short period of time, as when inspi-
    ration hits
Enjoy rolling up their sleeves (literally and figuratively) and getting the
    job done fast and accurately

Case Study

The authors believe that companies are people, too, and that some
kinds of people are more rare than others. Though we have worked
with hundreds of organizations and profiled dozens more for our
case study research, we have yet to come across an adequate representative of the "Working to Make a Difference" organization. If
the questionnaire produced this result, you should consider yourself special. Relying on the concept of personality preferences and
their dynamic interaction, we can present a fairly detailed description of your company's general characteristics: introverted, sensing, feeling, and perceiving.

As an introverted company, the "Working to Make a Difference" type draws its energy from the inner world of ideas and experience. In practice that means your organization comes off as reserved and conservative. In his book *The Character of Organizations,* William Bridges describes the ISFP organization as a highly individualistic group where talented people come together in a loose network of support and shared resources.[2] Employees perceive the company as a stage on which they perform their best work and win an audience. Mutual respect among individuals in this kind of company is the foundation of workplace harmony.

The reliance on sensory data is another characteristic of the type. These kinds of companies prefer information that is factual, real, and current, and rely on market research, review, and revisions to polish their products and services. This attention to detail provides the organization with one of its characteristic strengths: It is attuned to tiny variations in the needs and desires of its client base and makes minute adjustments for maximum effect. The combination of sensing and feeling as preferences means that total customer satisfaction makes a difference to the "Working to Make a Difference" company.

Because they are committed to making decisions based on values and their impact on people, "Working to Make a Difference" firms cultivate warm relationships. Loyalty and attentiveness prevail both within the organization and between the company and its clients.

The "Working to Make a Difference" preference for flexibility, spontaneity, and change leaves a visible imprint on the work environment. Standard operating procedures steer clear of hierarchy and rule in favor of informal, personal interactions. The company's ability to concentrate its resources to act on impulse allows it to respond effectively to new information and opportunities. Overall, this kind of organization is focused on the moment and ready to put its best face forward in any contingency.

"THRIVING ON RISKY BUSINESS"

Snapshot

- Focuses on information that is factual, real, and current
- Makes decisions using logic, analysis, and cause-and-effect reasoning
- Is energized by the outer world of people and activity
- Prefers a flexible, spontaneous, and changing environment

When you give this type of organization a problem to solve, stand back, because it will plunge right in at breakneck speed. The organization relishes the new, the exciting, the adventurous, and the risky. Constant action and involvement with new situations motivate it.

Expert at troubleshooting and crisis management, the organization enjoys the opportunity to "get its hands dirty." Uninhibited by rules and regulations, it will dive right in, taking whatever approach will solve the problem, *today!*

As far as the organization is concerned, work should be fun, not serious and full of rules. Flexible and adaptable, the organization lives moment to moment. Rules and regulations are seen as roadblocks, things that can and should change as needed. Sometimes the organization will change for the sake of changing—it just needs the stimulation and excitement of doing something new.

Employees who like a spontaneous environment and working autonomously will thrive in this environment. There is not likely to be too much formal training, either—employees are expected to forge ahead and learn by doing.

This organization is one of contrasts. For example, although it is friendly and fun, it is also impersonal and more interested in realistic data than in human ideas or motivations. Employees may wonder how their concerns can be dismissed so easily in the midst of all this pleasure and spontaneity.

Customers will be attracted to the organization's enthusiasm. Nonjudgmental and adaptable, this organization can work well with many different types of people.

The organization is expert at using its strengths and handling crisis and problem situations; however, it could benefit from some help with planning. Having staff members who can make long-term plans and goals and set up regulations and procedures the organization can live with (i.e., not too restrictive) would be a definite plus for the organization's long-term success.

Characteristic Strengths

Fearless risk taker, filled with optimism

Skilled at analyzing customer needs and wants in the short term

Adapts opportunistically to changing customer needs

Keeps its cool in a crisis

Capable of concentrating attention and resources for quick and powerful impact

Gifted at promotions and negotiations

Efficient problem solver, troubleshooter
Capitalizes on new opportunities by moving quickly

Characteristic Weaknesses

So absorbed in action and the moment that it may lose sight of goals
and the long term
Not uncommon to ignore people management
Propensity to change priorities may make it unstable
Occasionally creates crises where none exist
Occasionally needs help with long-term planning
Can become perplexed or miss opportunities by avoiding solutions
requiring innovation or dealing with ambiguity
Acting impulsively may cause some risk taking to be more like gambling
Can be so bored by routine that important activities go unattended
May apply a quick fix when a long-term solution is required

Work Environment

The company is a stage and work is a place to perform and create an
impact
Impulsive and spontaneous, sometimes chaotic
Focused in the moment
Fun and friendly, yet impersonal
Autonomy to respond to ever changing situations
Few formal meetings or communications
Risk taking permeates everything
Physically comfortable and attractive
Action abounds
Easygoing and cooperative; minimally structured or regulated
Conversations may be colorful

Values

Logic
Fun
Spontaneity
Risk taking
Autonomy
Challenge
Hands-on experience

Communication Style

Centers on the present in a logical and analytical way
Speech is colorful

Prefers to give directives and structure rather than information
Factual, concise, and contains concrete examples
Seeks to get to the point as quickly as possible
In meetings, seeks connection with the task first
Begins presentations with the details first

Sources of Energy

Opportunity to perform, especially in crises
Solving challenging problems in a practical and efficient way
Anything that requires an actionable response
Beating the system of rules and procedures

Signs of Stress

Charming Dr. Jekyll turns into demonic Mr. Hyde
Becomes excessively pessimistic, especially about the future
Becomes emotional
Decision-making capabilities erode

Behavior during Conflict

Not afraid to address conflict head-on, except in people issues
Will examine its systems to ensure that it can handle conflict rationally
Will seek to win with persuasion
If challenged, will become defensive

Approaches to Managing Change

Though a change agent, is uncomfortable with change imposed on it
Prefers continuity and stability, maintaining what is
Will seek information and advice from all sources
Will ask for proof that the change will work and is practical
Change comes from getting things to run more effectively
If the change honors its values, will try to persuade everyone to
change

Ideal Clients

Capitalizes on an opportunity with a narrow window for action
Involved in high-stakes activities requiring a performance, high-
profile image, and coolness under fire
Need a troubleshooter that can operate without a lot of structure or
formal communication
Value concrete and practical operating style
Need quick solutions based on logical analysis
Need a crisis solved immediately

Appreciate a problem solver not afraid to bend the rules
Thrive in a fast-paced, high-risk environment

Case Study

Our case study for companies that thrive on risky business is Winnebago Industries, the Iowa-based manufacturer of the world's most famous recreational vehicles. Winnebago is an extroverted, sensing, thinking, and perceiving organization. The company draws its energy from the outer world of people and activity, a preference that was manifested openly in the events surrounding its establishment in 1958. Citizens of Forest City, Iowa, concerned that their children were leaving home in order to find jobs, were determined to find a company to open a local facility. The success of this quest has recreated Forest City as a quintessential company town, and has guaranteed that Winnebago operates with an eye to the strengths, limitations, and desires of the local population.

Winnebago's pursuit of information that is factual, real, and current has provided one of the keys to its success in the complex recreational vehicle industry. RV manufacturing requires an ongoing investment in engineering and adaptation. Winnebago must strive for constant improvements in fuel efficiency and safety for one of the world's most awkward commercial vehicles. Winnebago laboratories work toward breakthroughs in materials and component design, building each element of the Winnebago RV on site. Extensive testing of vehicles indicates the typical behavior of a sensing organization.

In keeping with the legacy of founder John K. Hanson, Winnebago makes decisions using logic, analysis, and cause-and-effect reasoning. Hanson promoted a formula of eight business principles that he considered the foundation of success in manufacturing: adequate capital, facility, product, people, sales, purchasing, production, and accounting. Make the best choices in all of these categories, Hanson thought, and a successful company can run with minimal intervention from management.

In its commitment to flexibility, spontaneity, and a changing environment, Winnebago has embraced the best possible work style for its industry. The unpredictable price of oil exerts a strong influence on the popularity and sale of recreational vehicles, so Winnebago has a hard time executing long-range business plans. The company's ability to perceive the market outlook and to time its production and distribution schedules accordingly is an essential threshold for profitability. During very hard times—for example, the oil crisis of the 1970s—the flexible Winnebago organization proved its creativity in product licensing and adaptations of its proprietary technologies in new products.

"WE AIM TO PLEASE"

Snapshot

- Focuses on information that is factual, real, and current
- Makes decisions based on values and their impact on people
- Is energized by the outer world of people and activity
- Prefers a flexible, spontaneous, and changing environment

In this type of organization, taking care of customers' wants and needs is paramount. Whether it delivers a product or a service, an organization like this is very good at reading and knowing what the public wants and at responding to trends and opinions. With its zeal for performing, it will meet customers' needs with a sense of fun and entertainment, always presenting its best public face. It knows how to present a good image and is outstanding at public relations.

Perhaps the most generous of all the organizational types, this organization will be helpful and supportive to employees, customers, and staff in practical ways. Warm and gregarious, it is energized by group gatherings and personal interactions. Interactions may even include a little playful competition.

This organization doesn't handle stress well. Since it avoids dealing with tension for as long as possible (this type has the lowest tolerance for stress and anxiety of all the types), problems can build up and blindside the organization.

The organization thrives on a frantic pace. This fast pace may become too frantic for some staff members, especially those who need time to slow down and evaluate things. In addition, due to the lack of interest in planning and schedules, follow-through may be a problem.

Although this organization likes to have all the details before making a decision, it may delay making decisions because it also likes to keep its options open.

This type of organization is very vulnerable during times of change because of its orientation to the here and now. In addition, it is very tied into its public image, and it will regret any loss or changes to that image. Due to its people orientation, it will mourn any loss of personnel or changes that hurt the company's family atmosphere. It may rush through a transition period trying to get back to normal. Its goal during change will be to get back to the point where it can reestablish relationships with customers and find a place for the people in the organization to belong.

Characteristic Strengths

Excels at customer service
Sensitive to subtle market signals and to customers
Capable of concentrating attention and resources
Fearless risk taker, filled with optimism
Thrives in the spotlight and enjoys a good public image
Acts quickly to marshal human resources effectively in crisis
Creates a harmonious workplace that draws the best from people
Knows how to present a good image
Resourceful and efficient
Can find a quick fix for anything

Characteristic Weaknesses

Natural optimism and flair for risk may blind it to impossible situations
May use a quick fix when a long-term solution is needed
Not uncommon for feelings to overrule good business sense
Could be so absorbed in action that it loses sight of goals
Often lacks follow-through and attention to planning and schedules
May confuse action with data gathering
May find it difficult to set or keep to priorities
Overconfidence may propel it to disaster
Often lacks strategy and long-term plans for its tactics
May overly rely on image
Juggles too many balls and may drop some
May become distracted, forgetting the task at hand

Work Environment

The company is a stage and work is a place to perform and create an impact
Impulsive and spontaneous
Sensitive to the well-being of people
High interactivity with frequent meetings
Conversations abound and are light and entertaining
Harmonious: warm and friendly, supportive
Work is an adventure
Focused in the moment
Comfortable and attractive, stylish

Action-oriented, even frantic; hands-on
Minimum of structure, bureaucracy, and office politics

Values

Customer
Spontaneity
Fun
Excellence
Equality
Harmony

Communication Style

Centers on the present and on people
Language is concrete and specific and may be colorful
Prefers to give information rather than directives
Factual, detailed, friendly, and contains personal examples
Prefers face-to-face interaction
In meetings, seeks connection with people first, expressing points of
    agreement
Begins presentations with details first
Thinks out loud, and the pace is rapid

Sources of Energy

Opportunity to perform, especially in crises
Action, movement, and a fast pace
Constant flow of problems to solve
Engaging and serving people
Personal affirmations

Signs of Stress

Becomes emotional
Decision-making capabilities erode
Becomes excessively pessimistic, especially about the future
Becomes mired in details and unimportant facts

Behavior during Conflict

Prefers to avoid or deny conflict as long as possible
Will determine if the company is meeting people's needs
May seek to remedy the pain and discomfort being experienced
Will react viciously if a value has been trampled

Approaches to Managing Change

Welcomes internally developed change

Will seek information and advice from all sources

Will ask if the change is practical, has worked before, and is socially acceptable

Will consider the human aspect and whether all will benefit

If the change honors its values, will try to persuade everyone to change

Ideal Clients

Want the best possible customer service

Produce a product or service that contributes to the benefit of all

Appreciate showmanship and are sensitive to public image

Need immediate, though not long-term, solutions

Desire to capitalize on emerging trends with quick, focused effort

Appreciate and enjoy lots of personal and social interaction

Thrive on a demanding and quick pace

Case Study

Mary Kay Cosmetics illustrates the key components of this type of persona: extroverted, sensing, feeling, and perceiving. Like other organizations committed to direct sales, Mary Kay draws its energies (and profits) from interactions with a wide range of people. The company relies on small gatherings of potential customers in social settings for advertising and sales. The extroverted organizational focus of the company is further expressed in its open commitment to a social goal. More than any major company in the world, Mary Kay is devoted to the cause of women's empowerment.

Founder Mary Kay Ash, whose homespun wisdom continues to provide the moral foundation of the organization even after her death, urged sales representatives to think of everyone they met as wearing a sign that read, "Make me feel important."[3] In an indirect way, the maxim requires Mary Kay representatives to use their senses and their common sense to assess an individual's needs and desires. The company also expresses its preference for information that is factual, real, and current in more traditional methods. Mary Kay's extensive overseas expansion, for example, has proceeded in step with statistical research about emerging markets. Moreover, to accommodate international trade and tariff policies, the company employs extensive scientific and market testing of locally produced cosmetics.

In its reliance on values and their impact on people, Mary Kay epitomizes the "We Aim to Please" organization. In building what she called the "Dream Company," Mary Kay Ash gave first priority to the operation of the Golden Rule in business dealings: Do unto others as you would have them do unto you. In practice, that means personalized acknowledgments of milestones and achievements, from handwritten notes and birthday cards to the famous pink Mary Kay Cadillacs. Time and again, this kind of personalized attention and fair play has landed Mary Kay Cosmetics on business media lists of the best employers in the country.

Flexibility is another hallmark of the Mary Kay way. The perceiving work style preference reveals itself in all levels of the organization. Most significantly, the company offers employment opportunities to women who might otherwise have difficulty balancing demands of work and family, or to aspiring women taking on a second job. The direct sales method means that Mary Kay representatives control their own schedules and incomes, while one of the subsidiary principles of the company's version of the Golden Rule—no territories—means that sales reps are free to exploit opportunities without consulting corporate headquarters.

⑥ Profiles of Idealism

In this chapter, we group together four personalities that are highly interpersonal. These organizations share a tendency to subjectively evaluate concepts and abstract ideas. They are people-focused, with warm work environments that value harmony.

"Vision Driven by Values" companies are goal-oriented and committed to a greater good, while "Quest for Meaningful Work" companies make their decisions based on their impact on people. Companies with the "It's Fun to do Good Work" profile have endless enthusiasm for their work, and those with "Seeing the Big Picture in Human Terms" preferences are warm places to work.

"VISION DRIVEN BY VALUES"

Snapshot

- Focuses on the big picture, relationships, and connections between facts
- Makes decisions based on values and their impact on people
- Is energized by the inner world of ideas and experiences
- Prefers a structured, organized, and planned environment

If you ask members of this organization what it believes in, you're sure to get a quick (perhaps long) answer. It knows what it believes in; it's clear about its goals, and it lives by its values. It is highly committed to its beliefs, and its goals and strategies will be perfectly aligned with them.

Outsiders may not fully understand how the organization operates until they become more involved with it. The fact that it is a very creative, insightful place may not be immediately clear. It's an idea place where complexities and problems are seen as challenges. Using its powerful intuitive capabilities, the organization can often find hidden meanings and motivations that others wouldn't see.

Its strength lies in its ability to look down the road and find solutions that will ultimately help improve the situation. Possibilities are turned into answers in an organization like this because its people have the organizational skills to follow through on their grand plans and visions.

To outsiders, this type of organization appears somewhat serious and restrained, but those on the inside know that it's a place that's very interested in people, inside and outside the company. Inside the company, people benefit from its concern for their well-being, while outside, due to its love of learning, it exhibits an intense interest in new people and situations. Still, it will be most comfortable with a few long-term customers, rather than out in the world dealing with a variety of people on a daily basis.

Internally, there will be communication, both written and verbal, in order to keep everyone involved; however, there may be times when communication will fall off, giving the organization the chance to reflect and recharge its batteries. In keeping with the company's practical side, there will be systems and procedures in place, although individuals' concerns will be taken into account when necessary.

Employees of this organization can count on a supportive environment where their needs are considered. On the other hand, the organization will expect employees to be committed to its ideals in a big way. This intensity may be too much for some people.

People can also expect to receive support on the job in the form of training, developmental, and mentoring programs and similar activities. There may also be ceremonies and events that bring everyone together in an atmosphere of harmony.

Characteristic Strengths

Builds human potential through its vision of possibilities
Instinctively blends organizational and people goals
Builds enduring relationships internally and in the marketplace
Attracts superior problem solvers, particularly with human systems and organizations
Exceptional communications skills
Can be a critical observer without being judgmental, contributing to accurate market assessments
Able to clarify complex issues
Good at sensing trends and possibilities that others may miss

Able to set priorities and remain highly focused on a few critical projects

Capable of acting quickly, unencumbered by analysis paralysis

Characteristic Weaknesses

Could champion a cause to the detriment of operations and performance

Not uncommon for feelings or instincts to overrule good business

May need help translating concepts into reality

May become distracted by people problems

Frequently has difficulty juggling multiple priorities

May limit opportunities by avoiding data gathering and logical analysis

May allow people problems to become too controlling

Occasionally lacks details to communicate and implement vision

May jump to conclusions too quickly

Too rigid to respond to changing situations and opportunities

Work Environment

Built on core values and ideals

Encourages and supports growth and development, often through mentoring and coaching

Harmonious: people place, warm and friendly, supportive and appreciative

Quiet enthusiasm

Policies and procedures are in place, but not often insisted upon

Dedicated, serious, and hardworking; may be intense

Nonpolitical

Imaginative, Expressive

Positive, Highly motivating

Values

Innovation

Learning

Harmony

Sensitivity

Commitment

Insight

Communication Style

Centers on people and the future

Often discusses options, possibilities, and what could be, especially concerning people

Prefers to give directives rather than information
Prefers face-to-face interaction
Begins presentations with the big picture, goals, and objectives
Conceptual
Empathetic
Focuses on process over facts
May be prone to exaggeration and dramatics

Sources of Energy

Achieving the highest level of human potential
Establishing and maintaining corporate relationships
Engaging and serving people
Championing causes
Thinking and talking about what could be

Signs of Stress

Becomes overwhelmed with possibilities
Becomes obsessed with unimportant details
Preoccupied with irrelevant facts
Unable to decide between what is important to the people and to the
    company
Becomes overzealous about values
Loud arguments and emotional outbursts

Behavior during Conflict

Will avoid conflict if possible, but will defend values tenaciously
Ensures that corporate values are clearly articulated and understood
Conflict will come when values are violated or ignored
Would rather leave than win an argument
May reason with feelings rather than logic

Approaches to Managing Change

Enjoys predictability
Will consult internal data sources (data, experience, vision) and will
    involve everyone
Change must be consistent with values and vision
If change is consistent, will move quickly to implement
If change is not consistent, will become inflexible

Ideal Clients

Need an ingenious problem solver that prefers to play behind the
    scenes

Value an ethical and caring organization
Desire to build and maintain long-term relationships
Create or improve services or products that benefit people for the long
  term
Produce a product or service the organization believes in
Like a harmonious environment with little confrontation
Willing and able to give the organization time to develop its ideas

Case Study

In his study of the character of organizations, William Bridges described Johnson & Johnson, a representative of the introverted, intuitive, feeling, and judging type that mirrors the "Vision Driven by Values" profile. As an introverted company, the New Jersey–based pharmaceutical and health products manufacturer is energized by the inner world of ideas and experiences. You can see this preference in J&J's careful definition of its responsibilities as an organization, enumerated in the company's 100-year-old corporate Credo. Johnson & Johnson defines its work as a worthy end in itself, and ranks the needs of employees, communities, and stockholders below it. The J&J Credo insists on the integrity of the product itself—its ability to help alleviate pain and disease—as the chief imperative.

Many features of research, development, and marketing at Johnson & Johnson reveal the impact of the "Vision Driven by Values" focus on the big picture, relationships, and connections between facts. This intuitive preference is at the core of the R&D philosophy at J&J, captured in Robert Wood Johnson's famous statement that "[f]ailure is our most important product." Johnson & Johnson has indeed produced failures, but has also moved "accidentally" to conquer new and lucrative markets with unanticipated developments such as Band-Aid adhesives and Johnson's Baby Powder.[1] Another earmark of an intuitive approach to information gathering can be found in the company's ability to coordinate its offerings with emerging trends and tastes. In seeking a national market for Tylenol in the 1960s, for example, J&J foresaw the explosion of popular demand for name brand and over-the-counter pharmaceuticals.

The "Vision Driven by Values" organization expresses a strong interest in the well-being of people, both inside the company and in the larger human community. Evidence of this tendency can be found in the company's decision to build new offices in downtown New Brunswick, New Jersey, amid Rust Belt decline. The company's understanding of its responsibilities of citizenship required it to remain loyal to its hometown community.

In its embrace of a structured, organized, and planned environment, J&J reveals the often subtle impact of the judging work style preference. The company has evolved a remarkably decentralized divisional structure, with distinct but wholly owned subsidiaries producing some of its best-known products: McNeill Laboratories makes Tylenol, Ethicon makes surgical products, and Ortho handles contraceptives. This decentralized system allows each division to work at its own pace and establish its own procedures for marketing its products. The influence of the structured, planned environment of the J&J umbrella organization, however, ensures a high degree of consistency.

Like many "Vision Driven by Values" organizations, Johnson & Johnson has shown its willingness to champion a cause, even to the detriment of operations and performance. When confronting two consecutive incidents of Tylenol poisoning in the 1980s, for example, J&J stuck to its guns on behalf of its top-performing product, restoring public confidence in the Tylenol brand at a cost of more than $240 million. For all the short-term complications of staying true to its beliefs, the Tylenol rescue preserved for J&J a product that remains profitable and popular 20 years after the events. That's the kind of quiet enthusiasm that "Vision Driven by Values" firms bring to their work.

"QUEST FOR MEANINGFUL WORK"

Snapshot

- Makes decisions based on values and their impact on people
- Focuses on the big picture, relationships, and connections between facts
- Is energized by the inner world of ideas and experiences
- Prefers a flexible, spontaneous, and changing environment

This type of organization is a company on a quest. The most idealistic of all the organizational types, it has a private dream of creating a better world and bettering its profession. This vision is not always obvious to those outside the team, but it is nonetheless the central force behind many decisions.

This company cares, approaching its work with a kind of youthful optimism. Blessed with an innate ability to link unrelated concepts to form new ideas, this organization sees many possible solutions to any need. It is a good communicator, but does better as a force behind the scenes or in one-on-one persuasion than as a mass communicator.

If it can overcome a tendency toward disorganization and poor follow-through, it has the ability to develop cutting-edge work and imaginative service. It is a survivor.

These organizations are people oriented. Highly perceptive, they determine how things get done based on individual needs and today's concerns. The organization makes value-based decisions. One of those values is always harmony. It also is faithful to its obligations to clients or customers. When the work has meaning, the organization is truly inspired.

Anything new is exciting. These organizations learn by doing. Staff members tend to get the freedom to develop on a personal and professional level. There's plenty of encouragement and support. Ideas are genuinely welcomed.

This type is very trusting and hates confrontation. This can cause problems when vendors and others don't have the organization's best interest at heart. It's essential for a client to be a good match with the organization's values, or work may never get done. Meaningless work makes the organization unhappy and restless.

Characteristic Strengths

Draws strength from its ideals and vision for a better world
Grows the business by growing people
Builds beneficial and enduring relationships internally and in the marketplace
Good instincts about customer needs and what motivates them
Able to develop cutting-edge work and imaginative service
Able to clarify complex issues
Draws the best from people
Good at sensing trends and seeing possibilities that others miss
Strong communication skills
Able to capitalize on last-minute developments and options
Capable of acting quickly, unencumbered by analysis paralysis

Characteristic Weaknesses

Gift of imagination may remove it from reality
Not uncommon for feelings to overrule good business sense
May become immobilized by possibilities
Focus can be fragmented by too many projects, causing deadlines to be missed

Could champion a cause to the detriment of operations and performance
May need help with organization, follow-through, and schedules
Juggles too many balls and may drop some
Desire for perfection may delay critical actions or decisions
May allow people problems to become too controlling
Tendency to be weak at implementation

Work Environment

Encourages and supports growth and development
Harmonious: supportive and affirming
People can be seen working alone or in intimate groups
Unstructured, casual, minimally insistent on procedures
Considerable talking and listening, often centered on predictions
Significant contributions usually come from individuals
Quiet enthusiasm
Fun
Positive
Expressive
Hands-on
Teamwork and brainstorming often seen

Values

Innovation
Community
Diversity
Teamwork
Fun
Harmony
Integrity
Insight
Sensitivity

Communication Style

Centers on the future and people, with ideals
Prefers to give information rather than directives
Communicates at the conceptual level
May be prone to exaggeration and dramatics
Prefers face-to-face interaction
Language is verbally creative
Begins meetings with the big picture first
In meetings, seeks connecting with people first
Topics will vary widely, but will deal mostly with ideas

Conversations will jump from topic to topic
Options and possibilities will be communicated

Sources of Energy

Pursuing people possibilities and concepts that can help humankind
Idealistic relationships
Adopting and championing causes

Signs of Stress

Overwhelmed with possibilities, indecisive
Obsessed with unimportant details
Loud arguments and emotional outbursts
Becomes overzealous about values, or intense and vocal when they are
    not honored

Behavior during Conflict

Will avoid conflict if possible, but will defend values tenaciously
Ensures that corporate values are understood
Conflict will come when values are violated or ignored
May reason with feelings rather than logic

Approaches to Managing Change

Change will come from vision of the future
Will seek information and advice from everyone
Will ask if change is good for people
If changes honor its values, will try to persuade others
Change will be slow and evolutionary

Ideal Clients

Value an ethical and caring organization
Appreciate an organization that is honest and genuine
Willing and able to allow the organization time to develop ideas
Share a common focus on developing people
Appreciate keeping commitments
Like a harmonious environment with little confrontation
Value being part of creative, brainstorming activity

Case Study

Apple Computer provides our case study of the "Quest for
Meaningful Work" company—introverted, intuitive, feeling, and

perceiving.[2] Even people who have never used its products understand that Apple gets its energy from its own inner world of ideas and experiences. Unlike every other computer on the market, Apple machines operate using proprietary software. That means that Apple programs and applications can be used only on Apple machines, and that Apple machines can only use programs and applications adapted to Apple specifics. For Apple users—celebrated in company advertisements as individualists—this separation from the mainstream provides the foundation for a vibrant and insulated computer community.

Apple is focused on the big picture, relationships, and connections between facts. By recognizing the potential of computers to enrich all kinds of experiences for all kinds of individuals, company founders Steve Jobs and Steve Wozniak transformed a hobbyist's technology into an essential tool for office work and self-expression. The same preferences led the company to value the beauty and personality of Apple machines. Apple is so committed to its intuitive sense of what computer users want that the company rarely conducts market research for new products. Instead, each new computer appears to spring fresh and complete from the Apple imagination.

The intensity of Apple's quest for meaningful work derives in large part from its feeling decision-making preferences. As with all preferences, this emphasis on values and their impact on individuals in the workplace is a source of weakness as well as strength. Passion at Apple Computer, particularly under the leadership of Steve Jobs (who returned as CEO in 1997 after a 10-year hiatus), has sometimes caused the company to overestimate demand for its products, to introduce new hardware before it was perfected. On the plus side, however, this same enthusiasm has helped Apple create a strong sense of belonging—even faith—among dedicated users.

The quest for meaningful work at Apple does not proceed according to strict schedules and hardwired business plans. In the summer of 2000, for example, Apple executed a complex rearrangement in its education sales department that caused the company to miss deadlines for 2000–2001 school year budgets. More often, however, the spontaneity and decisiveness of the Quest type has yielded material benefits, including the original drive to market personal computers in the 1970s, which put Apple and the personal computer itself on the path to glory.

"IT'S FUN TO DO GOOD WORK"

Snapshot

- Focuses on the big picture, relationships, and connections between facts
- Makes decisions based on values and their impact on people
- Is energized by the outer world of people and activity
- Prefers a flexible, spontaneous, and changing environment

This type of organization radiates enthusiasm for its work. It tends to be the most vibrant, optimistic, and creative of workplaces. It wants to stimulate change in its industry and the whole world.

If they can overcome a tendency toward disorganization and poor follow-through, organizations with these characteristics have the capacity to produce cutting-edge work, imaginative products, and innovative services.

These organizations are also people organizations. Because they are so highly perceptive and able to understand people, they tend be excellent at solving problems and among the first to spot new trends. At their best, they shape trends; at their worst, they are trendy. This type prefers to improvise rather than to quantify its ideas with hard data or logic.

Anything new is always exciting, because these organizations like to learn by doing. This interest in the new and different can affect the organization's ability to hold onto clients and customers. The organization is always more interested in the next great challenge with a new customer than in maintaining a solid relationship with an older customer.

This organization makes value-based decisions. One of those values is always harmony. The organization hates confrontation. Therefore, it's essential for a client/customer to be a good match with the organization's values, or work may never get done.

These organizations focus the spotlight on themselves as often as possible, showcasing their unique, authentic identity. They want to be true to their vision and their dreams, wherever those dreams take them.

Characteristic Strengths

Big-picture visionary
Builds beneficial and enduring relationships
Creates a harmonious workplace that draws the best from people

Able to capitalize on developments and opportunities

Projects a desirable image through showmanship, salesmanship, and contagious enthusiasm

Has good instincts about customer needs and motivators

Good at sensing trends and seeing possibilities

Enthusiastic and capable leader of causes

Produces innovative, cutting-edge work, products, and services

Able to solve new, complex, and ambiguous problems

Has exceptional communication skills

Capable of acting quickly, unencumbered by analysis paralysis

Characteristic Weaknesses

May act prematurely or without adequate business logic or hard data to support decisions

Not uncommon for feelings or instincts to overrule good business sense

Tendency to drop current projects in favor of exploring new opportunities

May become distracted by people problems

Occasionally lacks details to communicate and implement vision

Could overly rely on intuition and fail to support it with proper critical analyses

Tendency toward disorganization, poor follow-through, and inattention to details

Occasionally will implement change for the sake of change, without sufficient rationale

May miss critical deadlines or delay critical decisions until the last moment

May spend considerable time in friendly conversation without a business connection

Juggles many balls and may drop some

Work Environment

Encourages and supports growth and development

Harmonious: people place, warm and friendly, supportive

Creative, imaginative

Considerable talking, listening, and brainstorming

Upbeat, full of energy and positive reinforcements

Radiates enthusiasm

Hands-on; learns by doing

Unstructured, relaxed, casual; may be chaotic

Spontaneous

Operates as a democracy

Values

Cooperation
Diversity
Teamwork
Fun
Innovation
Integrity
Harmony
Creativity
Equality
Relationships
Freedom

Communication Style

Centers on people and the future
Will often focus on process over facts
Prefers to give information rather than directives
Prefers face-to-face interaction
Language can be verbally creative, subjective, and evocative
In meetings, seeks connection with people first
Begins presentations with the big picture, goals, and objectives
Typically conceptual concerning options and possibilities
Expressive, enthusiastic, and may become emotional or redundant
Conversations will cover a variety of topics, often jumping quickly in
   a stream-of-consciousness manner

Sources of Energy

Pursuing people possibilities, concepts, and causes that can help
   mankind
Variety and change
Establishing and maintaining corporate relationships
Engaging and serving people; actualizing potential
Affirmation
Appreciation

Signs of Stress

Overwhelmed with possibilities; indecisive
Obsessed with unimportant details
Preoccupied with irrelevant facts

Behavior during Conflict

Prefers to avoid conflict at all costs if possible, but will defend values
   tenaciously

Will check that corporate values and principles have been clearly articulated and understood

Approaches to Managing Change

Is driven by love of change and will have an innovative aspect
Will seek information and advice from everyone
Asks if change is good for people
Will get everyone involved and will encourage extensive discussion, often centered on possibilities
If change honors its creative and action orientation, will try to persuade everyone to change

Ideal Clients

Want the flexibility to capitalize on last-minute developments
Share the company's values, especially those focused on people
Value enduring relationships
Require innovative possibilities; thinking grounded in meaningful customer needs
Require project work involving intense, challenging, and concentrated activity
Like a friendly, relaxed atmosphere
Energized by personal contact and the collaborative exchange
Believe in and appreciate teamwork

Case Study

Xerox Corporation provides a revealing example of the "It's Fun to Do Good Work" profile. The company's extroverted character is best conveyed by its history of intimate partnerships with independent and subsidiary firms. Well before Xerox was a success, it joined with an inventor at the Battelle Memorial Scientific Institute to develop the revolutionary process behind Xerox photocopying. Likewise, years later Xerox created a largely independent think tank, Xerox PARC in Palo Alto, to manage special research projects. The strong communications skills and leadership motivations of the "Fun" profile give companies like Xerox a concrete advantage in building partnerships.

Among many companies with intuitive information-gathering preferences, including Xerox, the commitment to research and development occupies a sacred place in the division of labor. The ten-year xerographic copying development project set the standard for a recurrent cycle of investment in R&D, some of which saw the company devote more of its resources than it could afford to pursuing its dreams. The leadership at Xerox justified the sacrifice by aligning it with the sweeping character of the company's ambitions. For example, Xerox's efforts to change the infrastructure of business offices led the company to pioneer new marketing techniques, such as leasing agreements that brought its complex and expensive first-generation copiers into thousands of workplaces.

Xerox's commitment to values and their impact on people has served simultaneously as a source of strength and as a burden. One reason for the company's fall from grace since its heyday in the 1960s and 1970s can be traced to the complications of human relationships and bureaucratic politics within the firm. Morale and momentum in the ranks has suffered due to a longstanding schism between Xerox's East Coast heart and the innovative minds behind the Palo Alto Research Center. Reflecting the importance of harmonious working relationships to the "Fun to Do Good Work" persona, tensions have exacted a high toll, most famously in the failure of Rochester and Stamford-based executives to put a premium on marketing PARC products. However, Xerox has also demonstrated the capacity for teamwork and salesmanship noted in "Fun" organizations. This ability to get back on track and working for the common good has brought the company back from the brink of disaster more than once.

Xerox's preference for a flexible and spontaneous work environment is the final dimension of its "Fun to Do Good Work" perspective. During the lean years before the introduction of the revolutionary 914 Xerox copier, the company refused to allow market deadlines to derail its painstaking effort to produce the very best in duplicating technology. The ultimate success of that technology confirmed the wisdom of the "Fun" type's commitment to perceiving the ripe time for action.

"SEEING THE BIG PICTURE IN HUMAN TERMS"

Snapshot

- Makes decisions based on values and their impact on people
- Focuses on the big picture, relationships, and connections between facts
- Is energized by the outer world of people and activity
- Prefers a structured, organized, and planned environment

Imaginative and entrepreneurial, this organization likes variety and new challenges. Ideas and vision are discussed here more than in any other organizational type. This organization likes to look at the big picture, even while juggling lots of things at once.

Harmony and cooperation are very important to this organization. It likes to organize people so everyone can get along and have fun. It truly wants workers to have warm relationships with one another and customers. There is a risk that the organization may become overly controlling in an effort to force harmony on people who don't want to work together as closely or as warmly as expected.

This organization is the master of face-to-face communication. Gracious and congenial, it uses tact and diplomacy to persuade others, making it excellent at public presentations. A natural leader, full of enthusiasm and even zeal for its own ideas, it's able to sell its ideas and programs with entrepreneurial style and flair.

Characteristic Strengths

Builds beneficial and enduring relationships internally and in the marketplace

Big picture visionary; good at sensing trends

Creates a harmonious workplace that draws the best from people

Highly focused on completing projects and major initiatives

Projects a desirable image through contagious enthusiasm

Capitalizes on its ability to foster teamwork

Can construct meaning and opportunity out of ambiguity and complexity

Good instincts about customer needs and what motivates them

Exceptional communication skills

Capable of acting quickly

Anticipates needs and marshals resources effectively

Characteristic Weaknesses

May act prematurely

Not uncommon for feelings or instincts to overrule good business sense

May ignore a few high-priority tasks in the desire to complete many tasks

Prone to be too rigid to respond to changing situations and opportunities

Occasionally lacks details to communicate and implement vision

Could overly rely on intuition and fail to support decisions with critical analyses

May become distracted by people problems, forgetting the task at hand

Work Environment

Encourages and supports growth and development, often through mentoring and coaching

Mildly scheduled, disciplined, and controlled, yet flexible to motivate individual growth

People place, warm and friendly

Fast paced

Creative, imaginative

Considerable talking, listening, and brainstorming, often centered on predictions

High level of interaction; lots of meetings

Upbeat, full of positive reinforcements, sometimes emotional

Encourages teamwork in problem solving

Minimal office politics

Values

Relationships

Creativity

Structure

Teamwork

Uniqueness

Harmony

Integrity

Communication Style

Centers on people and the future

Focuses on completion, using timetables and schedules

Highly interactive

Prefers to give directives rather than information

Prefers face-to-face interaction

Language can be verbally creative, subjective, and evocative

In meetings, seeks connection with people first, expressing points of agreement

Begins presentations with the big picture, goals, and objectives

Conversations will cover a variety of topics, often jumping quickly in a stream-of-consciousness manner

Flowing, exaggerated, and often redundant

Thinks out loud, and the pace is rapid

Sources of Energy

Pursuing concepts and causes that can help humankind

Personal affirmation and appreciation

Developing and realizing human potential
Ideas, vision, and creativity
Engaging and serving people
Dedication to causes

Signs of Stress

Loses ability to connect with employees and clients
Leads without listening or taking account of personal needs
Harmony turns to hypersensitivity
Looks for faults rather than solutions

Behavior during Conflict

Ignores conflict as long as possible
Will check that corporate values have been clearly articulated and understood
Conflicts become internalized and taken personally, draining energy and enthusiasm

Approaches to Managing Change

Will ask if change is good for people and if everyone will benefit
If questions are adequately answered, will move quickly to plan, organize, and administer change

Ideal Clients

Want the certainty that projects will be completed on time
Share the company's values, especially those focused on people
Value enduring relationships
Require innovative thinking grounded in meeting customer needs
Produce a product or service that contributes to the benefit of all
Energized by personal contact and the collaborative exchange of ideas
Nonconfrontational
Like a friendly, relaxed atmosphere
Believe in and appreciate teamwork

Case Study

In Southwest Airlines, we find a clear expression of the "Seeing the Big Picture in Human Terms" mind-set. Like other extroverted organizations, Southwest is highly attuned to conditions in its industry and the nature of the competition. After all, discount service—the airline's primary contribution to its market—is predicated on the existence of a high-priced alternative.

Southwest is also the model of an organization with intuitive information-gathering preferences, focused on the big picture. The discount ticket itself was a brilliant and risky innovation that defied the popular wisdom of the prevailing price structure. In fact, the U.S. Department of Transportation has identified a "Southwest effect" in the markets that it serves: Within 12 months after Southwest starts service, the price of air travel drops dramatically, while rates of air travel tend to double.[3] This strength reflects the "Seeing the Big Picture" organization's ability to see opportunity in ambiguous situations and to promote breakthrough achievement with the enthusiasm of a born entertainer.

Companies with "Seeing the Big Picture in Human Terms" preferences tend to favor feelings and values over thinking and logic when making decisions. Southwest's commitment to people—especially its employees—is one of the most visible characteristics of the organization. In its 30 years of business, the airline has never once laid off employees in the interests of cutting costs, and relations with the various unions that represent its staff and crews are unusually warm.

The airline's effort to plan and control all the dimensions of its business is consistent with the "Seeing the Big Picture" preference for scheduling, order, and structure. Southwest's low fares and consistent profits depend on the careful management of costs. Setting the industry standard with its 10-minute turnaround time, the airline saves significantly on airport fees and the costs of maintaining additional aircraft.

"Seeing the Big Picture" companies value relationships, creativity, structure, teamwork, uniqueness, harmony, and integrity. That's a checklist of the qualities and commitments that have made Southwest Airlines a festive, even joyous work atmosphere. While some employees and customers may find the cultlike culture at Southwest a little cloying, informed business leaders will recognize it as a springboard to greatness. It's one of the qualities that effective Big Picture organizations can mobilize in their effort to provide a platform for all their constituents to achieve their best.

⑦ Profiles of Competence

We turn in this chapter to personalities that are linked to their emphasis on valuing competence and setting high standards. These are companies who relentlessly pursue perfection, are found constantly testing the status quo, and conceptualizing change. Clear, precise communication and solid strategic planning are the norm with companies who share this style.

"Going All Out For Greatness" companies have a strong sense of their mission and self-worth. "In Pursuit of Intellectual Solutions" companies emphasize logical analysis, and "If We Can't Do It, No One Can" companies see problem-solving as their reason for being. "Driven to Lead" companies are adept at mobilizing people.

"GOING ALL OUT FOR GREATNESS"

Snapshot

- Focuses on the big picture, relationships, and connections between facts
- Makes decisions using logic, analysis, and cause-and-effect reasoning
- Is energized by the inner world of ideas and experiences
- Prefers a structured, organized, and planned environment

This type of organization is pragmatic and strongly independent. It's the most self-confident of organizations, and it absolutely worships achievement. This organization believes that anything and everything can be improved, and it thrives on the challenge. This is the key to its identity, making it a classic learning organization.

It is innovative, incisive, and even visionary. This organization excels at intellectual or scientific ventures, often acting as a pioneer in its field. It may focus on strategic planning and research, with most improvements concentrating on systems and ideas. Innovation is usually rooted in rational, intellectual logic.

Organizations with these characteristics see opportunities others don't. They are at their best when they can capitalize on new possibilities. They prefer to initiate change, and they detest change that is forced on them.

Strategy is a real strength for this organization. It will often enjoy the creative solution process more than the detail work that is necessary to make it all come together. There is often more interest in understanding things than in making things.

These types of organizations have very high standards for themselves and their employees. They expect the staff to multitask and to quickly understand what is expected and needed. People skills are usually lacking in an organization such as this, which makes its decisions based on facts, with little regard as to how they will impact people. The organization may not realize how its actions are affecting its employees' reactions, especially if they react with strong feelings. ("Isn't he overreacting?") It may also send employees mixed messages, where "Do what you think is best" could be translated into "Do it right or else—by this afternoon."

Speed is the operative word at this organization. This can be a strength, but it can also be a weakness because the employees may feel rushed and unappreciated.

Characteristic Strengths

Effectively combines big-picture vision and its parts (organization, theory, product)
Skilled at developing strategies to achieve long-term, visionary goals
Produces innovative, pioneering ideas and systems
Develops and capitalizes on its ever expanding knowledge base
Efficient
Able to clarify complex issues
Good at spotting trends and opportunities others miss
Avoids unforced errors by thinking before acting
Challenged by ambiguous problems
Constantly improving
Not distracted by emotional issues

Characteristic Weaknesses

May be overly conceptual and lose grasp of reality
Occasionally interprets thinking as action
Frequently has difficulty juggling multiple priorities

Ignores people management issues and individual needs

May need help translating concepts into action

At times, ignores the present for the future

Tendency to become complacent without complex challenges

Occasionally overly relies on logic and ignores or distrusts instincts

Can become immobilized with possibilities

May need help with short-term details

On occasion, can ignore the benefits of process, teamwork, and collaboration

Too rigid to respond to changing situations and opportunities

Work Environment

Quiet, efficient, fast-paced think tank

Very few meetings or team-building exercises

Clearly defined system and procedures

A place to acquire knowledge and competency, always open to discovery

Constant reminders of achievement and progress toward goals

Considerable thinking and theorizing

Private, contained, impersonal

Calm, cool, but may get intense and argumentative at times

Highly planned through schedules and agendas

Decisions made quietly and without much collaboration

Values

Learning

Logic

Innovation

Achievement

Competence

Independence

Pragmatism

Uniqueness

What could be

Communication Style

Centered on possibilities and logical improvements

Frequently terse and filled with goals and strategies, problems to be solved, possibilities

Prefers to give directions and structure rather than information

In meetings, seeks connection with the task first

Begins presentations with the big picture first

Logical, with cause-and-effect reasoning

Prefers writing and e-mail
Frequently conceptual; may seem arrogant
Contained, thoughtful, and reflective
Comments have already been thought through

Sources of Energy

Developing theories and vision
Solving complex and intellectually challenging problems
Constant learning and acquiring knowledge
Search for efficiency
Innovation

Signs of Stress

Loses objectivity
Becomes excessively pessimistic
Overwhelmed by fear of failure, resulting in too many plans and too
little action

Behavior during Conflict

Avoids emotional conflicts, but enjoys intense debate
Ensures that guiding vision and principles are clearly represented
Prefers to solve conflict with cool logic and reason
Becomes defensive and uses logical reasoning as a weapon

Approaches to Managing Change

Change is driven by the vision of the future and the joy of creating
something new
Will consult its internal data sources (data, experience, vision)
Will allow time to reflect and analyze
Thought will precede action
If the analysis is consistent with vision for the future, will move quickly
to implement the change

Ideal Clients

Seek visionary solutions to complex, ambiguous, and long-term
problems
Prefer to work independently rather than collaboratively
Appreciate a cool, logical, and detached approach
Value knowledge and the learning process
Value intellectual approach, competency, and zest for visioning possi-
bilities

Desire to clarify a complex market or industry change that is unprecedented and defies analysis

Enjoy debating, challenging, and questioning ideas and theories

Case Study

Nike Inc., the Beaverton, Oregon–based athletic company, provides a striking example of the "Going All Out for Greatness" personality.

Nike's introverted organizational focus can be seen in its ongoing effort to serve niche markets. What began as a direct appeal
from enterprising runners to other track-and-field types has
evolved into a company determined to serve the needs of athletes
as diverse as skateboarders and ballet dancers. The influence of
Nike's inwardness is also apparent in the company's celebration of
individual athletic achievers in its marketing and advertising campaigns, a tradition going back to the Olympic trials of 1972. As
individuals, athletes such as Mia Hamm and Michael Jordan provide examples of what the masses can aspire to with inspiration,
perspiration, and Nike gear.

"Just Do It," the well-known Nike slogan, encapsulates the
decisiveness and self-confidence of the intuitive type. With its
appreciation of the big picture, the fledgling company ventured
fearlessly into the uncharted market for athletic shoes in the
1970s, and Nike leadership pioneered new markets and techniques in subsequent decades. Part of the secret of Nike's success
has been constant innovation in performance and design. The
company's reliance on intuition pushes Nike shoes and gear to the
cutting edge of fashion and technology.

Nike has shown ample evidence of its reliance on logic, analysis,
and cause-and-effect reasoning in corporate decision making. In
particular, the thinking tendency manifests itself in Nike's manufacturing arrangements, which rely almost entirely on independent
contractors in factories around the world in order to accrue the
lowest possible costs for labor and overhead. It's only logical to
keep costs as low as possible, and Nike has been able to justify its
reliance on underpaid workers. In the face of rising protests among
Nike consumers against sweatshop practices, however, the company also used its thinking preferences to analyze the effects of a
fair labor boycott. Its efforts to ensure better working conditions
and pay for Nike subcontractors in recent years have confirmed its
rational, no-nonsense sensibility about suppliers and demand.

A second interpretation of the Just Do It maxim illustrates Nike's preference for a structured, organized, and planned work environment. Nike has proven its ability to stick with its program even in the face of opposition or obstacles. For example, the company defended its Air Jordan basketball shoe against the NBA's insistence that it had too much color, even when the league threatened to ban Nike's fledgling superstar rep from the game. The judging preference for planning and order has also created support for an innovative financing and production schedule that requires retailers to commit to "futures" of Nike product lines in advance of delivery dates. The result frees up capital for research and development—but only so long as Nike can ensure that it consistently fulfills its scheduled obligations.

"IN PURSUIT OF INTELLECTUAL SOLUTIONS"

Snapshot

- Makes decisions using logic, analysis, and cause-and-effect reasoning
- Focuses on the big picture, relationships, and connections between facts
- Is energized by the inner world of ideas and experiences
- Prefers a flexible, spontaneous, and changing environment

If you're looking for a company to create a new system or design or to understand and solve a complex problem, this type of organization is the perfect choice. Just don't expect the organization to follow through, especially if doing so requires a lot of routine work. Led by intellectual curiosity, this company simply enjoys analyzing any situation and looking for the logic behind it.

Complex, intellectual challenges intrigue and stimulate the organization. Analytical and pensive, it applies profound insight and intense concentration to every problem. Half-way is not good enough, and it will doggedly manipulate and explore every aspect of an idea until it completely understands the idea. Sometimes this is a negative thing because the organization won't let go of an idea, even if it proves unworkable.

Outsiders, clients, and even some employees may feel locked out. Private and somewhat mysterious, this organization has a loner quality about it. Communication with other organizations, clients, and employees is not a priority. Ideas are the important things, not personal communication or feelings.

Employees who do not like debate or who are offended by criticism may have a hard time working here. Combine poor communication skills with the fact that it's an idea place, not a people place, and, you get an environment where people may feel unappreciated or attacked.

Hunches and intuition lead the way, not policies and procedures. Practicality is not valued, so the workplace tends to be rather disorganized and sometimes chaotic. Although this organization is wonderful at long-range thinking and planning, the short term frustrates and stymies it.

Intellect and ideas are highly valued, and debate is a common means of communication. Debate and the criticism that goes with it are expected to be tolerated and even enjoyed. It's seen as just part of looking for answers and considering every possibility that might exist.

Characteristic Strengths

Strategic visionary with a firm grasp of the principles necessary for success
Able to clarify complex issues
Tenacious competitor when it comes to achieving destiny
Good at spotting trends and possibilities that others miss
Effectively combines big-picture vision with its parts (organization, theory, product)
Develops and capitalizes on its extensive knowledge base
Skilled at long-range planning, strategy, and problem solving
Constantly improving
Avoids unforced errors by thinking before acting

Characteristic Weaknesses

Love of learning may interfere with the necessity for action
Can set standards and expectations too high
Often ignores people management issues
May not drop unproductive ideas soon enough
Has difficulty translating concepts into action
May create problems where none exist
Could become complacent without complex challenges
May need help with short-term details and follow-through
On occasion, can ignore the benefits of process, teamwork, and collaboration

Work Environment

Acquires knowledge and competency; open to discovery
Calm, cool, but may get intense and argumentative at times
Frequently filled with debate and critical questioning
Prefers to make individual contributions
Casual, loosely structured
Private, contained, impersonal
Decisions are made quietly and without much collaboration
Disorganized and sometimes chaotic
Formal procedures often dismissed as too conventional or trivial

Values

Learning
Logic
Curiosity
Achievement
Creativity
Independence

Communication Style

Centers on patterns and principles
Language may be highly technical, complex, and detailed
Terse and filled with strategies and possibilities
Precise
Prefers to give information rather than directives
Brief and concise, often using graphics to aid comprehension
Fair, impartial, impersonal
In meetings, seeks connection with the task first
Begins presentations with the big picture first
Prefers writing and e-mail
Contained, thoughtful, and reflective

Sources of Energy

Developing theories and vision
Solving complex and intellectually challenging problems
Search for efficiency
Achievement, change, and constant improvement

Signs of Stress

Loses objectivity
Exposes raw emotions explosively
Becomes overly sensitive

Consumed by desire to achieve a goal
Overwhelmed by ambiguity
Stuck by fear of failure

Behavior during Conflict

Prefers to avoid conflict
Tenacious in defending the product of its valued thinking
Will ensure that guiding vision and principles are clear
Expects conflict to be resolved by logic and reason

Approaches to Managing Change

Change is driven by vision of the future and the joy of creation
Seeks to gather information about the change
Will evaluate information on the basis of its values or by logical analysis
Will allow time to reflect, analyze, and relate to historical frameworks
Change will come when justified by reason and logic
If the change is acceptable, will move forward on its own timetable
Will resist tenaciously any threat to its envisioned destiny

Ideal Clients

Need to create a new system or design, or to understand and solve a complex problem
Enjoy debating, challenging, and questioning ideas and theories
Value knowledge and the learning process
Appreciate a cool, logical, and detached approach
Value intellectual approach, competency, and zest for envisioning possibilities

Case Study

KFC Corporation, purveyor of Kentucky Fried Chicken, fits the model of the "In Pursuit of Intellectual Solutions" company—an introverted, intuitive, thinking, perceiving organization. KFC's introverted organizational focus is visible in the company's long-standing commitment to promoting individual upward mobility, a drive that can trace its origins to the ambition of the company's founder, Colonel Harland Sanders of Corbin, Kentucky. Like Colonel Sanders, who went into the business at age 65 as a means to supplement his Social Security check, owners of KFC franchises are the operational and emotional engines of the organization. Corporate culture at KFC celebrates the restaurant general manager, whose advancement as an individual earner and small business owner embodies the KFC promise. The ideas and experiences of this cadre of managers provide the restaurant chain's primary source of energy and success.

KFC shares with other "In Pursuit of Intellectual Solutions" organizations an ability to grasp the big picture, relationships, and connections between facts. At KFC, this intuitive knack is symbolized by the honored place of Colonel Sanders's Original Recipe for cooking chicken. Any cook could add 11 herbs and spices to batter to improve results, but at KFC the top secret combination of ingredients and cooking methods has made the difference for more than 50 years. The restaurant chain has continued to experiment with innovative culinary, marketing, and customer relations strategies. The most recent example of this intellectual quest—a move toward networked kitchen appliances whose use and maintenance can be monitored from corporate headquarters—confirms the company's visionary tinkering credentials.[1]

For all the human compassion evoked by the character of Colonel Sanders, who still dominates KFC marketing more than 20 years after his death, the company responds better to logic and analysis than to considerations driven by feelings. Like other "In Pursuit of Intellectual Solutions" organizations, KFC is committed to open debate, criticism, and impartial standards. A second recent example of KFC tinkering explores the potential of fingerprint technology for taking customer orders and payment—a far cry from the friendly, personalized service advertised by competing fast food chains.[2] Similarly, a statistical monitoring system calculates hard numbers about human errors in restaurants where workers compensation claims tend to run high.[3]

In its preference for a flexible, spontaneous, and changing environment, KFC completes the profile of the "In Pursuit of Intellectual Solutions" organization. The franchise system itself, pioneered in its first generation by Kentucky Fried Chicken and McDonald's in the 1960s, epitomizes the opportunistic bent of this kind of company. Sharing risk with enterprising individuals and taking advantage of demographic changes, the KFC franchise has grown when and where the market seems promising, and has trimmed operations as profitability lagged. In the twenty-first century, this kind of responsiveness has allowed KFC to lead U.S. chains in the exploration of overseas markets, where the Kentucky-based organization represents the American way as well as American food.

"IF WE CAN'T DO IT, NO ONE CAN"

Snapshot

- Focuses on the big picture, relationships, and connections between facts
- Makes decisions using logic, analysis, and cause-and-effect reasoning
- Is energized by the outer world of people and activity
- Prefers a flexible, spontaneous, and changing environment

Problem solving is at the heart of this organization. To see it at its very best, just throw a difficult problem or challenge its way and let it work its magic. Here, difficulties actually stimulate ideas and creativity. This organization will tackle even the most challenging projects—those that other companies might not touch. It's a master of innovation.

New and exciting challenges, and what can be done in the future, are much more exciting to the company than what's in the here and now; therefore, the work required to turn solutions into products or services isn't the company's strong suit. It may be chomping at the bit to move on to the next project and miss the opportunities it could capitalize on from the problem that's just been solved.

The energetic and exciting environment is ideal for those who like to work quickly and take risks. Unfortunately, those who work in a slow and calculated manner aren't tolerated very well.

Since everything is open to new possibilities, formal procedures and structures don't get much serious attention here. Everything is seen as open to change and reform, and, as a result, the practical side of the business can be disorganized and chaotic. Organizational, communication, and people management problems can lead to underachievement, and this organization may never reach its full potential without addressing those issues.

Exciting and stimulating, the company radiates a contagious enthusiasm for its ideas. A "we can do it" approach inspires confidence externally and internally. Optimism is a watchword. There's always another approach if something fails—try, try again.

Closure is difficult because there are always more possibilities to try. This also leads to constant debate. Discussion, inquiry, criticism, and challenges are all part of the game, and you had better learn how to play it if you want to fit in. There's a take-no-prisoners style that tends to be insensitive to those who get hurt in the sometimes contentious environment. Everyone is expected to quickly digest information and to become an active part of the ongoing debate.

Characteristic Strengths

Master of innovation, creating visionary products and services
Accepts challenges others won't touch
Able to capitalize on last-minute developments and opportunities
Skilled at long-range planning, strategy, and problem solving
Focused on constant improvement and fast solutions
Able to see possibilities that others miss
Always in command
Adept at mobilizing people
Able to clarify complex situations
Not distracted by emotional issues
Knows where it wants to go

Characteristic Weaknesses

Tendency to be weak at implementation
Often ignores people management issues and individual needs
Tendency to drop current projects
Juggles many balls and may drop some
May not convert all intellectual achievements into business successes
Can get bored with routine activities
So quick to move, may overlook important details
Occasionally lacks details to implement vision
May lack adequate systems and procedures to keep pace with rapid rate of change
Prone to lose interest or energy once the intellectual challenge disappears
May not always acquire knowledge for practical application

Work Environment

Resonates with energy and excitement
Radiates enthusiasm for ideas and theories
Fast paced
Minimal bureaucracy and structure
Change is welcomed
Filled with confidence and optimism
Spontaneous and improvisational
Risk-taking setting
Competitive

Contentious and often insensitive, may seem cold and distant
Casual, loosely structured
Meetings often include debate

Values

Intelligence
Creativity
Improvisation
Innovation
Logic
Learning
Efficiency
Excellence
Risk taking

Communication Style

Centered on ideas and the future
Often terse and filled with goals, strategies, and problems to be solved
Frequently involves discussion, inquiry, and criticism
Meetings feature lots of debate and "what if" games
Everyone is expected to become an active part of the ongoing debate
Prefers to give information rather than directives
Speech is energetic, precise, and may be colorful
In meetings, seeks to connect with the task first
Begins presentations with the big picture, goals, and objectives
Uses logical, cause-and-effect reasoning
Conversations will cover a variety of topics, often jumping quickly in
    a stream-of-consciousness manner

Sources of Energy

Developing theories and acquiring knowledge
Solving complex and intellectually challenging problems
Invention and improvisation
Change
Achievement
Innovation

Signs of Stress

Loses its sense of competence and confidence
Overwhelmed with possibilities
Obsessed with unimportant details
Preoccupied with irrelevant facts
Can't break problems into component parts

Behavior during Conflict

Will engage in lively exchanges, but prefers to avoid emotionalism

Will proceed based on guiding vision and principles

Will attempt to resolve conflict logically and rationally

May be seen as stubborn and arrogant

Approaches to Managing Change

Change is driven by the love of change and will have an innovative aspect

Will seek information and advice from all sources

Change must be logical and fit into a long-range vision

If the change honors the creative and action orientation, will try to persuade everyone to change

Ideal Clients

Value intellectual approach, competency, and zest for envisioning possibilities

Attracted to ability to do the impossible

Need a take-charge company to provide long-term vision

Require breakthrough concepts

Need a simple solution to a complex problem

Welcome a rational and objective perspective on sensitive issues

Case Study

Among participants in Companies Are People, Too workshops, two successful organizations have been identified as "If We Can't Do It, No One Can" organizations: the Museum of Science and Industry in Chicago and a similar institution, Heureka, in Finland. For our case study, however, we're going to look at a more popular company: Atari Corporation, the computer games pioneer that has been recently resurrected as a division of the French company Infogrames. Atari's outward-looking organizational focus is evident in the interactive nature of its products. The extroverted tendency of the company also helped it to create a community of Atari enthusiasts who have remained committed to the company through thick and thin.

Like many technology-based companies, Atari has demonstrated its ability to see the big picture. Atari founder Nolan Bushnell made the improbable intellectual connection between the capacities of high-tech Defense Department computer systems and computer-simulated action appropriate for games. No kind of market testing or research could have predicted the incredible success of Pong, a computer version of tennis, which was Atari's first commercial product.

Companies with the "If We Can't Do It, No One Can" profile prefer to use logic, analysis, and cause-and-effect reasoning when making decisions. This tendency toward thinking rather than feeling—in combination with Atari's perceiving work style—means that employees are empowered to take risks and compete with one another. At times during the company's heyday in the 1970s and early 1980s, this competitive atmosphere created tensions in the workplace. One the whole, however, the "If We Can't Do It, No One Can" spirit creates a stimulating and fast-moving work environment.

Atari got its break by moving quickly to market with whimsical adaptations of hard science. This ability to recognize an opportunity and act on it is characteristic of companies with a perceiving work style preference. Atari has consistently favored allowing computer game projects to develop at their own pace of weeks, months, or years. Organizations with this outlook rarely get tied down to schedules, rules, and procedures. If we can't do it on our on terms, participants might say, we'd prefer not to do it at all. Accordingly, the "If We Can't Do It, No One Can" personality steers clear of rules and regulations and gives employees free reign to experiment and conquer on their own terms.

"DRIVEN TO LEAD"

Snapshot

- Makes decisions using logic, analysis, and cause-and-effect reasoning
- Focuses on the big picture, relationships, and connections between facts
- Is energized by the outer world of people and activity
- Prefers a structured, organized, and planned environment

This organization wants to be in charge, directing its staff, vendors, customers, and, with any luck, its industry. It can be very visionary, able to see what should be done and to move quickly to do it. This organization is at its most inspired and energized when it is creating plans, developing prototypes, and designing strategies.

This type of organization is all about boldness. It has willpower and imagination. Inventive and intuitive, it tends to be quite curious, a place where questions are encouraged. The organization tends to think logically, with a strong respect for what the data reveals. At the same time, it respects its own gut feelings. This gives it good antennae for discovering upcoming opportunities in the industry.

What's more, this organization is often good at communications, so it can share its vision with others. Yet, it may think that some things are obvious, not bothering to explain them. This can result in the organization running too far ahead of its own customers or clients.

This kind of company loves good ideas, its own and others'. It can recognize a good idea, build enthusiasm for it, and work to turn it into reality. This makes it a natural to pioneer in new areas and to design ingenious programs and products.

This organization can be better at ideas and strategy than at tactics and implementation for one key reason: its people skills. This organization can be about as warm and cozy as a bulldozer. Only a section of the population is willing to work for or with an organization that commands—and demands—respect without seeming to return the favor. As a consequence, turnover tends to be high. Whenever plans go awry, it is often due to miscalculations regarding the human element in the equation.

If the organization can overcome its natural problems with understanding people, allowing it to plan more realistically, it can succeed in any arena. It has its best chances in industries that need a cool, detached, and logical approach.

This organization tends to develop and implement smooth systems. Inefficiency, ineffectiveness, and confusion are the enemy. It works within its own standard procedures as long as they are working. Procedures that do not produce the desired results get an overhaul.

This organization tends to remember and honor its commitments. It believes in its own integrity. This makes it willing to stand on principle, no matter what the consequences.

Characteristic Strengths

Always in command with a take-charge, decisive manner
Highly focused on competing tasks and major initiatives
Able to see possibilities that others miss—visionary
Can decide quickly
Skilled at long-range planning, strategy, and problem solving
Pioneers in the development of new products, services, and markets
Focused on constant improvement

Brings resources and people together effectively
Good at communication
Results oriented
Not distracted by emotional issues
Values its intellectual approach, competency, and zest for visioning possibilities

Characteristic Weaknesses

Tendency to decide too quickly, leaving too little time for reflection
Often ignores people management issues and individual needs
May be overly conceptual and lose grasp of reality
Can get bored with routine activities and leave them unattended
May occasionally supply few details for follow-through
At times, ignores the present for the future
Prone to be too rigid to respond to changing situations and opportunities
May not always acquire knowledge for practical application

Work Environment

Calm, cool; perhaps even cold and detached
Has a controlled intensity, often the result of impatience
Well organized
Change is constant
Lively debates are enjoyed and questioning is encouraged
Frequent communications—meetings, phone calls, e-mail, and written communication
Competitive
Purposeful and focused

Values

Intelligence
Logic
Efficiency
Excellence
Learning
Instinct
Innovation

Communication Style

Centered on organization and improvement
Frequently terse and filled with goals, strategies, and problems to be solved

Prefers to give directives and structure rather than information

Speech is energetic, precise, and may be colorful

Conversations often include the question "Why?"

Seeks to get to the point as quickly as possible

In meetings, seeks connection with the task first

Begins presentations with the big picture, goals, and objectives

Uses logical, cause-and-effect reasoning

Avoids emotional issues but is passionate in debates

Sources of Energy

Developing theories and vision

Solving complex problems

Constant learning and acquiring knowledge

Attaining higher and higher levels of competency

Innovation

Signs of Stress

Loses objectivity

Explosively exposes raw emotions

Becomes overly sensitive

Becomes overwhelmed by fear of failure

Behavior during Conflict

Will engage in lively exchanges, but prefers to avoid emotionalism

Will proceed based on guiding vision and principles

Will attempt to resolve conflict logically and rationally

When confronted will seldom back down

May be seen as stubborn and arrogant

Approaches to Managing Change

Prefers continuity and stability, maintaining what is

Change is driven by the love of change

Will engage in critical questioning

If questions are adequately answered, will move quickly to plan, organize, and administer the change

Ideal Clients

Appreciate a cool, logical, and detached approach

Provide long-term vision and plans

Desire to clarify a complex market or industry change that is unprecedented and defies analysis

Need to move quickly and decisively to harness resources and people

Require breakthrough concepts
Enjoy debating, challenging, and questioning ideas and theories

Case Study

America Online, the lead component of AOL Time Warner during
the merger of the two giant media firms in 2001 and afterward, provides a classic illustration of the decisiveness of the Driven to Lead
type. Despite widespread fears that technology stocks, including its
own, were overvalued, AOL managed to transform its high price
into hard currency with the purchase of Time Warner shares at bar-
gain rates, and moved quickly to take over top management posi-
tions. In 2002, as AOL executives took the heat for the downward
spiral of the stock, the AOL division of the conglomerate also
demonstrated vividly another earmark of this kind of organization:
high turnover, stemming in part from grave miscalculations of Time
Warner's human responses to all the swashbuckling.

The personality preferences at work in the "Driven to Lead"
profile demonstrate the wellsprings of AOL's business vigor. The
company sees itself as deeply integrated into the AOL community
of national and international network of Internet users. In other
words, it takes its energy from the outer world of people and activity, even though this exchange and engagement take place in a
solitary medium. But, for all the hype about community, there is
little of the family feeling among "Driven to Lead" organizations.

Also strongly at work in the "Driven to Lead" organization is
the influence of its intuitive side. Like many intuitive organizations, the AOL division aspires not only to pioneer new territory
but also to uncover secrets capable of transforming the way people
live. The AOL vision is for the power of technology to enrich and
unite the human experience.

Companies with this personality preference bring a brass-
knuckles sensibility to the workplace; at AOL Time Warner, for
example, AOL types openly flaunted the quick cash they took
from the merger and mocked their Time Warner counterparts as a
species of dinosaur. The inevitable backlash has typified the
"Driven to Lead" persona's tendency toward recurrent personnel
problems.

In matters of rhythm and work styles, "Driven to Lead" organizations tend to strike an effective balance between order and oppor-
tunism. Though it favors structure, organization, and planning in the
work environment, a company like AOL is analytical and alert enough

to act decisively at a critical juncture. This preference also underwrites AOL's considerable mastery of the intricacies of scheduling. Like other "Driven to Lead" shops, AOL tends to implement effective and efficient operating systems. This kind of talent may bode well for the larger project of integrating AOL Time Warner's sprawling capabilities toward collective goals. If multimedia synergy is capable of taking communication to a new plateau of connectivity, the AOL division is driven to lead the company toward that achievement.

Now that you've discovered your company's personality, the final chapters of this section are devoted to revealing your personal leadership style. In the next parts of the book, "Articulate" and "Live," we'll marry all of these concepts and show you how to align the personalities that comprise your company.

⑧ Discover Your Leadership Personality

LEADERSHIP: IT'S NOT JUST ABOUT YOU

In the aftermath of the boom-and-bust stock market of the turn of the twenty-first century, businesses in the United States have reevaluated the high price of top-gun talent in the executive ranks. The abuse of stock options, insider information, and personal loans by rogue corporate officers—to say nothing of multi-million-dollar compensation packages uncoupled from performance standards—has cast the harsh light of scandal on the previously venerated position of the CEO. While the nation's most respected business leaders have emerged from the ordeal with reputations intact, a veil of mistrust has separated the boardroom from shareholders and the general public. Critics have denounced what some call the talent myth, calling into question the wisdom of investing great power and privilege in the careers of the corporate elite.[1] Can leaders be trusted to guide and protect an organization? Or are they more likely to give their own interests first priority?

The Great Executive Ego Audit of the twenty-first century has provided a healthy corrective to the somewhat irrational exuberance about corporate leadership during the boom years. But public scrutiny of boardroom shenanigans has also served to underscore the fundamental importance of integrity and stewardship in corporate management. Today's organizations recognize the need for managers who can distinguish between their needs as individuals and their responsibilities as professionals.

Understanding companies as people can help leaders tell the difference between their personal goals and the interests of the organization. And it goes beyond integrity and accountability! Understanding personality allows corporate leaders to recognize the way preferences and choices work to organize the workplace. If they accept the organization as an independent personality, managers can recognize the influence of personality preferences in a range of important choices. Rather than leading from their (default) preferences, they can lead the company according to its preferences and values. By focusing on the company as a living entity, leaders of organizations can step out of the spotlight in order to illuminate the enterprise as a whole.

If you're the leader of an organization, team, or division, you might be excused for thinking the company revolves around you and your strengths and weaknesses. There are healthy consequences that can result from this kind of thinking. After all, if you feel like you carry the world on your shoulders, you are much more likely to work hard to shoulder its weight. Your example of commitment and pride may serve to inspire your employees and coworkers. If you take it personally when the company fails, you are likely to exert tremendous energy on behalf of helping it win.

But your business is not just about you, and, except for the weakest cases, your effort is not the only thing that sustains it. The idea behind *Companies Are People, Too* is that organizations have a life of their own and that individual employees in an organization are participants in an enterprise greater than the sum of its parts. When you think of the company as a living entity, you can see the way your job fits into the complex networks of activity that power the corporate body. When it's not about you, you can more easily recognize what's necessary to keep the corporation alive and thriving.

With this proviso, we're about to introduce you to a dimension of the Companies Are People, Too method that *is* about you. In Figure 8.1, you'll find a CAP2 questionnaire designed to uncover the personality preferences of leaders in organizations. If you complete it, you'll find a CAP2 mini-profile that tells you more about your own personality type. And for those who already know about their type from the Myers-Briggs Type Indicator or another diagnostic, we've included the four-letter designations that correspond to each CAP2 profile. Personality profiles for individuals offer insight into the dynamic interaction between leaders and the corporate persona, and showcase the diversity of work styles within the organization. Individual personality type analysis is the subject of many books, articles, newsletters, and Web sites.[3] For now, we hope you'll use what you learn about yourself to better adapt your work to the preferences of the organization. Recognizing differences—and even polar oppositions—in work style preferences can help you to understand and overcome the frustration of trying to force your will on a noncompliant system. When they lead according to the organization's preferences instead of their own, managers instinctively put the interests of the organization at the top of the list. This kind of understanding can be the wellspring of integrity and effective leadership.

HOW TO DETERMINE YOUR LEADERSHIP STYLE

In the questionnaire that follows, complete the following questions about the four dimensions of personality: focus of energy, information gathering, decision making, and work style. If you find some of the questions difficult to answer, try to think about which choice seems more natural. Focus on the way you usually feel about things, the kinds of choices you would make if you were sure no one was looking. As you can see, we're asking you to choose between polar opposites, one side represented by the letter A and the other by the letter B. At the end of each of the four sections of the questionnaire, you will add up the number of answers in each column to calculate your score. Those of you familiar with the type may recognize our A and B columns as representative of one of the letter categories associated with the eight preferences in the four dimensions: extroverted (E) or introverted (I) preferences for focus of energy; sensing (S) or intuitive (N) for information-gathering preferences; thinking (T) or feeling (F) for decision-making preferences; and judging (J) or perceiving (P) for work style. We use numbers to indicate the same division. When you complete the questionnaire, you will use the numbers from each of the four sections to determine your results. In the final component of the diagnostic, you will consult your CAP2 Leadership Profile to learn more about your personality preferences as a leader. For comparative purposes, we've included the four-letter designations that correspond to each of our CAP2 Leadership Profiles, so that if you already know about your preferences, you can identify your CAP2 counterpart. Special thanks to Henry L. Thompson, PhD, president and CEO of High Performing Systems, Inc., for preparing the Leadership Profiles for this book.

Circle A or B

Focus of Energy

You would rather have:
A. lots of friends, seeing each one less often
B. a small circle of friends you see often

Your telephone conversations tend to:
A. stretch out longer than necessary
B. be as short as possible

Among a group, you:
A. start talking first
B. wait for someone to talk to you

When you have something important to say, you:
A. just start the conversation
B. practice what you want to say

Being the center of attention is:
A. wonderful
B. rather unpleasant

At gatherings, you often:
A. stay late
B. leave early

You prefer to communicate with coworkers:
A. in person or over the telephone
B. by memo, letter, or e-mail

You tend to:
A. introduce your friends and associates to each other
B. think "networking" is unimportant

Total number of As circled: _____
Total number of Bs circled: _____

If As are the highest number, write #1 below.
If Bs are the highest number, write #2 below.

Focus of energy: _____ (#1 or #2)

Circle A or B

Information Gathering

You have more fun:
A. doing hands-on work
B. daydreaming

You prefer to read:
A. practical how-to books
B. lyrical prose

You most appreciate your:
A. practical common sense
B. rich imagination

You are more interested in:
A. the basics of a situation
B. the nuances of a situation

You are more interested in:
A. a specific case
B. a general trend

You tend to be:
A. more pragmatic than innovative
B. more innovative than pragmatic

FIGURE 8.1   CAP2 Questionnaire.

You prefer to work with:
A. extensive facts
B. reasonable suppositions

You would prefer to:
A. produce goods and services
B. do research and development

You tend to be more:
A. down to earth
B. visionary

You like:
A. accurate information
B. intriguing conjecture

You would tend to trust more:
A. common sense
B. a gut feeling

You wish you had more time:
A. to do practical work
B. to daydream

You tend to pay more attention to:
A. what a person said
B. what a person meant

You prefer to work with:
A. data
B. concepts

You like to work with:
A. details
B. theories

You prefer writers who:
A. write exactly what they mean
B. express ideas creatively

You are:
A. more practical than imaginative
B. more imaginative than practical

You are more interested in:
A. what actually is
B. what could be

You see yourself as a:
A. realist
B. philosopher

You tend to do things:
A. the traditional way
B. in a unique way

You would be more interested in:
A. a sensible, cost-effective idea
B. an ingenious idea with possibilities

Total number of As circled: _____
Total number of Bs circled: _____

If As are the highest number, write #3 below.
If Bs are the highest number, write #4 below.

Information gathering: _____ (#3 or #4)

(continued)

Circle A or B

Decision Making

You prefer to be known for your:
A. just decisions
B. compassion

You tend to:
A. impartially uphold the rules
B. make exceptions to the rules

When forming opinions about people, you:
A. try to be completely objective
B. give them the benefit of the doubt

It is more important to have:
A. clear thinking
B. good will

It is more important to:
A. see things clearly
B. feel things deeply

You tend to be more:
A. dispassionate
B. understanding

You are more comfortable when you:
A. are totally objective
B. feel personally involved

You most appreciate your ability to be:
A. firm
B. affectionate

You feel the most satisfaction when you:
A. reach a firm agreement
B. discuss an issue in detail

Your actions tend to be governed by:
A. what you think
B. how you feel

You tend to:
A. stand firm for what you believe
B. see both sides of an argument

It is easier for you to verbally:
A. criticize someone's work
B. appreciate someone's work

You tend to have:
A. a cool head
B. a warm nature

It is more important to:
A. achieve justice
B. show mercy

You are naturally:
A. objective
B. caring

In forming an opinion, you are more:
A. impartial
B. emotional

It's easier for you to:
A. treat people fairly
B. be pleasant to people

Your first conversations with a person tend to be:
A. more impersonal
B. more personal

It is better to be:
A. fair
B. kind

You are more:
A. detached
B. sympathetic

You are more likely to:
A. ask a lot of questions about a situation
B. go along with what other people want

Total number of As circled: _____
Total number of Bs circled: _____

If As are the highest number, write #5 below.
If Bs are the highest number, write #6 below.

Decision making: _____ (#5 or #6)

Circle A or B

Work Style

You prefer gatherings that are:
A. scheduled
B. spontaneous

You tend to be:
A. more cautious than easygoing
B. more easygoing than cautious

You often:
A. plan which events to attend
B. attend events on the spur of the moment

You tend to:
A. do what you've planned
B. do what you feel like

You would rather:
A. be in control
B. go with the flow

You like to:
A. make decisions
B. put off decisions

You feel more comfortable with:
A. final decisions
B. lots of options

You feel better:
A. after you've made a decision
B. before you've made a decision

Your telephone conversations tend to:
A. stretch out longer than necessary
B. be as short as possible

(continued)

You keep a schedule and a to-do list:
A. as much as possible
B. as little as possible

You prefer a room to:
A. have everything in its place
B. look a little lived in

You are more proud of your:
A. organizational skills
B. adaptability

You value:
A. structure
B. flexibility

You feel more comfortable:
A. planning a meeting
B. putting off a meeting

You feel more comfortable when:
A. all the decisions are made
B. you have options to select

A detailed schedule for the weekend makes you:
A. feel more relaxed
B. feel unhappy

You are:
A. generally on time
B. often late

An approaching deadline tends to:
A. make you tense and uncomfortable
B. give you a burst of energy

You:
A. prefer to have deadlines
B. resent deadlines

You are more likely to:
A. follow your action plan
B. follow your impulses

When you undertake a project, you tend to:
A. make a step-by-step plan at the beginning
B. believe that the best thing to do next will be evident as you proceed

Total number of As circled: _____
Total number of Bs circled: _____

If As are the highest number, write #7 below.
If Bs are the highest number, write #8 below.

Work style: _____ (#7 or #8)

Determine the Results

From each of the four preceding sections, record your chosen number from the bottom of the column.

_____	_____	_____	_____
Organizational focus (1 or 2)	Information gathering (3 or 4)	Decision making (5 or 6)	Work style (7 or 8)

The four-digit number corresponds with one of the 16 leadership personalities described on pages 116 through 120.

1357 = The Controller
1358 = The Troubleshooter
1367 = The Harmonizer
1368 = The Coach
1457 = The General
1458 = The Entrepreneur
1467 = The Catalyst
1468 = The Explorer
2357 = The Organizer
2358 = The Risk Taker
2367 = The Traditionalist
2368 = The Mobilizer
2458 = The Architect
2459 = The Systems Builder
2467 = The Motivator
2468 = The Crusader

To assist you in finding your profile and its corresponding four-letter type, refer to Figure 8.2, then read the descriptions that follow.

The Organizer (ISTJ)	The Traditionalist (ISFJ)	The Motivator (INFJ)	The Systems Builder (INTJ)
The Risk Taker (ISTP)	The Mobilizer (ISFP)	The Crusader (INFP)	The Architect (INTP)
The Troubleshooter (ESTP)	The Coach (ESFP)	The Explorer (ENFP)	The Entrepreneur (ENTP)
The Controller (ESTJ)	The Harmonizer (ESFJ)	The Catalyst (ENFJ)	The General (ENTJ)

FIGURE 8.2   Leadership Profiles and corresponding four-letter types.

CAP2 LEADERSHIP PROFILES

The Organizer (ISTJ)

- Energized by the inner world of ideas and experiences
- Focused on information that is factual, real, and current
- Makes decisions using logic, analysis, and cause-and-effect reasoning
- Prefers a structured, organized, and planned environment

These leaders seek to ensure that all the pieces fit together. They try to focus the energies of the workplace in a coordinated campaign, and take action only after they have implemented their strategy across the board. At times, they may appear to move slowly and to be resistant to change.

The Traditionalist (ISFJ)

- Energized by the inner world of ideas and experiences
- Focused on information that is factual, real, and current
- Makes decisions based on values and their impact on people
- Prefers a structured, organized, and planned environment

These leaders are low-key, practical, and organized. They give their energies to preserving and interpreting the legacies of the past and tend to be cautious in the face of change. Nonetheless, they remain passionately engaged in day-to-day operations.

The Motivator (INFJ)

- Energized by the inner world of ideas and experiences
- Focused on the big picture, relationships, and connections between facts
- Makes decisions based on values and their impact on people
- Prefers a structured, organized, and planned environment

These leaders quietly motivate people to be all that they can be. They are articulate and precise. Because they are inspired to meet the challenges of the future, they can articulate the larger implications of business decisions and effectively communicate their enthusiasm to coworkers.

The Systems Builder (INTJ)

- Energized by the inner world of ideas and experiences
- Focused on the big picture, relationships, and connections between facts

- Makes decisions based on logic, analysis, and cause-and-effect reasoning
- Prefers a structured, organized, and planned environment

These leaders see the future and build complex systems to achieve their visions. They believe in the efficiency and power of organizational systems. Independent and determined, Systems Builders will resist business decisions that impair the effectiveness of recognized standards and procedures.

The Risk Taker (ISTP)

- Energized by the inner world of ideas and experiences
- Focused on information that is factual, real, and current
- Makes decisions based on logic, analysis, and cause-and-effect reasoning
- Prefers a flexible, spontaneous, and changing environment

Risk Takers are quiet, action oriented, and pragmatic. They are keen observers, blessed with the ability to identify the root causes of problems. Because of their self-confidence, they are often able to assess an opportunity and act on it without hesitation.

The Mobilizer (ISFP)

- Energized by the inner world of ideas and experiences
- Focused on information that is real, factual, and current
- Makes decisions based on values and their impact on people
- Prefers a flexible, spontaneous, and changing environment

These leaders work to coordinate their coworkers to accomplish the organization's goals. Their great strength is the ability to recognize what has to be done as well as to match particular needs with individual interests and skills. Without fanfare, they can champion a team effort and produce results.

The Crusader (INFP)

- Energized by the inner world of ideas and experiences
- Focused on the big picture, relationships, and connections between facts
- Makes decisions based on values and their impact on people
- Prefers a flexible, spontaneous, and changing environment

Crusading types rally the commitment of their coworkers by

articulating a compelling vision of the organization's mission. They love to generate ideas. Because of their visionary idealism, they tend to serve as a moral conscience in the workplace.

The Architect (INTP)

- Energized by the inner world of ideas and experiences
- Focused on the big picture, relationships, and connections between facts
- Makes decisions based on logic, analysis, and cause-and-effect reasoning
- Prefers a flexible, spontaneous, and changing environment

These leaders are the consummate designers of models and systems. They see patterns in organizations. Insightful and resourceful, they have a knack for problem solving. They not only can design systems, but can also adjust and improve them to enhance overall performance.

The Troubleshooter (ESTP)

- Energized by the outer world of people and activity
- Focused on information that is factual, real, and current
- Makes decisions based on logic, analysis, and cause-and-effect reasoning
- Prefers a flexible, spontaneous, and changing environment

Troubleshooters are the folks to call when the going gets tough. No type is better suited to the task of putting out fires and resolving crises. These leaders are bold and clever—two qualities that make them well suited to make the best out of difficult circumstances. These leaders thrive on action.

The Coach (ESFP)

- Energized by the outer world of people and activity
- Focused on information that is factual, real, and current
- Makes decisions based on values and their impact on people
- Prefers a flexible, spontaneous, and changing environment

These leaders are enthusiastic, action-oriented, *people* people. Coaches tend to serve as mentors in both their official and their unofficial capacities at work. As keen observers of other people, they are capable of recognizing strengths and building confidence to get the job done.

The Explorer (ENFP)

- Energized by the outer world of people and activity
- Focused on the big picture, relationships, and connections between facts
- Makes decisions based on values and their impact on people
- Prefers a flexible, spontaneous, and changing environment

Explorers see connections that other kinds of leaders miss. They are skilled at generating ideas and motivating other people to bring ideas to life. Leaders of this type move quickly to articulate the larger meaning of particular responsibilities and to energize their colleagues to accomplish the organization's mission.

The Entrepreneur (ENTP)

- Energized by the outer world of people and activity
- Focused on the big picture, relationships, and connections between facts
- Makes decisions based on logic, analysis, and cause-and-effect reasoning
- Prefers a flexible, spontaneous, and changing environment

These leaders are enthusiastic about the big picture, seeing all the possibilities for success. Entrepreneurs excel at recognizing opportunities and resources, but their true talent can be found in their ability to motivate others to implement their visions.

The Controller (ESTJ)

- Energized by the outer world of people and activity
- Focused on information that is factual, real, and current
- Makes decisions using logic, analysis, and cause-and-effect reasoning
- Prefers a structured, organized, and planned environment

These leaders try to control all dimensions of their work through the organization and administration of key resources. They are systems masters, taking detailed information into account even as they monitor ideas and events in every aspect of the operation.

The Harmonizer (ESFJ)

- Energized by the outer world of people and activity
- Focused on information that is factual, real, and current

- Makes decisions based on values and their impact on people
- Prefers a structured, organized, and planned environment

These leaders are first and foremost *people* leaders. They rank the welfare of the members of the organization as more important than the work itself. They will go to extremes to create harmony and morale. Inspired by the past, they work to maintain a sense of tradition and community in the workplace.

The Catalyst (ENFJ)

- Energized by the outer world of people and activity
- Focused on the big picture, relationships, and connections between facts
- Makes decisions based on values and their impact on people
- Prefers a structured, organized, and planned environment

These leaders are warm, friendly, and enthusiastic. They are focused on the growth needs of the organization and of the individuals who participate in its work. Leaders of this type have a natural charisma that helps them reach out to coworkers and employees and overcome skepticism or fears about the future.

The General (ENTJ)

- Energized by the outer world of people and activity
- Focused on information that is real, factual, and current
- Makes decisions using logic, analysis, and cause-and-effect reasoning
- Prefers a structured, organized, and planned environment

Generals marshal all internal and external resources available and create strategies that bring these assets to bear on existing challenges. They are bound and determined to achieve their vision of the future. Generals stay well informed about operational details, but not at the expense of the big picture.

Each leader brings his or her individual personality to the organization. There are 16 basic leader personalities, which, at the individual level, are very similar to the organizational personalities described earlier. As shown in Figure 8.3, the leader personalities can be grouped into four categories: Leaders who structure, Leaders who harmonize, Leaders who innovate and create, and Leaders who value.

	Task Focused	**People Focused**
Structured	Leaders who structure	Leaders who harmonize
Flexible	Leaders who innovate and create	Leaders who value

FIGURE 8.3 Personality quadrants.

Leaders who structure create structure around the organization's mission and vision and mobilize resources to realize the mission and vision. They take people into consideration, but it is secondary to getting the job done. Leaders who harmonize focus on structuring the organization so as to create harmony among the members. They tend to be warm and friendly people-focused leaders. Leaders who innovate and create are action oriented, move fast, and make the most of the resources available—or create new resources. They are the crisis managers and entrepreneurs. Leaders who value tend to be flexible, action oriented, and values focused. They lead with their values and quickly establish the moral conscience of the organization. The individual characteristics of each of these types of leaders are detailed in Figures 8.4 through 8.7.

In his study of leaders who took their companies from *Good to Great*, Jim Collins observed that the most effective chief executives are overwhelmingly modest about their contributions at work. The rectitude of good-to-great executives in his study was truly striking. For all their achievements at companies such as Wells Fargo, Gillette, Kimberly-Clark, and Philip Morris, leaders in the Collins study demonstrate humility about their success as individuals. Time and again, they gave the credit to the quality and drive of the organization, and praised the individuals lower on the corporate ladder.[i] Good-to-great leaders also tended to take the blame upon themselves for any disappointments. Personal humility such as this is what Collins calls Level 5 Leadership, the very best effort that the very best managers can provide. When combined with intense professional will, as it was in the cadre of chiefs in the Collins study, this sense of modesty equips leaders to drive their organizations toward greatness.

Understanding personality can help you get to Level 5 by teaching you to be less conspicuous about your leadership role. When you recognize the company as a personality in its own right,

	The Controller (ESTJ)	The Organizer (ISTJ)	The General (ENTJ)	The Systems Builder (INTJ)
Focus	Controlling Stability The past Mission Operations	Service The past Stability Mission Operations	Controlling Creating the future Change Vision Strategy	The future Creating a structure Improvement Vision Strategy
Values	Logic Consistency Predictability Caution	Tradition Efficiency Responsibility Reality	Logic Intelligence Initiative Effectiveness	Independence Competence Pragmatism Knowledge
Style	Gregarious Confident Rule based Tactical	Reserved/hard to read Rule based Detailed Tactical	Gregarious Confident Strategic Takes charge	Reserved/hard to read Deliberate Confident Impersonal
Communication Style	Logical Past focused Impersonal Long answers Businesslike	Logical Past focused Impersonal Long answers Businesslike	Logical Big picture Blunt Long answers Intellectual	Logical Big picture Blunt Long answers Intellectual

Conflict Style	Confrontation Quick to intervene Argumentative Wins with logic	Avoidance or offensive Past focused Wins with logic	Confrontation Quick to intervene Argumentative Wins with logic	Avoidance or offensive Future focused Wins with log
Decision Making	Quick decisions based on past Rigid	Time to think Based on past Rigid	Quick decisions based on the future May change mind	Quick decisions based on the future May change mind
Blind Spots	Impact of decisions on people Slow to change "Pushy"	Past focused Slow to react Too detailed Slow to change	Demanding Fast to react May be seen as arrogant	Demanding Withholding May be seen as arrogant Aloof
Under Stress	Uncontrolled emotions Questions self-worth Takes criticism personally Aggressive and mistrustful	Loses touch with reality Compulsive Focuses on negative possibilities Reads into the situation	Uncontrolled emotions Questions self-worth Takes criticism personally Aggressive and mistrustful	The future is now Sensory overindulgence Fact focused Easily angered Loner

FIGURE 8.4 Leaders who structure.

	The Harmonizer (ESFJ)	The Traditionalist (ISFJ)	The Catalyst (ENFJ)	The Motivator (INFJ)
Focus	Harmony The past Facts The outer world of people	The past People needs Harmony Low-key environment Practicality	The future People needs of the organization Structure Making things happen	The future Building human potential Structure Core values and ideals
Values	Harmony Strong work ethic Tradition Family Structure Socializing	Harmony Efficiency Loyalty Tradition Structure Control	Relationships Uniqueness Creativity Family Structure Socializing	Independence Relationships Uniqueness Creativity Structure Control
Style	Gregarious Enthusiastic Sensitive to others Organizes everything	Reserved/hard to read Determined Action oriented Organized	Gregarious Enthusiastic Fosters teamwork Coach/mentor Creativity	Reserved/hard to read Builds relationships Clarifies complexity Confident Action oriented
Communication Style	Outgoing People focused Past focused Direct personal feedback Hesitant to say no Face to face	Reserved People focused Past focused Direct personal feedback Hesitant to say no Face to face	Outgoing Excellent communicator People focused Future focused Face to face	Reserved People focused Future focused Face to face

Conflict Style	Avoidance or offensive Establishes harmony	Avoidance or personal attack Establishes harmony	Avoidance or offensive Establishes harmony	Avoidance or personal attack Establishes harmony
Decision Making	Quick decisions Rigid Values based Experienced based	Quick decisions, but may change mind Values based Experienced based Sets priorities	Quick decisions Rigid Values based Future based	Quick decisions, but may change mind Values based Future based Sets priorities
Blind Spots	Takes on too much Rigid Quick decisions about people Feelings overrule logic	Skeptical of change Rigid Low collaboration Feelings overrule logic Controlling	Takes on too much Feelings overrule logic May ignore factual data Fast to react Rigid	Takes on too much Feelings overrule logic May ignore factual data Controlling
Under Stress	Loses connection with people Overwhelmed Faulty logic Hypersensitivity Finds fault/blame	Emotional Loses touch with reality Hypersensitivity Faulty logic Loner	Loses connection with people Overwhelmed Faulty logic Hypersensitivity Finds fault/blame	The future is now Fact focused Emotional Loner Faulty logic

FIGURE 8.5 Leaders who harmonize.

	The Troubleshooter (ESTP)	The Risk Taker (ISTP)	The Entrepreneur (ENTP)	The Architect (INTP)
Focus	The present Fixing the immediate crisis Creating an impact	The present Continual improvement Efficiency Optimization Immediate impact	The future Big picture The organization The vision Strategy	The future Building a model Big picture Strategy Patterns
Values	Cleverness Action Innovation Risk taking Low structure	Risk taking Pragmatism Precision Innovation Low structure	Action Creativity Knowledge Change Low structure	Autonomy Learning Competence Pragmatism Low structure
Style	Troubleshooter Problem solver Calm under pressure Resourceful Flexible	Reserved/hard to read Pragmatic Logical Calm under pressure Flexible	Creative Action Mobilizes resources Impersonal Flexible	Confident Impersonal Precise Competitive Flexible
Communication Style	Gregarious Present focused Fact focused Literal Colorful	Reserved Present focused Fact focused Literal Blunt	Gregarious Logical Big picture Rambles Blunt	Reserved Big picture Ideas Logical Blunt

Conflict Style	Head-on Persuasive Wins with logic Defensive	Avoids or becomes defensive Wins with logic	Quick to engage Stubborn Wins with logic Argumentative	Avoids or becomes defensive Wins with logic Argumentative
Decision Making	Quick decisions Cause and effect Short term Practical	Cause and effect Short term Practical Efficient	Quick decisions, may change later Flexible, then rigid Logical	Slow decisions Little collaboration Flexible, then rigid Logical
Blind Spots	Absorbed in the moment Creates crises Impulsive Dislikes rules Applies quick fixes Lack of follow-through	Short-term focus Changes direction quickly Ignores people issues Applies quick fixes Lack of follow-through	Implementation People issues Overcommitment Lack of follow-through Loses interest easily Translating future into action	Implementation People issues Overcommitment Lack of follow-through Loses interest easily Translating future into action
Under Stress	Mystical Suspicious Hair splitting Anxious Compulsive	Easily influenced Hypersensitivity Feels like a victim Feels unappreciated Emotional	Dire consequences Psychosomatic Phobias Compulsive	Easily influenced Hypersensitivity Feels like a victim Feels unappreciated Emotional

FIGURE 8.6 Leaders who innovate and create.

	The Coach (ESFP)	The Mobilizer (ISFP)	The Explorer (ENFP)	The Crusader (INFP)
Focus	Action oriented The present Facts, reality People Crisis management	The present Facts, reality Crises Harmonious workplace Opportunities	Big picture The future Concepts, possibilities Needs of people Harmony	Big picture The future Concepts, possibilities Ideas Harmony
Values	Personal values Harmony Equality Cooperation Flexibility	Personal values Action Harmony Personal dignity Cooperation	Personal values Spontaneity Cooperation Creativity Freedom	Personal values Uniqueness Equality Freedom Flexibility
Style	Risk taker Resourceful Spontaneous Socializing Enthusiastic	Reserved/hard to read Attention to details Mobilizes people Resourceful Opportunistic	Risk taker Spontaneous Creative Socializing Enthusiastic	Reserved/hard to read Creative Spontaneous Supportive Unstructured
Communication Style	The present People Thinks out loud Face to face Action oriented Factual	The present People Sensitive Face to face Action oriented Factual	The future People Thinks out loud Face to face Rambles Possibilities	The future People Sensitive Face to face Rambles Ideas

Conflict Style	Avoids as long as possible Reacts strongly to trampled values	Avoids as long as possible Reacts strongly to trampled values	Avoids as long as possible Reacts strongly to trampled values	Avoids as long as possible Reacts strongly to trampled values
Decision Making	Quick decisions Impact on people Values based Impulsive Solves immediate problems	Impact on people Values based Impulsive Solves immediate problems	Quick decisions Impact on people Values based Impulsive	Slow decisions, may change mind Impact on people Values based
Blind Spots	Absorbed in the moment Impulsive Dislikes rules Poor follow-up Feelings overrule logic	Absorbed in the moment Impulsive Dislikes rules Poor follow-up Feelings overrule logic	Bored by details Overcommitment Feelings overrule logic Acts too quickly Misses deadlines	Bored by details Overcommitment Feelings overrule logic Lack of follow-through
Under Stress	Mystical Suspicious Hair splitting Anxious Compulsive	Lost in facts Compulsive Faulty logic Rigid Questions self-worth	Dire consequences Psychosomatic Phobias Compulsive	Lost in facts Compulsive Faulty logic Rigid Questions self-worth

FIGURE 8.7 Leaders who value.

you can choose to set aside your own personality preferences in the interests of the organization. More important, you direct attention away from yourself and toward the collective enterprise, which can only be encouraged, not distracted, by the white heat of the spotlight. Auditing your ego as a leader helps you to conceptualize anew your role as a manager and as an example to employees. It's the threshold to working in harmony with the character of your organization.

⑨ Personality and Cultural Diversity

Since the rise of civil rights and feminism in the 1960s, leaders of organizations have struggled with the issue of cultural diversity in the workplace. Differences in this arena can serve simultaneously as a source of weakness as well as strength, conflict as well as harmony. The task of leadership is to direct the energy of diverse points of view toward a common objective, while minimizing the tensions inherent in cooperation. The leader's mantra—"We shall overcome"—rallies employees to set aside their differences on behalf of a sweeping, united objective.

Regardless of what executive rank you hold or what kind of industry you operate within, you have to recognize that your personality preferences are no more valid and no more important than anyone else's. Your organization depends on the endeavors of a diverse array of types to achieve its goals. Where would Systems Builders be, after all, if they didn't have Crusaders and Entrepreneurs to help them envision an end to the company's means? We hope you'll use the CAP2 Leadership Diagnostic as an exercise in building tolerance, and perhaps as the foundation for a new appreciation of people not like yourself.

From the perspective of Jungian psychology, which forms the intellectual foundation of Companies Are People, Too, leaders of organizations might be seen as agents of transcendence—that is, as mediators whose wisdom and creativity help to diminish the tensions between the extremes of personality preferences. Just as a reflective, resourceful individual is capable of transcending type and tapping into the power of opposing forces, a company with resourceful leaders can overcome conflict in diversity in order to exploit both sides of every argument. The process requires awareness of company personality, your own personality preferences, and the leadership profiles of key members of the staff. Equipped with knowledge about typical behaviors, irritants, and goals—the company's, your own, and your coworkers'—you can glide past a potential crisis or rise to an occasion when an unusual opportunity knocks.

As you and your organization learn and grow, you may emerge as a workplace multi-culture, where you recognize the *gifts differing* (to borrow a phrase from MBTI pioneer Isabel Myers) of everyone equally. Multi-culture lets management borrow techniques and perspectives that are not usually associated with the company's dominant preferences. Leadership might propose an interlude of introverted assessment during a time of transition, or commit to developing a more humane environment after a series of layoffs. Individual employees feeling overwhelmed by deadlines can make a case in favor of spontaneity and observation. In a workplace multi-culture, decision makers automatically know the power of the tactical reverse in the face of stubborn problems. Is your client antagonized by the slow pace and limited goals of the services you have proposed? Then it's time to set aside your company's preferences for factual information gathering and rely more on intuition. A tactical reversal of your company's dominant preference in this instance may produce the kind of bold vision your client demands. Understanding personality preference offers decision makers the opportunity to select from a wide range of management tools for articulating and implementing business strategy. While the character of the corporation (and its people) remains consistent, the process of transcendence channels the power of the full range of personalities on behalf of your business.

MAKING THE COMPANY YOUR CLIENT

In the autobiographical *My Years with General Motors,* which experts have described as the best management book ever written, longtime GM chief Alfred P. Sloan Jr. observed that a good manager treats his or her business as if it were a client. Sloan, who more than any business leader of his generation defined what it meant to be a professional, indicated that this special relationship is the only thing that makes management a profession in the same sense as medicine, the ministry, or the law. The responsibility to fulfill or exceed the expectations of the company as client, in Sloan's view, is the single, all-encompassing mission of the professional manager.[1]

Understanding companies as people helps you conceive of your business as a client by providing a recognizable persona to represent the organization. Once you have imagined the organization as a distinct personality, it is simple to imagine what it expects of you or how it will react to what you and your coworkers do. CAP2 lets managers envision the company as client in detail. When you can understand and anticipate the company's response to your initiatives, you confront every challenge with an action plan. This approach gives texture and meaning to the concept of professionalism, emphasizing the personal dimension of your commitment to your work.

Another pearl of wisdom from Alfred Sloan: Professional managers cannot afford to rely on their own preferences when making decisions about business.[2] Understanding personality gives leaders a moral compass for distinguishing individual motivations from the needs and aspirations of the company as a whole. Our advice to leaders of organizations: Try to lead to the company's personality preferences instead of your own. Even when it cuts against the grain of your personal habits and values, it pays to adapt to the environment. If the company is committed to spontaneity and flexibility, for example, you will fight an uphill battle if you want to impose a more rigorous structure. You can succeed, but only when you choose your battles carefully and adapt your tactical strategy to prevailing conditions. Imagining the company as your client helps you to make judgments about personality preferences in conflict. Be persuasive; worry about what might make the organization turn away; remember that, in the final judgment, the company as customer is always right.

The new news in *Companies Are People, Too* is that you can enhance your effectiveness by taking your own views less seriously and surrendering some of your leadership prerogatives to something larger than yourself. When you discover and embrace your company's personality, you bring a new senior partner into the office. This discovery also provides additional incentives and tools for you and your colleagues to do your very best work. When you treat your job with the same energy and respect you show your clients, you instinctively put the interests of the whole organization first. That relationship is the foundation of professionalism, integrity, and achievement.

ARTICULATE

Your company personality profile probably tells you a lot of things about the company that you're ready to hear. For one thing, you should be able to recognize the broad contours of your company's character in our description. Moreover, the profile may help you appreciate strengths you never knew you had. Even the bad news is good news! When you can anticipate problems or controversies before they get started, you minimize the negative impact. For most companies that complete the diagnostic in workshops, the process of identification creates a kind of thrill. Suddenly, you understand your reasons for being the way you are.

But discovery is only part of the process. In fact, it's the easy part. It's no achievement to have a personality. What sets a successful organization apart from the crowd is its ability to translate self-awareness into sound business practices and attitude. Now that you know your company has a personality, we'll use this section of the book to help you articulate it and weave it into the very core of what you stand for and how you behave. Can understanding personality create tangible benefits for your company? We believe personality holds the key to a healthy corporate culture and a strong brand identity. It can help you unlock your ambitions and advance to the next level of achievement.

⑩ Personality and Culture: A Cautionary Tale

Understanding and embracing your company's personality is a crucial first step toward defining its corporate culture. While personality, culture, and brand are very different elements of corporate identity, successful companies acknowledge a high degree of interdependence among the three. *Companies Are People, Too* provides useful tools for understanding these relationships, beginning with some important definitions.

Personality is the fundamental basis of corporate identity, encompassing a company's origins, experience, and infrastructure and the current composition of its employees, clients, products, services, and physical plant. Personality manifests itself in preferences and presentation styles; taboos and sacred cows within the organization; inclinations in hiring, staff promotion, and decision making; and susceptibility to a range of ideals and rhetorical postures. The personality of a company—like that of an individual—is enduring, if not permanent. While a company can adapt its culture, and even its brand identity, its core personality preferences will usually remain intact.

Culture is the sum of an organization's behaviors, values, and goals. Culture is the environment a corporate entity creates for itself and operates within. If a company's personality can be compared to a fish, its corporate culture is like the water in which the fish swims—surrounding and sustaining it, sometimes a source of contamination, but more often the secure and essential setting for living and thriving. At best, corporate culture reflects and reinforces the winning dimensions of the company core. Signs of culture confusion can indicate a basic failure of self-awareness or even low self-esteem.

Brand identity is the face an organization projects to the outside world. While all companies have personality and most operate within a recognizable corporate culture, brand identity is a prized and elusive quality. Personality is personal—fundamentally private and internal—and corporate culture is created at the nexus of personality and the operating environment. Brand identity, in contrast, emerges only in the context of communication with the public. By definition, a brand is the way a company or its products and services become familiar to strangers. A brand encompasses a company's reputation, style, and promise to the consumer. Companies that engage in branding attempt to convey a specific sensibility or image about what they offer. Branding succeeds when this image is consistent with the corporation's culture and personality. Recognizing and nurturing that identity is an essential component of branding strategy.

The experience of two of the best-known American companies illustrates the intersection of personality, corporate culture, and brand identity. Southwest Airlines and The Gap share a number of enviable characteristics. Both are Forbes 400/Fortune 500 companies with nationally or globally famous brand names. Both are recognized as innovative and dynamic, known for a record of achievement in two of the most tumultuous and least profitable industrial sectors—air travel and retail fashion. Southwest Airlines (established in Texas in the late 1960s) and The Gap (established in San Francisco in the late 1960s) have benefited alike from strong and enduring leadership. Southwest's longtime CEO and founder Herb Kelleher is an outrageous, charismatic champion whose fierce determination propelled his company into the top ranks. During his nearly 20 years of service at The Gap, CEO Mickey Drexler's brilliant eye for fashion and merchandising helped to reshape the way Americans and many others shopped, dressed, and integrated fashion into their lifestyle. Southwest

Personality: The basis of corporate identity, encompassing a company's origins, experience, infrastructure, preferences, and behaviors. Often manifested in the current composition of its employees, clients, products, services, and physical plant.

Culture: The sum of an organization's behaviors, values, and goals. The environment that keeps the personality alive.

Brand identity: The way a company or its products and services become familiar to strangers, encompassing a company's reputation, style, and promise to the consumer.

Airlines and The Gap rounded the turn of the twenty-first century in the full bloom of prosperity and optimism for future expansion and profits, with soaring stock prices and high visibility. Both confronted leadership transitions as Kelleher and Drexel brought their careers at their respective companies to a close. The transitions revealed fundamental differences between these two great American companies.

Southwest Airlines entered a new era under new leadership with little turbulence. Despite the twin setbacks of the terrorist attack on American air travel and the overall economic downturn of 2001–2002, the company continued to prosper and expand. Southwest inaugurated its first cross-country flights in 2002 and continued its controlled expansion into new American markets. More impressive still, the airline has sustained its practically unrivaled record of profitability. In the spring of 2003, if all goes well, Southwest will post profits for the 120th consecutive quarter—a landmark 30th anniversary of achievement. While profitability is hard to predict even in the best of times, the odds are decidedly in favor of the company's ability to maintain its other practically unrivaled perfect record. Between 1971 and 2002, Southwest Airlines did not lay off a single employee. The loyalty and enthusiasm of the company's staff has stimulated similar emotions among passengers and shareholders.

The corporate fabric of The Gap, meanwhile, has in recent years shown unmistakable signs of unraveling. The Gap excelled in categories that did not even exist for fashion retailers when Drexler took the reins in 1983. Drexler's stores made a stunning market transition from a teenager's emporium of cheap jeans with a radio jingle to a sleek purveyor of affluent style. The winning strategy featured beautiful merchandising—persuasive arrays of color in a large stock of sizes—as well as top-dollar advertising campaigns that tapped a rich vein of cool. Above all, The Gap owed its success to the excellence of its casual garment collections, and here Drexler's contributions were invaluable. Scrutinizing thousands of items of clothing in almost obsessive detail, he and his team managed to select fashions with broad appeal and a lasting impact on American style. As The Gap, Banana Republic, and Old Navy (established in 1993) expanded into over 4,000 venues in North America, Europe, and Asia, the nice-shirt-and-khakis Gap look became emblematic of the contemporary lifestyle and workplace sensibility. The Gap (and, to a lesser extent, Banana Republic and Old Navy) became a recognizable look, a feat previously reserved for haute couture design houses or high-end retailers like Ralph Lauren. The Gap brand took its place alongside such classic American labels as Disney, McDonald's, and Coca-Cola, while the company's stock returns outperformed the giants and the S&P 500 by significant margins.

Riding high in the late 1990s, The Gap veered into a sharp down cycle well before the onset of the 2001–2002 recession. A series of flat fashion choices, compounded perhaps by a sense of overkill, hit The Gap's sales at a vulnerable juncture. Having recently financed a huge global expansion (in 2000, after years of rapid growth, the three brands increased their total square footage by 30 percent), the company experienced a cash crunch of devastating proportions. Forced by creditors to reduce inventories, The Gap found its stores with a comparatively sparse offering of comparatively unattractive clothing. Shoppers felt betrayed. Stock prices fell. Wall Street downgraded The Gap's debt to a junk rating.

The Gap organization revealed significant strains. Once the envy of the industry on the technological frontier, The Gap's logistics and distribution system was starting to fail. After years of success with its in-house advertising shop, the company hired and fired independent advertising agencies. Its system of financial and operating controls proved woefully inadequate to its new global dimensions. In 2000–2001, top executives quit their jobs, and unfavorable stories began to appear in the press. "The CEO is accountable for results and doing well," Drexler said. He announced his resignation and departure in May 2002. Prospects for a turnaround under Drexler's as yet unnamed successor remain mostly grim.

The crisis at The Gap reflected the company's failure to sustain a healthy and effective corporate culture. In the process of becoming one of America's best-known brands, The Gap seemed to lose track of its true identity. The transition from its hippie roots (the San Francisco store sold only Levi's jeans and record albums) to the urban professional market had proceeded smoothly, with few indications of resistance or discontinuity within the organization. In fact, the company's origins in the youth market and the mechanics of its transformation seem to have been largely forgotten—absent from The Gap's merchandising and advertising, interviews and magazine profiles, and even from the "Milestones" section of the company Web site. Stories about The Gap published in major business outlets in the 1980s and 1990s were inevitably about Drexler's genius for merchandising and its landmark impact on retail fashion. His controlling influence on all matters Gap became a media legend. The *personalismo* of Drexler's leadership style was reinforced by his failure to groom a successor or build up a powerful management infrastructure. He even eschewed written memoranda and e-mail in favor of voice mail messages, a narrow and ephemeral medium for building a collective sense of purpose. "Can Drexler's [merchandising] vision be turned into a formula?" asked a reporter in a 1998 profile. "Can he institutionalize his art?"[1] The Gap's performance in the new millennium seems to indicate that Drexler never made time for this important task. Uninformed about their company's history and disengaged from the center of real power in the organization, The Gap's 166,000 employees have not served as an effective counterpart to the cultural impact of the chief. As his sense of direction faltered in 2000 and 2001, the company confronted an internal credibility gap.

Herb Kelleher's glorious ride into the Southwest Airlines sunset, in contrast to Drexler's clouded departure from his post at The Gap, can serve as an indicator of the relative strength of their organizations. While Kelleher himself was a larger-than-life CEO— whose antics and uproarious humor made him a leader with a higher public profile than Mickey Drexler—"Big Daddy-O" Kelleher cultivated an image as the head of a growing and rambunctious corporate family. Southwest built its reputation around the idea that air travel can be fun. At Southwest Airlines, 1970s-style fun featured shuttle service among the big Texas cities ($20 from Houston to Dallas) that served free booze during daytime flights and gave a bottle of whiskey to passengers during fare wars. Benefiting from airline deregulation, Southwest secured a monopoly at Dallas's downtown Love Field and endorsed "LUV" as the company theme. Stewardesses in hot pants, employee "Heart" awards, and Valentine decor conveyed the image to the airline's boisterous clientele. As lifestyles changed in later decades, the airline broadened its concept of fun to include jets painted like killer whales, Kelleher in Elvis costumes, and wisecracking flight attendants. Flying fun tended to make Customers happy (the capital C became a traditional flourish) and to nurture high morale among the employees. The no-layoffs policy and a high percentage of worker stock equity reinforced the effect. As service expanded and the company attracted media attention, audiences in geographic markets not yet served by Southwest Airlines were already getting insights into the unique character of the organization. The national brand identity that emerged in the 1980s and 1990s reflected the clarity and appeal of corporate culture at Southwest as much as its reputation for value and superior service.

The strong sense of identity at Southwest was the result of purposeful, creative business strategy. Herb Kelleher and his team placed a premium on self-awareness and team building at all levels of the corporation. As managers, Kelleher's executive team cultivated common knowledge about their craft. They donated the cocktail napkins on which they scribbled their original plans for Southwest to the National Business Hall of Fame. As told by the irrepressible Kelleher, the story of the founders' legal wrangles, drunken revels, and fisticuff encounters with competitors became the stuff of legend. Employees and managers throughout the corporation live up to the Big Daddy standard with help from an elaborate screening, training, and personnel management program. The University of People at Southwest's Love Field headquarters conveys the essentials of the Southwest Way in organized fun and games, video satires starring Herb Kelleher, and serious strategic workshops. For Kelleher, the investment in building corporate culture was a guaranteed winning venture in an industry beset by takeovers and fierce competition. "Our esprit de corps is the core of our success," he noted in an April 2000 interview. "They can [buy] all the physical things," he said, but no rival airline could hope to imitate or intimidate Southwest.[2]

Is your company more like Southwest Airlines or more like The Gap? If you feel like you understand what can't be imitated or intimidated about your company, you may have the kind of confidence and self-awareness that keeps Southwest Airlines at the head of the pack. Our cautionary tale illustrates the potential hazards where personality, corporate culture, and brand identity intersect. In the case of The Gap, the company's failure to know itself as an entity independent of its product created serious structural problems. In the end, Mickey Drexler and his staff created an oversized role for The Gap's powerful brand in the corporate culture. When they could have and should have been focused on building harmony and continuity within the organization, they became preoccupied with momentary, market-based considerations. At Southwest Airlines, in contrast, the company's brand strategy has consistently reflected the inherent character of the organization. And more important, corporate culture at Southwest has remained faithful to the same spirit, cultivating a strong sense of the company's identity in all its employees.

The case of Southwest underscores the importance of building your organization from the bottom up. Get to know your company, and then you'll recognize the procedures and general atmosphere that complement its goals and requirements. Companies Are People, Too provides a simple and painless method for getting in touch with your company's core characteristics—the foundation for its mission, vision, and values. Once you've mastered that core, you can create clarity, consistency, and alignment in your organization's corporate culture and brand identity.

⑪ Finding a Face for Your Personality

Once you have completed the CAP2 diagnostic and consulted your company personality profile, you should have a fairly good sense of your organization's identity. Your next challenge is to bring the company persona to life as a fully dimensional character in the workplace. The linchpin of the Companies Are People, Too method joins the timeless and essential elements of your work to everyday choices and patterns of behavior on the job site. To achieve this feat, your company must commit itself to mining for insight in the uncharted depths of your company persona. You'll find that ongoing processes maximize the benefits of self-discovery. Get up close and personal with the organization, and integrate what you find into daily routines, and you'll remain true to your company's best working rhythms and professional values. In this chapter, we outline commonsense applications of Companies Are People, Too as a comprehensive decision-making framework and marketing tool. In the process, we show you how to help your company persona articulate its motivations and priorities.

Companies that have worked with Fekete + Company on the Companies Are People, Too program commit considerable time and energy to the project of creating a persona to represent the organization. We're talking about imaging a human being, complete with a name, appearance, and lifestyle, to serve as the embodiment of the company's personality. Creating a persona gives a human face to the otherwise intangible dimensions of organizational identity. The personality profile provides a foundation for building a detailed, recognizable company persona. When you visualize a person instead of a bureaucracy, you make it easier for employees, clients, and business partners to relate to the company on a personal level. The relationship raises the stakes for understanding and accommodating the organization's unique purposes, strengths, and aggravations.

The effort to humanize the company can take place in a workshop, in the context of workday assignments, or on the individual level. What's important is that participants think creatively about possible personal characteristics of the company or institution. Once you have worked out a recognizable character for your company, you'll learn to use the character to enrich your company's brand identity, to develop products and services consistent with your company's personality, and to align your everyday activities with the core interests and purposes of the organization.

To get you started, we've included some Up Close and Personal Profiles for well-known companies prepared for *Companies Are People, Too* as an exercise for an MBA class. Figure 11.1, on pages 146 and 147, profiles corporate giants Nike, Target, IBM, and Microsoft. These well-known companies have immediately recognizable brand identities. Our MBA class examples tend to be more like caricatures than characters. That's because these famous companies' well-developed brand identities are the type that your company is probably still struggling to establish. Articulating who you are as an organization can bring that kind of clarity to your public persona, and to the internal deliberations of your company as well. Remember to consult the CAP2 profile for your company when you work on getting up close and personal. After all, we're asking you to articulate the priorities and tastes derived from this basic worldview. When you're done, you can welcome a new presence in the workplace whose perspective represents the interests and intricacies of the whole.

The final exercise in this section asks you to fill in the blanks for your own organization and to create a compelling representative of your company. Make copies of this form and work together in groups to come up with your company's persona. Review the in-depth profile beforehand, and highlight key attributes. Have each group tackle three to five of the categories and report back to the whole team. Assign a facilitator to help you arrive at a consensus.

CARE AND FEEDING OF THE NEW YOU

You tap into the power of personality only when you take care to cultivate what you've learned about your company's profile. We

Get Up Close and Personal with NIKE

Pet:	Cheetah
Mate's strength:	Aggressive
Favorite dinner:	Surf and turf
Favorite drink:	Tequila shot
Casual clothes:	Sports gear
Work uniform:	Polo shirt with swoosh
Most prized possession:	Awards and trophies
Fitness regime:	Three times a day
Just can't stand:	Losing
For relaxation:	Running
Favorite books:	Self-help
Car(s):	Sports car
Best trip ever:	Cross-country drive
TV show:	*Extreme Sports*
For inspiration:	Team building
Likes most about self:	Winner
Name:	Olympus

Get Up Close and Personal with TARGET

Pet:	Spuds McKenzie
Mate's strength:	Hip and forward-thinking
Favorite dinner:	Nachos
Favorite drink:	Diet Mountain Dew
Casual clothes:	Cargo pants
Work uniform:	Red golf shirt
Most prized possession:	Bullseye
Fitness regime:	Kickboxing
Just can't stand:	Kmart or Wal-Mart
For relaxation:	Hot tub
Favorite books:	Oprah's book club recommendations
Car(s):	Jeep Liberty
Best trip ever:	Las Vegas
TV show:	*Friends*
For inspiration:	Shopping
Likes most about self:	Home decor
Name:	Dot

FIGURE 11.1   Up close and personal examples.

Get Up Close and Personal with IBM

Pet:	Furby
Mate's strength:	Longevity
Favorite dinner:	Steak and potatoes
Favorite drink:	Martini
Casual clothes:	Khakis
Work uniform:	Dark suit and tie
Most prized possession:	Palm Pilot
Fitness regime:	Jogging
Just can't stand:	Change
For relaxation:	Computer games
Favorite books:	Reference
Car(s):	Volvo
Best trip ever:	Space and Rocket Center
TV show:	*Star Trek*
For inspiration:	Internet
Likes most about self:	Everything
Name:	John

Get Up Close and Personal with MICROSOFT

Pet:	Electronic
Mate's strength:	Smart and innovative
Favorite dinner:	Sushi
Favorite drink:	Energy drink
Casual clothes:	Khakis and polo
Work uniform:	Khakis and polo
Most prized possession:	Palm Pilot
Fitness regime:	Treadmill
Just can't stand:	Government
For relaxation:	Sci-fi movies
Favorite books:	*Lord of the Rings*
Car(s):	SUV
Best trip ever:	Mushrooms
TV show:	*The Simpsons*
For inspiration:	Astronomy
Likes most about self:	Brain
Name:	Seth

encourage participants in CAP2 workshops to designate the care and feeding of the company persona as an ongoing responsibility for employee teams. Usually, teams are assigned by drawing a number from 1 to 12. If there are 36 people in the room, there are three sets of 12 numbers. In this scenario, there will be 12 teams of three people each. Each team takes responsibility for keeping the company persona alive during the month corresponding to its team number (for example, team #3 is March). This ensures that specific people will be accountable for initiating something that will remind everyone about the personality of the company.

Keepers of the company persona attempt to add dimension and vitality to the human image of the organization by continuing the process of conceptualization after the Up Close and Personal exercise. More important, keeper activities can help make the company persona a meaningful presence in the daily life of the workplace by sponsoring activities in the persona's name. Keeping the spirit of the corporation alive in the image of the company persona is a straightforward and effective way to boost the esprit de corps in your office. To keep fresh ideas and enthusiasm flowing, you would do well to rotate keeper responsibilities regularly among teams or members of your staff. (In one of the more successful applications of the keeper technique, the most creative teams received a prize for the year's best keeper activities.) Figure 11.2 includes a list of keeper ideas to help you get started.

SELLING YOUR TRUE SELF

When you start to understand your company as a person with preferences and values, you establish a foundation for marketing your true self to a wider audience. The company persona itself can be adapted to represent the company in advertisements and other business communications. Or a symbol consistent with the character of your organization can serve in its stead. However you choose to project your self-image to the public, understanding personality provides a level of insight into your strengths and capacities that you can readily communicate to others. The concept can bring consistency and depth to your marketing strategy.

The experience of Elford, Inc., a Columbus, Ohio–based commercial construction firm, demonstrates a subtle way to use the power of personality for marketing and brand identity. Founded in 1910 by Edward "Pop" Elford, the company decided to participate in the Companies Are People, Too workshop as a prelude to

The Companies Are People, Too Keeper's Guide

Congratulations! You get the enjoyable and essential task of serving as the keeper for your company's personification. The following suggestions are based on ideas that have worked successfully for other keepers.

Please begin with the ideas under "Getting Started." Then, feel free to use the other ideas that you think appropriate. Let us know about your successes or any innovations that you make as keeper.

Getting Started

1. Get a scrapbook or journal. You could pick out one that your personification would select or decorate a three-ring binder. Make sure you have a loaded camera at your desk.
   - Record your keeper activities with dates.
   - Note any changes that you observe in your company as a result of Companies Are People, Too. Record personality-based decisions (i.e., those that result when you ask, "What would _____ do in this situation?").
   - Take pictures of the staff and the personification activities.
   - When clients are in the building, take their pictures, too! Send copies to them.

2. Make it visual. Select a common area of your office to devote to your personification. (Many companies use the break room.)
   - Place objects mentioned in the Up Close and Personal exercise, such as clothing, music, car models, pictures from TV shows and movies, recreational items, and so on, in the area.
   - Put up a bulletin board and/or a write-on board devoted to the personification. Encourage the staff to post or write questions, concerns, compliments, etc.
   - Create a poster with your core ideology, purpose, values, and personification for your personification's bulletin board.

3. Select a symbol or create an illustration of your personification.
   - Hold a creative session with other staff members to select a symbol for your personification from the Up Close and Personal profile and/or core ideology. Or, you can pick one yourself. (Examples from other companies: Fekete + Company's Smart Marketing core ideology is symbolized with hats. Elford Construction's symbol for its personification "Pop" is a work boot.)
   - An alternative is to have a talented artist in your company create an illustration or caricature of your personification.
   - Display this symbol prominently in your office as the sign that you are the keeper. This can become a trophy or sign as the keeper duties rotate.
   - This symbol or illustration can be used on your marketing materials, too!

4. Establish benchmarks for profitability, growth, and turnover, so you can see what the program does for you.

(continued)

FIGURE 11.2 Keeping your company persona alive.

Building on Your Personification

1. Create a visual impression that reflects your personification's interests. Cut out magazine pictures that reflect the activities, food, clothes, entertainment, and so on that your personification enjoys. Or use some actual items.
   - Make a mini-scrapbook of these pictures kept in your personification's space.
   - Create a collage from the pictures.
   - If you have the equipment, you can create a "home movie" that may be a compilation of movie or other clips that reflect your personification. (For example, Dixon Schwabl Advertising put together clips of Indiana Jones in action to illustrate their company's personification, Jaz, and core ideology, "We Make It Happen.")

2. Hold a scavenger hunt, breaking the staff into teams to search for items that represent your personification. You can make a list, or just give them Up Close and Personal category answers to use in making their selections. The items can be displayed in the personification's personal space.

3. Write out a more detailed description of your personification, such as "a day in the life of _____."

4. Expand the journal idea by creating a "baby book" or "memory book" with firsts for your personification. You can use the birth certificate you receive in this project.

5. Make and post signs that say "What Would (your personification's name) Do?" (i.e., "What Would Jaz Do?") and "What Would (your name) Say?"
   - Make them into professional-looking posters and place them in visible areas.
   - Have magnets made with the phrase on them. Give to staff members.

6. Develop T-shirts or hats with your personification for the staff to wear.

7. Give your personification an e-mail address, if your company uses e-mail extensively.
   - Assign a mailbox to the personification if your company sends notes via mailbox extensively.

8. Do what is necessary to include Companies Are People, Too jobs in your system so they get done. For example, if you assign client and job numbers to get projects on a schedule, assign a client number to your personification.
   - Turn the action list into your personification's task list, assigning dates to get things done.

9. Create a "Memo from (personification name)" letterhead template on the computer. Use it to send out weekly or monthly reminders about your core ideology, purpose, values, and goals, as well as to announce events.
   - You could spend a few hours with quotation books, compiling a list of quotes that your personification would say. This can be a resource for you and other keepers to follow.

Keeping the Discussion Alive in Staff/Creative Meetings

1. Use staff or creative meetings to continue to review and polish your core values, converting them into appropriate behaviors for each job category in your company. Use these in hiring and in performance evaluations. Every

person in the organization must have a copy of the appropriate behaviors for his or her job.
- Have everyone think of the person in the job who most exemplifies the chosen core value.
- Have everyone write down three behaviors that person does that reflect this.
- Compile the behaviors to make the appropriate behaviors list.

2. Complete the strengths and growth opportunities worksheets in your packets. Write down examples that articulate each strength and an action list to work on reflecting your growth opportunities.

3. Review your current marketing materials and your competitors' to see if you clearly differentiate in your positioning.

4. Develop a profile of your ideal customer (the ones who would find you irresistibly attractive) based on your Companies Are People, Too results.
- List behaviors of these customers.
- Check the list against your current customer base.
- Check the list against your prospect list.
- Brainstorm new companies that you can add to your prospect list.

5. Develop a description of what people can expect when working with your company based on the profile. You could include a description for:
- Clients
- Vendors
- Employees

6. Develop a creative platform based on your symbol and personification. It could include ideas, headlines, and visuals for all marketing areas, interior decoration, and special events.

7. Review your action list quarterly to check for progress and to add new items to it.

Team Building

1. Pair up opposites in your company for a week or more to be teams.
- Have them develop a team name.
- Have them get to know their teammate and purchase a personality-based item for $10 or less for that person's office.
- Have them assign each other one task from their jobs, so they see what the other does.
- Have a wacky Polaroid contest with each team trying to communicate the personification's image.
- Have them dress like the other person for a day.
- Try Friday sessions for team-building communication games, such as Taboo, Pictionary, and so on. (One company gave a day off to the winning team in the company tournament.)

2. Take your personification on a field trip.
- Have everyone write down a location they would like to visit, including places that your personification might visit, such as clients' offices and places that spark creativity. Put the slips of paper in a jar.
- Pull out a slip to plan a quarterly lunch or afternoon out for part or all of your team. (If you send out departments, be sure to rotate.)

3. Create your personification's traveling gift basket. Select a nice basket that goes from person to person on the staff.

(continued)

- As the keeper, you fill the basket for the first time. Put in something that reminds you of the personification (food, a picture, a book, a video, anything under the dollar limit you set), a quote from your personification, and a note that tells the person who is receiving the basket what you most appreciate about having them as a coworker. Each person keeps the contents of the basket, fills it anew, and sends it on to the next person on the list on the next Monday morning.

4. Develop a "(personification) in a box" to give to new employees, including:
   - The Up Close and Personal exercise
   - The appropriate behaviors for the job description
   - The symbol

5. Put out a yearbook or annual report on your personification for employees and for clients who would appreciate it.

6. Hold a monthly staff lunch to deal with the company's business only (no client talk). It could be a party given by your personification with appropriate decorations, food, and music.
   - Give awards to employees who have done something outstanding that reflect the organization's core values.

7. Put out desk or door signs that reflect individual personality types.

8. Create a gift package from your personification to give to staff members and even clients on their birthdays.
   - Appropriate small toys
   - A homemade card featuring the symbol or illustration

9. Compile a box or scrapbook of work that you are particularly proud to do. It can be your "Greatest Hits" package.

Marketing

1. Review your corporate materials to find ways to incorporate your personification.
   - Create a fax cover sheet with your personification.
   - Create a holiday card with your personification.
   - Create a monthly newsletter sheet to fax to clients, including the personification.

2. Introduce your clients to your personification.
   - If your clients would enjoy it, hold an open house for them to meet your personification, send out a birth announcement, or do a broadcast fax about the personification and your core ideology.
   - Hold a meeting of the minds with clients to discuss Companies Are People, Too.

3. Create a direct mail piece or campaign based on your personification to use with prospects.

4. Look at the interior decoration of your office to find ways to incorporate the personality into it.

Operations

1. Hold a contest to develop cost savings ideas. You can assign points for how much will be saved with each idea. The staff member with the idea or ideas for saving the most money wins a free day off.

preparing a strategic plan. Though Elford had used management and marketing consultants many times in the past, and had worked hard to define its mission and values in other workshops, the experience with Companies Are People, Too resulted in something special. Participants immediately recognized Elford in the CAP2 description of the "Playing by the Rules" personality profile. The profile soon became the foundation for an especially productive application of the Up Close and Personal exercise (see Figure 11.3). Nicknamed "Pop" in a nod to the company founder, the Elford persona has emerged as a fictional yet factual representation of the character of the organization.

While the name is the same, Elford's Pop represents the company as a whole rather than Edward Elford himself. Pop embodies Elford's commitment to integrity, values, performance, and professionalism. In his fatherly, orderly way, the character is a mirror for the no-nonsense, "Playing by the Rules" Elford personality. The Elford team has worked hard to bring the character of Pop to life within the company. In addition to the keeper activities outlined in Figure 11.2, Elford has sponsored a Pop theme awards banquet (complete with Popsicles, popcorn, and popping party favors), a Pop Elford display case for the office, and an annual Pop Elford Quality Award for employees. Even more successfully, Elford has discreetly integrated the Pop persona into communications with customers and the public.

Elford chose the work boot as a symbol for Pop and the company as a whole. The selection illustrates the way you can adapt information from your CAP2 profile to your company's public persona. As a "Playing by the Rules" organization, Elford is committed to thorough, consistent performance and follow-through. The slogan "We're with you every step of the way," seemed to capture the essence of that commitment. The work boot analogy also allowed Elford to bring the Pop persona into its marketing strategy, with the claim that "Pop Elford put himself in the customer's shoes, and Elford, Inc., follows in his footsteps today." The statement emphasizes the company's commitment to understanding the customer's needs and to meeting those needs with integrity and professionalism. A graphic designer prepared an image of boot tracks for use in the company newsletter, while photographers took shots of Elford employees' boots for promotional materials. At a party to celebrate the opening of new offices, Elford asked guests to leave their own tracks on a Walk of Fame and distributed shoeshine kits as party favors. Other slogans, such as "We walk you through it," and "We

Get Up Close and Personal with Elford, Inc.

Pet:	Mixed-breed, obedient dog named Dammit
Mate's strength:	Independent, supportive, good listener, practical, organized
Favorite dinner:	Rare steak, wings, dessert
Favorite drink:	Cold beer
Casual clothes:	Jeans
Work uniform:	Work boots, Elford golf shirt, jeans
Most prized possession:	Reputation
Fitness regime:	Beer and wings workout, intense cardio
Just can't stand:	Dishonest, unethical, unprofessional people
For relaxation:	Sports, fishing
Favorite books:	Adventure and mystery
Car(s):	Pickup truck
Best trip ever:	Fishing trip to Canada
TV show:	*60 Minutes, Late Night with David Letterman*
For inspiration:	Surrounding people
Likes most about self:	Professionalism
Name:	Pop

FIGURE 11.3   Up close and personal with Elford.

always put our best foot forward," extend the metaphor of the work boot as a symbol of Elford's values and strengths.

THE PERSONA AS AN ICON

An example that everyone will recognize incorporates the company persona in a more explicit way. The image of Colonel Harland Sanders of Kentucky as the human face of KFC is more a part of the identity of the international restaurant chain than the Kentucky Fried Chicken that made the company famous. While KFC has tipped its hat to the supposedly prevailing distaste for fried food by dropping the words *Kentucky Fried Chicken* from its name, the colonel's white suit and string tie are perpetually in style. His persistence as the company mascot is not without irony. Seventy-five years after he founded the company, the Colonel's conservative Southern persona could be seen as out of step with the global corporation's progressive, multicultural values. But his native charm and natty appearance—to say nothing of his mastery of the art of cooking chicken—continue to carry the day. Whether fixing chicken at a roadside restaurant in real life, or playing basketball as a stylized cartoon in a worldwide advertising campaign, Colonel Sanders serves up a symbol of something as American as fried chicken itself. Those of you who think that a cartoon is a marketing cliché might do well to take a closer look at your own Up Close and Personal profile!

In Figure 11.4, fill in the blanks for KFC, a well-known company with an existing persona, Colonel Sanders.

Can your personality profile help you put your company's best foot forward like Elford? We believe there's a natural fit when your marketing strategy reflects your true self. Whether it's a persona that you bring to life using animation or actors, or a drawing or object that serves as a symbol of your values and taste, your marketing strategy can bring out the winning dimensions of your company personality. Your audiences will appreciate the authenticity.

UP CLOSE WITH YOUR CUSTOMERS

Once you've become proficient at creating the persona to represent your organization, you might try to adapt your new skills to the task of envisioning your ideal customers. In this era of niche marketing, the more clearly you perceive your customers and their wishes, the more information you collect to use to your company's advantage.

Get Up Close and Personal with KFC

Pet:

Mate's strength:

Favorite dinner:

Favorite drink:

Casual clothes:

Work uniform:

Most prized possession:

Fitness regime:

Just can't stand:

For relaxation:

Favorite books:

Car(s):

Best trip ever:

TV show:

For inspiration:

Likes most about self:

Name:

FIGURE 11.4   Up close and personal with KFC.

Many businesses and nonprofit organizations target their products and services at a narrowly defined group of people, often a single age group or income bracket. Creating a persona helps you to create a fuller picture of the preferences of your target group.

To illustrate the benefits of creating a persona to represent your customers, let's look at an exceptionally successful concept developed by the creators of Tommy Bahama brand clothing and retail services. Many of you may know Tommy Bahama menswear (and a related line of women's clothes) as a line of fine-quality sportswear with a vaguely tropical theme. If you've been fortunate enough to visit one of the Tommy Bahama theme restaurants in select resort locations, you'll probably know Tommy as something infinitely more complex. The founders of the Tommy Bahama brand have created a fully dimensional character to represent their offerings and to guide them in merchandising and marketing their line. With the question, "What would Tommy do?" in mind, they have developed a detailed composite of the priorities and tastes of the men and women targeted for Tommy Bahama sales. The results have been encouraging. Only 10 years after establishment of the brand, revenues for the company have exceeded $300 million annually—a significant accomplishment in the low-margin, highly competitive garment industry.[1] With Tommy Bahama as our model (see Figure 11.5), we can get some practical advice on how to create a persona to represent your customers and serve as a guide to business decisions.

Before there was Tommy Bahama sportswear, the company founders are quick to observe, there was Tommy Bahama. The idea for the character was born long before two friends with neighboring beach condos decided to go into business using Tommy's name. After a particularly satisfying vacation in Florida, Tony Margolis and Bob Emfield began speculating about what it would be like if they didn't have to go back to work. They began joking about a character who didn't have to go to work, and who spent all his time living large on the beach and in other fun settings.[2] Over time, Margolis and Emfield, both veterans of the fashion industry, began to understand their fictional friend as the foundation for a great brand. By imagining Tommy and the kinds of things he would do and buy, they were able to project the tastes and wishes of a select demographic of well-to-do and fun-loving men, ages 35 to 55 and even older. Margolis and Emfield pooled their savings and teamed up with a designer in 1992 in an effort to bring Tommy Bahama—and his wardrobe—into sharper focus.

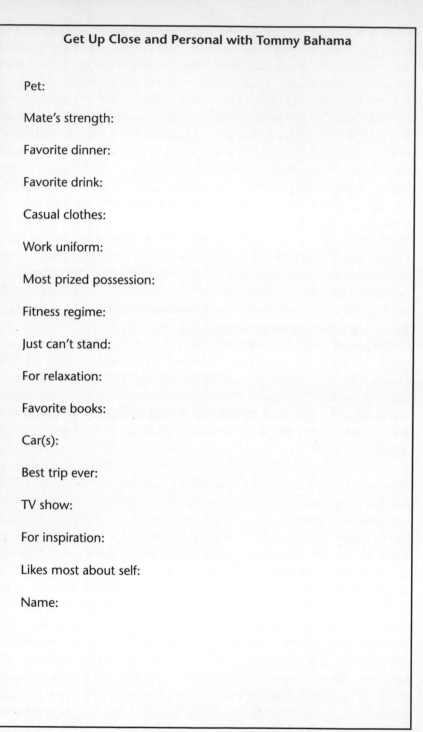

Get Up Close and Personal with Tommy Bahama

Pet:

Mate's strength:

Favorite dinner:

Favorite drink:

Casual clothes:

Work uniform:

Most prized possession:

Fitness regime:

Just can't stand:

For relaxation:

Favorite books:

Car(s):

Best trip ever:

TV show:

For inspiration:

Likes most about self:

Name:

FIGURE 11.5   Up close and personal with Tommy Bahama.

For a fledgling clothing company, the most important question to answer is how to get the product line within sight of the public. Department stores and smaller retailers—when they bothered stocking the product at all—tended to display Tommy Bahama clothes indifferently alongside other items. For Margolis and Emfield, who understood their jobs as "purveyors of the island lifestyle," it was important to present Tommy Bahama clothes as part and parcel of the rarified world that Tommy himself would inhabit. To ensure that the clothes appeared against the proper backdrop, they began to explore opening a retail outlet of their own. When the search for space blossomed unexpectedly into an opportunity to open a restaurant and bar alongside a shop in Naples, Florida, the opportunities for Tommy to express himself increased exponentially. Spurred on by the sales and sensibilities created in the Naples compound, the Bahama brand has expanded to include six theme restaurants, 12 retail outlets, and licensing agreements to sell tasteful and sometimes tropical items as diverse as home furnishings, sunglasses, and microbrew beer.

At the heart of the merchandising and planning process is the question, "What would Tommy do/wear/eat/drink/think about this choice?" Along the way, the character of Tommy Bahama has gained detail and depth. For example, the company has given serious thought to the kind of cars he would drive (a Porsche and a woody station wagon), what he likes to drink (Bahama beer), his favorite foods (to be found on the menu at a Tommy Bahama restaurant), and what kinds of music he likes. This up close and personal awareness of Tommy's tastes has simplified decisions on important questions, such as the quality of fabrics for the clothes and advertising venues. For example, Tommy Bahama has invested considerable resources in the sponsorship of sports events that Tommy himself might enjoy, including auto races, golf tournaments, and equestrian events. The result is a natural fit between the brand and its business applications.

You can get this same easy fit when you conceive of your ideal customers and the kinds of services they want from your organization. The Up Close and Personal exercise gives you a ready format to adapt to this task. Imagining your customers and the services you can offer them gives you more than just a detailed sense of what they want. When you imagine a persona to represent your customers and another well-developed character to represent your company, you have created the foundation for a meaningful interpersonal relationship—the very essence of a brand identity.

Take control of your brand by filling out the dimensions of your company's relationship with its customers at the up close and personal level. Like the creators of Tommy Bahama, you might find the key to a successful brand in your own imagination (see Figure 11.6).

UP CLOSE TO THE HEART AND SOUL OF YOUR ORGANIZATION

Brands and marketing strategy are vital components of the work of an organization, but the first responsibility of any organization is to articulate the focus of its collective efforts and its strategy for achieving its most important goals. Getting up close and personal with your company helps you to fulfill the number one responsibility of leadership: recognizing what it takes to make your organization grow and thrive. When you create a persona based on your company's history and envisioned future, you introduce an eminent decision maker into the executive ranks. We can concede the marketing savvy of asking what a brand character like Tommy Bahama might wear or listen to, and yet recognize more gravity in asking what Elford's Pop or Microsoft's Seth might do when faced with an important management decision. A sober Up Close and Personal persona, paired with information from the CAP2 profile, provides a point of departure for the discussion of the heart and soul of your organization. Think of the persona as a living member of the discussion group that will define your company's vision, mission, and values for a 100-year strategic plan. Wouldn't you want to make a place at the conference table for someone with this kind of commitment, insight, and expertise?

In the next chapter, we'll recreate some of the components of the Companies Are People, Too workshop for our readers as leaders of organizations. With the CAP2 profile and the Up Close and Personal persona as our guides, we'll get your company started toward understanding and implementing its potential as a dynamic, living organism. In the process, we ask you to keep your self-discovery alive by contemplating the personality and preferences of your company. Give them all a seat at your table! When you get up close and personal, you give a voice to the opinions that matter most.

Get Up Close and Personal with Your Company

Pet:

Mate's strength:

Favorite dinner:

Favorite drink:

Casual clothes:

Work uniform:

Most prized possession:

Fitness regime:

Just can't stand:

For relaxation:

Favorite books:

Car(s):

Best trip ever:

TV show:

For inspiration:

Likes most about self:

Name:

FIGURE 11.6   Your up close and personal worksheet.

⑫ Defining Vision, Mission, and Values

Understanding companies as people makes it easier to recognize the idealistic side of an enterprise. While living companies must be profitable to survive (and nonprofit institutions have to satisfy their own bottom line), almost every organization aspires to something greater than revenues and growth. Many of the best business books published in the last decade have talked a lot about vision, mission, and values, developing concepts such as core ideology and the mission statement for use in strategic planning. Seen as part of a trend toward the soft side of management, some of these ideas have fallen out of fashion or even become the subject of ridicule at the office. We at *Companies Are People, Too* understand why some of these methods have fallen short of expectations. In search of something that sounds right, too many businesses have embraced statements of purpose or values that have no organic connection to the heart and soul of the organization. What's more, too many managers have failed to link their idealistic precepts to concrete behaviors that bring ideals to life.

When you get up close and personal with your company profile, you encounter the true voice of your organization. Speak your dreams and aspirations out loud in this voice, and your employees and business partners will hear them. The concept of personality also creates a natural fit between business idealism and workplace routines. Attuned to the four mental processes and orientations affected by personality preferences, the CAP2 leader can integrate values into the rhythms and tastes of the organization. A large part of the promise of CAP2 is its effectiveness in helping businesses articulate vision, mission, and values. We're dedicating this chapter to exercises and examples that will show you how.

From the Fekete Files

An article in the May 1995 issue of Inc. *magazine by James Collins reinforced my belief that companies have their own personalities. The article described the research findings presented in* Built to Last, *written by Collins and Jerry Porras. The article was only two pages long, but it announced loudly and clearly that if a company knows itself and lives true to itself, it has a greatly improved chance at longevity compared with companies that don't do these things.*

Collins and Porras talk about core ideology. I interpreted it as core personality. They said, "[A] deeply held core ideology gives a company both a strong sense of identity and a sense of purpose beyond just making money.[1]"

They talked about "clock building." I understood it to mean that the CEO's personality is not the company's personality, and that the great CEO stands for the company, not for him- or herself. They wrote, "[T]he primary accomplishment of leaders who build great companies is not the implementation of a great idea, the expression of a charismatic personality, or the accumulation of wealth. It is the company itself and what it stands for."[2]

They talked about a "cultlike culture." I interpreted it as a spirit that emanates from companies that know who they are, what they stand for, and where they are going.

Collins and Porras's work gave credence to the foundation on which CAP2 was built. I realized then that CAP2 was a beginning, not an end. It answers the leaders who read Built to Last *and say, "I want that for my company. Where do I start?" The answer is, you start with getting a consensus about who your company is and what it stands for by using CAP2 in your organization. Then, you work hard to dig deep into the fabric of the company—into its core—to articulate your aspiration, your business, and your values. Finally, you breathe life into that profile by weaving it into the behaviors—the actions—of everyone, every day, every way.*

ITINERARY

There's an energy at work inside your organization that transcends the here and the now and operates on its own volition. You can see the organization as it sees itself when you contemplate its motivations as a personality. We are not going to create your core; rather, we are going to help you unearth it. It's already there, deep inside the organization, and you've begun to bring it out by looking hard at its personality.

Imagine you're going on a trip. What drives your organization today and for the next 100 years? What aspiration does it strive to achieve? That core ideology or vision is your ultimate destination.

Next, think about what vehicle will get you to your destination. That will be the business you're in—your core purpose. Finally, what will you hold onto throughout the journey? What is there that you fight to preserve, even if it kills you? Those will be your core values.

As you proceed through the exercises in this chapter, keep this trip tik in mind. Use it in group discussions. It'll help you stay on track!

IDENTIFY YOUR VISION

As individuals, most of us have a strong sense of personal identity and a feeling of belonging to a larger, cosmic whole. Companies, too, possess self-awareness and a sense of their place within an industry or a community. In *Built to Last,* Jim Collins and Jerry Porras argued that the most respected and successful corporations nurtured a core ideology about the company's destiny and purpose. Among the built-to-last companies they studied, employees at all levels could summarize this organizing vision in just a few words. Merck Pharmaceuticals, for example, aims to preserve and improve human life, while Disney is committed to making people happy. Mary Kay aspires to give unlimited opportunity to women; 3M to solve unsolved problems innovatively; Johnson & Johnson to alleviate pain and disease; Wal-Mart to give ordinary folks the opportunity to buy the same things as rich people.[3] At Fekete + Company, our vision is to help companies find and keep customers. Elford's is to exemplify professionalism.

In articulating your company's core ideology or vision, it is helpful to think back to the founder. What was the aspiration that started the company? It should be very much alive today and able to stand as your aspiration 100 years from now. Use Figure 12.1 to define your vision.

IDENTIFY YOUR MISSION

If you've defined your aspiration—your ultimate destination—the next step is to identify the vehicle that will get you there—your core purpose, also known as your mission, or, in other words, the business that you're in. This is the nuts and bolts on which the organization will base its survival. It's what you do beyond making money.

Understanding mission gives a sense of purpose to your organization's daily grind and can serve as a guide for decision making.

Define Your Vision

Write your company's core vision in the space below. If you get stuck, review the examples on page 164. This is effectively done in a workshop format, breaking into small groups and reporting back to each other.

- It's your company's aspiration for the next 100 years (the destination on your itinerary).
- It often goes back to the founder, so talk to the founder, call on someone who was there at the time, or refer to company history.
- It never changes.
- It's almost sacred and is pursued with religious zeal.
- You should be able to say it in three to five words, but it's not an exercise in wordsmithing or sloganeering.

FIGURE 12.1   Define your vision.

The next workshop exercise in this series (Figure 12.2) helps you square your company's core purpose with its core ideology and personality preferences. Once again, it's a matter of uncovering hidden dimensions of the company as a personality.

Let's look at some examples. Disney's core ideology or vision is to make people happy. The vehicle that will get it there—the business it is in—is entertainment. Fekete + Company's core ideology is to help Companies get and keep customers. The business we're in is smart marketing. Both examples encompass a wide playing field. Disney's business of entertainment does not limit it to theme parks. Fekete + Company's business of smart marketing allows us to venture into many realms. Both cases will be valid in 100 years. And both will help us decide what to do and not do. For example, if my company were approached to develop a prototype for a new dog food, we would walk away from the opportunity because it would not fit within our core business of smart marketing.

- Your mission should inspire people within the company.
- Like your vision and values, it should still be valid in 100 years.
- By placing work within the broadest context, the mission should leave room to explore new opportunities for growth.
- A clear statement of purpose can also help you decide what not to do.
- Your mission should be authentic—that is, true to the real you.

IDENTIFY YOUR VALUES

In *Built to Last,* Collins and Porras quote Ralph Larsen, CEO of Johnson & Johnson, the company with perhaps the best-known statement of values in corporate America. "The core values embodied in our Credo might be a competitive advantage," Larsen said of J&J's most sacred company text, "but that's not why we have them. We have them because they define for us what we stand for, and we would hold them even if they became a competitive *dis*advantage in certain situations."[4]

Like your vision, statements of values should convey a timeless commitment—these are principles that you hold dear even when prevailing trends would nudge them aside. But most of us find it difficult to conceptualize our work in such sweeping terms; hence the conundrum of mission statement idealism. In CAP2 workshops, we give participants a checklist about values gleaned from *Built to Last.* We think it helps them conceptualize

---

Define Your Mission

This is the business you're in. Since your vision is what you aspire to be, think of your mission as the vehicle that will get you there. It should accommodate a wide playing field, and it doesn't need to be long (Disney's mission is entertainment, which will help it achieve its vision of making people happy.)

1. Write your company's vision from the previous exercise (your destination).

   _____

   _____

2. Describe your organization's work (the vehicle that gets you to your destination).

   _____

   _____

3. Next, write down why you think that work is important. What does it accomplish for humankind? How does it make life better?

   _____

   _____

Finally, write a statement of your company's mission.

   _____

   _____

   _____

   _____

   _____

   _____

   _____

   _____

   _____

   _____

   _____

   _____

   _____

FIGURE 12.2   Define your mission.

Disney's Core Values[5]

1. No cynicism
2. Nurturing and promulgating wholesome American values
3. Creativity, dreams, and imagination
4. Fanatical attention to detail
5. Preservation and control of the Disney magic

the link between the company's core beliefs and the commitments and behaviors that give them life. As you think about values for the next exercise (Figure 12.3), keep our checklist for identifying values in mind.

- Your company's core values will never change.
- You would be willing to sacrifice customers to uphold your core values.
- Almost everyone in your company upholds these principles almost all of the time.
- Hundreds of people in your company making thousands of decisions every single day can use these values for a guideline.
- Behaviors are the true manifestation of your company values. If it's truly a core value, 99 percent of your people behave according to that value 99 percent of the time.

One more tip for identifying core values: Study your company personality profile. You'll see a list of basic values that reflect personality preferences. The profile list is general, designed for use by companies that may have nothing in common except for their personality preferences. You'll need to elaborate on the significance of these values for your particular organization. See Figure 12.4 for a list of some values common to each CAP2 type.

Values, like values systems, cannot be manufactured. They either exist or they don't. Many times, we've seen companies in our workshops list a value that couldn't pass the ultimate test: If you aren't already doing it, it's not a core value! For example, people from one firm stated that continuous learning was a core value. If that were so, they would have been be able to cite several examples of behaviors that support that statement (tuition reimbursement program, internal learning program, budget allocated to seminars and workshops, etc.).

Identify Your Company's Core Values

- Will *never change.*
- Willing to sacrifice customers to uphold them.
- Entire company behaves this way 99 percent of the time.
- Most companies have 3–5 core values.

Write your core ideology/vision (your aspiration; your destination).

_____

_____

Write your core purpose/business (the vehicle that will get you to your destination).

_____

_____

Now list the values that make up your value system, referring to the checklist and the general values listed in your CAP2 profile.

_____

_____

Test each value by asking the following questions:

_____

_____

If the circumstances changed and penalized us for holding this core value, would we still keep it?

_____

_____

A company does not change its core values to respond to market changes. It changes markets, if needed, to keep its core values. It changes clients (whom have you fired?). It changes markets. How has your target market changed?

_____

_____

_____

_____

_____

_____

FIGURE 12.3   Define your values.

Solid as a Rock	You Can Count on Us	Vision Driven by Values	Going All Out for Greatness
Excellence	Customers	Innovation	Learning
Hard work	Responsibility	Learning	Logic
Tradition	Tradition	Harmony	Innovation
Achievement	Loyalty	Sensitivity	Achievement
Customers	Quality	Commitment	Competence
Efficiency	Harmony	Insight	Independence
Control	Control		Pragmatism
Responsibility	Family		Uniqueness
			What could be

Action, Action—We Want Action!	Working to Make a Difference	Quest for Meaningful Work	In Pursuit of Intellectual Solutions
Excellence	Excellence	Innovation	Learning
Autonomy	Action	Community	Logic
Quality	Harmony	Diversity	Curiosity
Efficiency	Personal dignity	Teamwork	Achievement
Logic	Hard work	Fun	Creativity
Spontaneity	Cooperation	Harmony	Independence
Independence		Integrity	
Risk taking		Insight	
Integrity		Sensitivity	
Challenge			

Thriving on Risky Business	We Aim to Please	It's Fun to Do Good Work	If We Can't Do It, No One Can
Logic	Customers	Cooperation	Intelligence
Fun	Spontaneity	Diversity	Creativity
Spontaneity	Fun	Teamwork	Improvisation
Risk taking	Excellence	Fun	Innovation
Autonomy	Equality	Innovation	Logic
Challenge	Harmony	Integrity	Learning
Hands-on		Harmony	Efficiency
Experience		Creativity	Excellence
		Equality	Risk taking
		Relationships	
		Freedom	

Playing by the Rules	Doing the Right Thing	Seeing the Big Picture in Human Terms	Driven to Lead
Logic	Customers	Relationships	Intelligence
Efficiency	Community	Creativity	Logic
Tradition	Teamwork	Structure	Efficiency
Achievement	Dependability	Teamwork	Excellence
Accuracy	Harmony	Uniqueness	Learning
Caution	Family	Harmony	Instinct
Predictability	Fun	Integrity	Innovation
	Loyalty		
	Efficiency		
	Integrity		
	Tradition		

FIGURE 12.4 Values common to CAP2 personalities.

SIGNAL BEHAVIORS: THE MANIFESTATION OF VALUES

The final step in the Articulate exercise is also the most important one. This is where the rubber meets the road—how you define what you will do now that you know who your company is, what it stands for, and where it is going. 3M proves that one of its values is innovation by insisting that every employee spend 15 percent of his or her time innovating. Your company's behaviors are its fundamental values translated into action.

We refer to these behaviors in CAP2 workshops as *signal behaviors,* because doing them should signal what you value as an organization. Defining your company's signal behaviors will give people in your organization a path to learn how to choose behaviors that align with the company's values. Empowered with this knowledge, they can independently make decisions about what action(s) to take hour by hour and day by day. In fact, we advocate that the signal behaviors become integral to your job descriptions and performance standards, as has happened at Elford Construction (See Figure 12.5).

Making your behaviors true to your values enables you to live out the potential of your organization. In the process, you may discover that your presumed core values are not really core values at all. If they are, this next step should be fairly easy. If you struggle with defining behaviors for any of your values, pause to ponder whether you've selected a bogus value. Just as you didn't fabricate your vision, purpose, or values, you won't need to make up your behaviors. They're already there.

The most successful CAP2 companies are those that have completed this final step and then lived it. In the next section, we'll discuss how to live in harmony with your personality. But first, let's invest some time identifying behaviors for each of your core values. Use the blank core chart (Figure 12.6) to fill in your company's core ideology, core business, and core values. Then, write in behaviors that support each core value. A good place to start is to think of the one person in your organization who best exemplifies each value. Then ask yourself what that person does, and write it in the space provided under each core value. Also, be sure to think about existing procedures and policies that support the value and write them down.

When you know who you are and where you're going, you get a better sense of what you can achieve and how to do it. In the next section, we'll outline ways to bring your behaviors and your work environment into alignment with vision, purpose, and values.

ELFORD CONSTRUCTION CORE CHART

Personality:
Playing by the Rules

Personification:
Pop

Vision:
Exemplify professionalism

Mission:
Make construction a positive experience

Core Value	Core Value	Core Value	Core Value	Core Value
Be trustworthy	Build lasting relationships	Build community	Work hard, work smart	Keep learning

Signal Behaviors:

Be Trustworthy
- Do the right things at the right time for the right reasons.
- Hire the best people.
- Develop workable plans and realistic budgets.
- Show up on time.
- Demonstrate consistent excellence in workmanship.
- Clean up.
- Keep promises.
- Keep the customer informed so there are no surprises.
- Provide accurate information.
- Spend all the time necessary to do the job right.
- Deliver when you say you will.
- Accept responsibility for the end result.
- Do whatever it takes to finish the job as promised.

Build Lasting Relationships
With customers:
- Develop lifelong relationships with customers.
- See things from the customer's point of view.
- Put construction decisions into perspective for customers.
- Encourage and solicit input.
- Foster relationships on a personal, rather than purely business, level.
- Encourage more than one employee to develop a relationship with a customer.
- Understand the customer's expectations.
- Seek continual feedback.
- Be prepared to assume at least some financial responsibility to fix a situation that may damage a long-term relationship.
- Behave as if we were spending our own money.

FIGURE 12.5   Elford core chart.

With vendors and subcontractors:
- ☐ Treat them with fairness and respect.
- ☐ Encourage and solicit input.
- ☐ Use subcontractor programs and other means to build mutual trust and appreciation.

With employees:
- ☐ Make good hiring decisions to promote a solid team of high caliber.
- ☐ Ensure safe working conditions and practices with a hazard-free job site.
- ☐ Pay fair wages.
- ☐ Reward employee loyalty.
- ☐ Be fair but firm in enforcing rules.
- ☐ Recognize and reward hard work.
- ☐ Be discreet with personnel policies.
- ☐ Encourage and solicit input.
- ☐ Take the time to listen.
- ☐ Foster an extended family environment.
- ☐ Hold company events and functions.
- ☐ Honor achievements.

Build Community
- ☐ Encourage employee involvement in civic groups.
- ☐ Participate in community initiatives.
- ☐ Provide financial contributions and support for important causes.

With the industry:
- ☐ Become actively involved in industry groups to build the industry.

Keep Learning
- ☐ Be a technological leader in the construction industry.
- ☐ Develop new systems using automation and computerization.
- ☐ Actively seek new knowledge about construction through industry groups and other areas.
- ☐ Encourage workers to continue their education as construction professionals.

Work Hard, Work Smart
Meticulously maintain equipment.
- ☐ As much as possible, control the sequence of events.
- ☐ Track the cost, status, and schedule of every task and detail.
- ☐ Develop and use logical systems that enhance the efficiency of each task without compromising workmanship.
- ☐ Hire experienced supervisors and managers who are able to balance the needs for caution, quality, and timeliness.
- ☐ Hold efficient meetings.
- ☐ Document decisions.

Blank Core Chart for Your Company

Personality Type:

Personification:

Vision:

Mission:

Core Value   Core Value   Core Value   Core Value   Core Value

Signal Behaviors:

Core Value

Behaviors:

Core Value

Behaviors:

Core Value

Behaviors:

Core Value

Behaviors:

Core Value

Behaviors:

FIGURE 12.6   Core values exercise.

Meanwhile, we hope these exercises have helped you speak in your company's voice about matters close to its heart.

Companies Are People, Too provides a model that lets you cultivate the visionary qualities in your organization. You can use our technique to replicate the strategies of the brightest and best U.S. companies for strengthening corporate culture, brand identity, and ambition. Simply keep in mind the interests of your organization as a distinctive living entity, and personality will guide you toward a vision that endures and values that transcend habits and routines. It's an in-the-moment decision-making framework that everyone at your company can appreciate and use.

LIVE

In these final chapters of the book, we'll show you how to make the most of your new-found self-awareness. Armed with this knowledge, you'll then be ready to maximize and grow your company's personality.

Part of realizing who you are is to discover how to act upon your company's values. In the next chapters, we'll discuss how you can create strategic objectives based on your core vision, mission, and values. We'll also show you how to adapt your behaviors in support of these goals. At the end of the book, you'll have a one-page strategic plan for your company that reflects your personality and values and outlines your goals for the future.

Another aspect of personality and values is how a company fulfills its physical needs. Companies need an architecture or space that allows them to build their culture in line with their needs and goals. We'll show you how to build a work environment that will support your company's preferences.

We'll also discuss strategies for dealing with change. This is obviously a crucial question with our volatile economy, and we cover ways to mitigate organizational change. Luckily, when you know yourself well, you can anticipate change and determine the best course of action that's in line with your strengths.

We conclude the book with other applications for the Companies Are People, Too methodology, such as assessing a rival or anticipating how you might work with a partner company. We'll also reveal ways to accept your personality and to compensate for your weaknesses. These final chapters will show you how to align everything with your company's strengths, from your values and goals to your working systems and partnerships.

⑬ Living in Harmony with Your Company's Values

I t's essential to know who you are as an organization if you hope to achieve and sustain success. Even more important, you have to find ways to be yourself with incredible clarity and consistency, whatever the demands of the moment, and in spite of your individual preferences. We've shown how you can use the CAP2 personality profile to articulate the core of your business or organization: your core ideology (or vision); the core (purpose and mission) of the enterprise; and the fundamental values that shape your company's behavior every day. In the final section, we'll talk about how to implement—how to live—what you've learned about your organization. Companies Are People, Too helps you discover ways to express your company's innermost ambitions and preferences and project that knowledge outward into every aspect of your operations. It's not some kind of planning model that sits in a drawer—it's a *doing* model that helps you answer questions and take action every day.

Living and working in harmony with personality lets your company find a natural balance and rhythm. Know and be yourself as a company, and you'll know how best to respond in the face of adversity, crisis, change, and growth. Companies Are People, Too is a guide to self-awareness, but it's also a program for doing. It's not what you know, after all, but how you use that knowledge. CAP2 is a system for knowledge management. It helps you access relevant data and interpretation for everyday decision making. As your company becomes familiar with its organizational persona—someone you get to know up close and personal—you can give a voice to the unseen energy that exerts its will in your workplace. You can embrace a new member in your community, whose contribution represents the best hope and whole interest of the enterprise.

"What would the company persona do?" If your employees can conceive of the answer, they've tapped into the power of personality for the here and now. To introduce the CAP2 Decision Making Framework—your company's program for being itself on purpose—we've borrowed some ideas from Roy Shafer, an Ohio-based organizational coach, who has used the Companies Are People, Too approach in work with dozens of nonprofit institutions, universities, and businesses. Shafer's concept of a doing model puts your company personality to work in the development of a 100-year strategic plan. The doing model helps you envision your company's future as an organization and also sets up an ongoing in-the-moment decision-making framework for your work in the immediate term. Most important of all, the doing program integrates that vision into your daily work by tapping into the power of personality.

Most people find themselves at ease in the company of people they know. When you gain this kind of intimacy and insight into your organization as a living entity, you'll find it easier to gauge the most natural course of action. Understanding personality can help your organization capitalize on its strengths and differentiate itself from the competition. It helps you recognize your blind spots and weaknesses and build your organization's sense of community and consensus. Above all, perhaps, the technique provides a straightforward, natural way to measure the results of your efforts. Are you living in harmony with your company's personality? Think about what your company persona would do and do it. You'll gain clarity, alignment, and consistency in everything you do.

DO THE RIGHT THINGS THE RIGHT WAY

Books and workshops on business strategy have tended to focus on strategic planning for organizations, but *Companies Are People, Too,* coupled with Shafer's model, offers a method for strategic doing. Does your company or organization aim at greatness? Then you need to develop effective mechanisms for sustainable success. The doing model helps you link your values and aspirations to the company's daily operations. It's a way to make personality part of the mechanism that drives your organization every moment of every day. We'll help you begin to create your own doing model in this section using the core statements of ideology, business, and values (Shafer's terms for the vision, mission, and values from the exercises in the preceding chapter). When you're done, you'll have a more concrete way to live your organization's personality; everyone, every day, every way.

Figure 13.1 shows a visual model of the Decision Making Framework.

CORE IDEOLOGY

In Chapter 12, you identified your company's enduring, 100-year aspiration—its core ideology—in three to five words. In the next exercise, we'll help you articulate how to best pursue this over-arching aspiration in the more immediate term (the next three to five years) and finally in the next annual plan/budget cycle. To guide you in this effort, we'll rely on an example drawn from one of Shafer's CAP2 clients, the Museum of Science and Industry (MOSI) in Tampa, Florida.

MOSI identified its core ideology as "making a difference in people's lives," its core business as "making science real," and its core values as integrity/honesty, growth, flexibility, and being 'MOSIfied'." Its personality preferences were ideally suited to this enlightened aspiration: "It's Fun to Do Good Work," an extroverted, intuitive, feeling, perceiving organization. Since its establishment in 1962, MOSI had relied on the organization's scientific expertise to

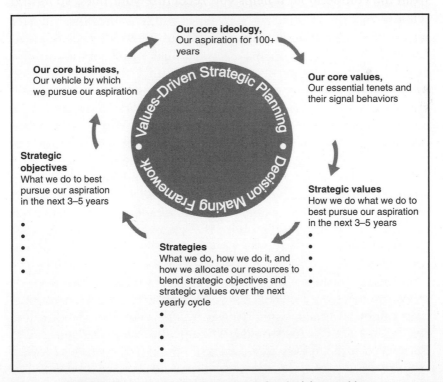

FIGURE 13.1 CAP2 framework for decision making.

pursue its aspiration. Its exhibits were long on factual material and interpretation and short on features that allowed patrons to form their own judgments about the natural world.

Equipped with insight into its personality preferences—especially the individualism and drive of its intuitive sense—and its aspiration of making a difference in people's lives by making science real, the institution came to understand its relationship to scientific knowledge in a new way. Old exhibits and events at MOSI had sought to convey the breadth and detail of scientific knowledge to the visitor. New MOSI programs instead emphasized people discovering the science themselves through interactive programs and facilities—making science real. The shift not only gratified the organization's preference for intuition over sensory data, but also complemented MOSI's outward-looking, extroverted orientation. By asking visitors to connect the dots of scientific cause and effect themselves, the institution's persona, "MAX," got up close and personal with its public.

MOSI's adaptations provide a successful example of how to use personality to create your own company's doing model. The model includes a set of strategic objectives and strategic values that help you pursue your long-term aspiration in the more immediate term of next three to five years. MOSI found that the best way to make a difference in people's lives by making science real was to help all its visitors discover the thrill of invention and discovery on their own terms. MOSI personnel also resolved to be more inventive in their efforts to convey this thrill to their various audiences. As it happens, striving for continuous improvement is another key trait of the "It's Fun to Do Good Work" personality profile. Because what's new is always exciting to organizations with this preference, MOSI needed to commit itself to building more, discovering more, and reaching more and bigger audiences with its message. The new emphasis resulted in the construction of indoor and outdoor installations that challenged and delighted the public, including a high-wire bicycle exhibit that lets visitors test their faith in science in a personal way, and other innovative programs.

You can use the MOSI model to come up with your own set of strategic objectives. Look back at your core vision, core mission, and core values and their signal behaviors. Then think of three to five strategic objectives that would best help you bring your core to life in the next three to five years, and write them in the space provided (Fig. 13.2).

Strategic Objectives

Write down what you will do to best pursue your aspiration in the next three to five years.

_____

_____

_____

_____

_____

_____

_____

_____

_____

_____

_____

_____

_____

FIGURE 13.2   Strategic objectives exercise.

STRATEGIC VALUES

Core values represent the enduring essential tenets of your organization and the vital source for its signal behaviors. They are your instincts and your reflexes. They are pervasive across the organization. Strategic values, on the other hand, are those values and their signal behaviors that you believe are present in the organization but not pervasive. Many times they are values that do not pass the core value test; however, there is agreement that if you work on them through their signal behaviors, it will help you become better at what you do, especially over the next three to five years. If strategic objectives are what you will do, think of strategic values as how you will do what you will do. With the doing model and CAP2, you can identify what is most important to your organization's core in its current operations. Insight from personality can help you align how you do what you do to what you value most.

To continue with examples from the Museum of Science and Industry in Tampa, let's look at MOSI's core values and their signal

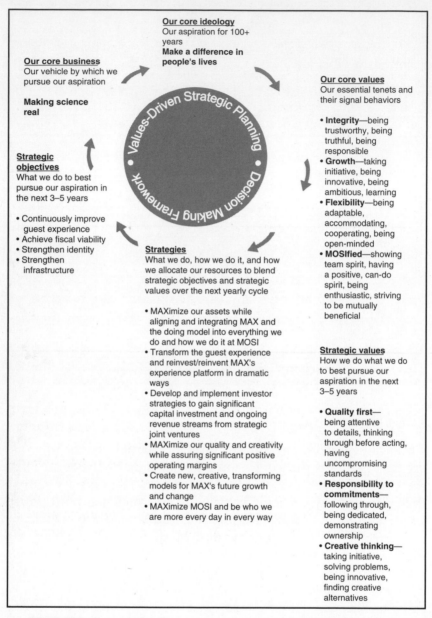

FIGURE 13.3 MOSI's complete framework for decision making.

behaviors. (See Figure 13.3.) In one of the CAP2 sessions, MOSI
determined that its core values and their signal behaviors included
"Being 'MOSIfied'—which they defined as having a positive,
can-do spirit; being enthusiastic with a win-win attitude; growth,
being ambitious, curious, adaptable, accommodating, cooperative,
and open-minded; always learning; and remaining committed to

Strategic Values

Write how you will do what you will do to best pursue your aspiration in the next three to five years. For each strategic value, you will also want to define signal behaviors that demonstrate what you mean. (For example, one CAP2 client identified personal responsibility as a strategic value with behaviors that include doing what you say you'll do, taking ownership of your work, being loyal, and being accountable.)

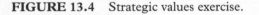

FIGURE 13.4   Strategic values exercise.

integrity and honesty, which MOSI staffers identified as a hallmark of good science. MOSI's case illustrates the sometimes profound differences between an organization's unchanging core values and the strategic adaptations that may better suit its work over the next few years. Flexibility, for example, is a core value that is strongly identified with the perceiving work style preference of "It's Fun to Do Good Work" organizations. In pursuit of opportunity, however, the museum had recently found itself overwhelmed with obligations taken on in the spirit of spontaneity. MOSI adopted quality first—being attentive to details, thinking before acting, and upholding uncompromising standards—as one of the organization's strategic values. Putting quality first lets the organization temper flexibility with stewardship and good service. The museum hopes to reinforce its core commitment to making science real by being more creative in the immediate term, participating more directly in the process of discovery itself. The strategic emphasis on responsibility to commitments also links MOSI's current programs to its core values of integrity and honesty.

As you think about your organization's strategic values, we urge you to look again at the CAP2 profile and the notes on core values from the earlier chapter. Write down three to five values and their signal behaviors that you can use in the immediate term of three to five years to best pursue your core (Fig. 13.4).

BEHAVIORS

As we discovered in the previous chapter, values are simply words unless and until you "behavioralize" them. Once we identify signal behaviors that demonstrate what we value, we can work on making those behaviors and values more pervasive across the organization. It's the key to sustainable success. Adapting your behaviors to your core is the most important lesson of *Companies Are People, Too.* When you make your behaviors true to your values, you live out the potential of your organization. More than any other factor, your behaviors are the *do* in the CAP2 doing model. Just as you defined signal behaviors for your core values, you must do so for your strategic values.

Let's look again at MOSI and see how its people have tried to behave in accordance with the museum's personality. The MOSI staff members decided to take the most literal interpretation of their core commitment to education and collaboration: In partnership with two local charter school programs, the museum transformed part of its extensive site into full-time charter schools. It also invested more in its commitment to flexibility by joining with a non-profit organization in a research project on the nature of risk—a subject with an undeniable appeal to the "It's Fun to Do Good Work" eye for opportunity. Overall, these behaviors have helped raise the profile of the organization in the Tampa community, while remaining consistent with its fundamental character and values.

STRATEGIES

In the CAP2 Decision Making Framework, we call on leaders to build the foundation for a strong collaboration with the character of their organizations. The last element in the doing model is to decide on and commit to what your company will do for the next yearly cycle, how you will do it, and how you will allocate your resources to it. Select from the three- to five-year strategic objectives and values, and zero in on those that will receive the highest priority in the next year. These strategies are the final step in the doing model. You will now have a one-page strategic plan for your company that is completely aligned with who your company is, what it stands for, and where it's going.

⑭ The Physical Dimensions of Your Company

J ust as human beings are made up of the same elemental ingredients as the earth itself, corporations exist on the level of the
physical environment. While your company is decidedly more
than the sum of its assets, it nonetheless consists of tangible,
fundamentally perishable physical parts.

Companies and institutions occupy real estate and transportation
routes—globally, in airports and waterways; locally, on interstates,
parking lots, and office parks—and confront an array of unpredictable material forces. The physical footprint of your organization
reveals aspects of its personality preferences. What's more, companies and institutions use physical processes, including methods of
communication, to conduct their business. Communication preferences and other choices can reinforce company's strengths but can
also perpetuate bad personality habits. As illustrated in the doing
model, your company's choices on small or material matters can
have grand implications when they capitalize on your strengths and
actualize your values. The CAP2 profile for your organization can
help you bring the organization into greater harmony with the
environment.

THE WORK ENVIRONMENT

Like any other living organism, an organization possesses a distinct physical appearance in the form of its offices, factories,
grounds, and other facilities. A company's physical plant tends to
reflect personality as well as the requirements and amenities of
doing business. In designing and occupying their physical spaces,
companies can build awareness, morale, and brand identity
for employees and the general public. The personalized work

environment is an ideal medium for revealing an organization's inner motivations and goals.

A broad range of expressions marks the physical face of a company or institution. At the simplest level, company personality is often revealed in office decor. At the corporate headquarters for Cranium, Inc., makers of the popular board game borrowed the game's signature colors for their own interiors, with brightly colored walls and purple carpet that evokes Cranium modeling clay. The colors symbolize the young company's irreverent sensibility and reinforce its emergent brand identity.[1] Special facilities at other firms accentuate personality preferences that cut to the heart of the corporate identity.

At Ben & Jerry's, for example, the ice cream company's physical plant symbolizes its commitment to building a sense of community with fellow Vermonters. The Waterbury, Vermont, manufacturing plant reinforces this commitment by incorporating a tour route that showcases the production process. The plant, which draws more than 250,000 visitors each year, is Vermont's number one tourist attraction.

At the Nike World Campus in Beaverton, Oregon, facilities and layout reflect the apparel manufacturer's passion for sports and competition. Its various buildings are named after Nike spokespersons from the world of sport, celebrating the athletic heroism of celebrities such as Mia Hamm and Michael Jordan. The heroics of everyday athletics are featured in state-of-the-art facilities for Nike's favorite sports, including basketball and tennis courts, an aerobics studio, and a track and field complex.[2] The facilities reinforce the central messages of Nike advertising and also provide opportunities for employees to "just do it" by integrating fitness and athletic striving into the working day.

Companies seeking to live in harmony with personality can begin with similar efforts to create facilities that reflect their inner character. Dixon-Schwabl Advertising, Inc., in Rochester, New York, found an opportunity to do this when a snowstorm collapsed the roof of the company's old offices in 1999. The company took personality into account in the design of its new building. Working with Fekete + Company, Dixon-Schwabl had recently participated in the Companies Are People, Too diagnostic and identified its personality profile as "It's Fun to Do Good Work." The new building highlights the showmanship, salesmanship, and contagious enthusiasm typical of the Fun profile. In a three-story glass atrium, a 16-foot curving slide connects the top-floor loft (home to the agency's creative division) with the lobby, where a wall of water adds a visual and audible dimension. In a nod to the emotionalism associated with the "It's Fun to Do Good Work" profile (and perhaps also its inclination to avoid conflict at all costs), the agency installed a padded primal scream room as a place for employees to blow off steam. A two-story conference room, complete with kitchen and fireplace, embodies Dixon Schwabl's essential sociability and casual atmosphere. The customized setting creates an environment in which the agency can concentrate on living in harmony with personality.

Another Fekete + Company client, Elford, Inc., took its CAP2 profile ("Playing by the Rules") and the Up Close and Personal description of "Pop" directly to the designer when the company began making plans for a new headquarters. With that kind of insight into the company's priorities, they were told, the designers could proceed to interior design concepts without further consultations with the Elford management.

Take a look around your physical plant. Does it communicate your company's personality? In Figure 14.1, we've extracted elements from the work environment section of each CAP2 profile that describe what the physical surroundings might look and feel like.

HOW DO YOU SAY . . .

Communication—a physical process rather than a place—also reveals characteristics of company personality. While the physical dimension is not the only aspect of communication style that is shaped by personality, the act of giving and receiving information is a manifestation of preferences that is simple to explain and relatively easy for leaders to adapt to new priorities. At AOL Time Warner, for example, the use of Instant Messaging (IM) technology for in-house communication represents more than simply the creative application of a proprietary technology. AOL's rapid-fire, one-on-one online connection, popular among teenagers but still being developed for use by the broader business community, is a perfect match for the troubled conglomerate's "Driven to Lead" personality profile. Reliance on IM reflects the fascination with innovation that "Driven to Lead" companies—and not just those that develop online communications—tend to share. Instant Messaging also conforms to this type's prototypical demand for quick, terse, to-the-point communications.

Solid as a Rock

Maintains a high work ethic; the company is always very busy

Serious, with little room for chitchat

Traditions are prominent; corporate culture is important and celebrated

Maintains a discreet, low-key, and conservative public image

Structured, analytical, and observant: predictable

Sees the world in black and white

You Can Count on Us

People orientation combined with common sense and practicality

Decisions may be made quietly and without much collaboration

Exhibits a high work ethic; the company is always very busy

Traditions and corporate culture are prominent and celebrated

Individual responsibility has high visibility

Vision Driven by Values

Built on core values and ideals

Harmonious: people place, warm and friendly, supportive and appreciative

Quiet enthusiasm

Dedicated, serious, and hardworking; may be intense

Imaginative

Positive

Expressive

Highly motivating

Going All Out for Greatness

Quiet, efficient, fast-paced think tank

Very few meetings or team-building exercises

A place to acquire knowledge and competency; always open to discovery

Will see constant reminders of achievement and progress toward goals

Private, contained, impersonal

Calm, cool, but may get intense and argumentative at times

Action, Action—We Want Action!

The company is a stage and work is a place to perform and create an impact

Impulsive and spontaneous, with freedom of action

Work is an adventure

Largely a closed universe with little contact with the outside world

Prefers personal accomplishments to team accomplishments

Action abounds, hands-on

Working to Make a Difference

The company is a stage and work is a place to perform and create an impact

Work is play or friendly competition

Impulsive and spontaneous

Optimistic, cheerful, friendly

Filled with the spirit of risk taking

Exudes the creative element

Easygoing, upbeat, and exciting

Physically attractive and comfortable

Quest for Meaningful Work

Harmonious: people place, warm and friendly, supportive and affirming

Will frequently see people working alone or in small, intimate groups

Unstructured, loose, casual, minimally insistent on rules and procedures

Quiet enthusiasm

Fun

Positive

Expressive

Hands-on

In Pursuit of Intellectual Solutions

A place to acquire knowledge and competency; always open to discovery

Calm, cool, but may get intense and argumentative at times

Casual, loosely structured

Serious, with little room for chitchat

Private, contained, impersonal

Disorganized and sometimes chaotic

FIGURE 14.1 CAP2 work environments.

Thriving on Risky Business

The company is a stage and work is a place to perform and create an impact

Impulsive and spontaneous, sometimes chaotic

Work is an adventure and each day is unique

Fun and friendly, yet impersonal

Risk taking permeates everything

Physically comfortable and attractive

Action abounds

Hands-on

We Aim to Please

The company is a stage and work is a place to perform and create an impact

Impulsive and spontaneous

Sensitive to the well-being of people

High interactivity with frequent meetings

Harmonious: people place, warm and friendly, supportive and appreciative

Work is an adventure

Fun, socially interactive, exciting, even hilarious

Comfortable and attractive, stylish

Action oriented, even frantic, and hands-on

It's Fun to Do Good Work

Harmonious: people place, warm and friendly, supportive

Creative, imaginative

Considerable talking, listening, and brainstorming

Upbeat, full of energy and positive reinforcements, sometimes emotional

Radiates enthusiasm

Hands-on

Unstructured, relaxed, casual, and may be chaotic

If We Can't Do It, No One Can

Resonates with energy and excitement

Radiates enthusiasm for ideas and theories

Fast paced

Filled with confidence and optimism

Spontaneous and improvisational

Risk-taking setting

Competitive

Contentious and often insensitive; may seem cold and distant

Casual, loosely structured

Playing by the Rules

Strong work ethic; the company is always very busy

Traditions are prominent; corporate culture is important

Predictable, stable, orderly

Serious, with little room for chitchat

Harmony achieved through teamwork

More like a community than a workplace

Work is done with a steady energy

Doing the Right Thing

Exhibits a strong work ethic; the company is always very busy

Harmonious: people place, warm and friendly, supportive and appreciative

Respects hierarchy, norms, and rules

Socializing and corporate events are commonplace

Strong service orientation

Teamwork and group contribution flourishes

Family-like culture

Seeing the Big Picture in Human Terms

Harmonious: people place, warm and friendly, supportive and appreciative

Fast paced

Creative, imaginative

High level of interaction; lots of meetings

Upbeat, full of energy and positive reinforcements, sometimes emotional

Driven to Lead

Calm, cool, perhaps even cold and detached

Has a controlled intensity, often the result of impatience

Well organized

Change is constant

Lively debates are enjoyed and questioning is encouraged

Competitive

Solid as a Rock

Centers on logic and links with the past

Language is functional and will often refer to tasks and duties

Prefers to give directives and structure rather than information

Fair, impartial, impersonal

In meetings, seeks connection with task first

Begins presentations with details first

Brief and concise, dealing with concrete issues on a realistic level

Prefers writing and e-mail to meetings

You Can Count on Us

Centers on people in a way that addresses relationships and the past

Language is functional and will often refer to tasks and duties

Prefers to give information rather than directives

Fair, impartial, impersonal

Prefers face-to-face interaction

Concrete, step-by-step, sequential, and highly detailed

In meetings, seeks connection with people first

Begins presentations with details first

Structured

Contained, thoughtful, and reflective

Vision Driven by Values

Centers on people and the future

Often hear about options, possibilities, and "what could be," especially concerning people

Prefers to give directives rather than information

Prefers face-to-face interaction

In meetings, seeks connection with people first, expressing points of agreement

Begins presentations with the big picture, goals, and objectives

Conceptual

Empathetic

Focuses on process over facts

May be prone to exaggeration and dramatics

Going All Out for Greatness

Centered on possibilities and logical improvements

Frequently terse and filled with goals and strategies, problems to be solved, possibilities

Prefers to give directions and structure rather than information

Brief, concise, and can be blunt

In meetings, seeks connection with task first

Begins presentations with the big picture, goals, and objectives

Logical, with cause-and-effect reasoning

Prefers writing and e-mail

Frequently conceptual, may seem arrogant

Contained, thoughtful, and reflective

Comments have already been thought through

Action, Action—We Want Action!

Centers on the present in an analytical and logical way

Language may be colorful, but most likely concrete and realistic

Prefers to give directives and structure rather than information

Working to Make a Difference

Centers on the present and on people

Language is concrete and specific and may be colorful

Prefers to speak through actions and results

Quest for Meaningful Work

Centers on the future and people, with ideals

Prefers to give information rather than directives

Communicates at the conceptual level

In Pursuit of Intellectual Solutions

Centers on patterns and principles

Language may be highly technical, complex, and detailed

Terse and filled with goals and strategies, problems to be solved, possibilities

Thriving on Risky Business	We Aim to Please	Its Fun to Do Good Work	If We Can't Do It, No One Can
Factual, concise, blunt, specific, and contains concrete examples	Factual, direct, detailed, friendly, and contains personal examples	May be prone to exaggeration and dramatics	Precise
Prefers writing and e-mail	Prefers face-to-face interaction	Prefers face-to-face interaction	Prefers to give information rather than directives
Logical, with cause-and-effect reasoning	Structured	Language is verbally creative	Brief and concise, often using graphics to aid comprehension
In meetings, seeks connection with task first	In meetings, seeks connection with people first	Begins meetings with the big picture first, expressing points of agreement	Fair, impartial, impersonal
Begins presentations with details first	Begins presentations with details first	Topics will vary widely, but will deal mostly with ideas	In meetings, seeks connection with task first
Structured	Contained, thoughtful, and reflective	May be expressive, enthusiastic	Begins presentations with the big picture first, then goals and objectives
		Conversations will jump from topic to topic	Cool and dispassionate
		Options and possibilities will be communicated	Prefers writing and e-mail
		Focuses on process over facts	Contained, thoughtful, and reflective
Thriving on Risky Business	**We Aim to Please**	**Its Fun to Do Good Work**	**If We Can't Do It, No One Can**
Centers on the present in a logical and analytical way	Centers on the present and on people	Centers on people and the future	Centered on ideas and the future
Speech is colorful	Language is concrete and specific and may be colorful	Will often focus on process over facts	Often terse and filled with goals, strategies, and problems to be solved
Prefers to give directives and structure rather than information	Prefers to give information rather than directives	Prefers to give information rather than directives	Frequently involves discussion, inquiry, and criticism
Factual, concise, blunt, specific, and contains concrete examples	Factual, detailed, friendly, and contains personal examples	Prefers face-to-face interaction	Meetings feature lots of debate and "what if" games
Seeks to get to the point as quickly as possible	Prefers face-to-face interaction	Language can be verbally creative, subjective, and evocative	Everyone is expected to become an active part of the ongoing debate
In meetings, seeks connection with task first			

(continued)

FIGURE 14.2 Communication styles of the CAP2 personalities.

Thriving on Risky Business (*cont.*)	**We Aim to Please** (*cont.*)	**If We Can't Do It, No One Can** (*cont.*)
Begins presentations with detail first	In meetings, seeks connection with people first, expressing points of agreement	Prefers to give information rather than directives
	Begins presentations with details first	Speech is energetic, precise, and may be colorful
	Thinks out loud, and the pace is rapid	In meetings, seeks to connect with the task first
		Begins presentations with the big picture, goals, and objectives
		Uses logical, cause-and-effect reasoning
		Seeks to get to the point as quickly as possible
		Conversations will cover a variety of topics, often jumping quickly in a stream-of-consciousness manner

Playing by the Rules	**Doing the Right Thing**	**Its Fun to Do Good Work** (*cont.*)	**Seeing the Big Picture in Human Terms**	**Driven to Lead**
Centers on logic and links to the past	Centers on people in a way that addresses relationships and the norms of society	In meetings, seeks connection with people first, expressing points of agreement	Centers on people and the future	Centers on organization and improvement
Language is functional and will often refer to tasks and duties	Language is functional and will often refer to tasks and duties	Begins presentations with the big picture, goals, and objectives	Focuses on completion, using timetables and schedules	Frequently terse and filled with goals, strategies, and problems to be solved
Prefers to give directives and structure rather than information	Prefers to give information rather than directives	Typically conceptual, concerning options and possibilities	Highly interactive	Prefers to give directives and structure rather than information
Concrete, specific, and brief	Language is concrete and specific	Flowing, exaggerated, and often redundant	Prefers to give directives rather than information	Speech is energetic, precise, and may be colorful
Logical, with cause-and-effect reasoning	Prefers face-to-face interaction	Expressive, enthusiastic, and may become emotional	Prefers face-to-face interaction	Conversations often include the question "Why?" and are often along intellectual lines
In meetings, seeks connection with the task first	In meetings, seeks connection with people first	Thinks out loud, and patter is rapid	Language can be verbally creative, subjective, and evocative	
		Conversations will cover a variety of topics, often jumping quickly in a stream-of-consciousness manner		

Begins presentations with the details first	Begins presentations with details first	In meetings, seeks connection with people first, expressing points of agreement	Seeks to get to the point as quickly as possible
Prefers writing and e-mail	Thinks out loud, and the pace is rapid	Begins presentations with the big picture, goals, and objectives	In meetings, seeks connection with task first
		Conversations will cover a variety of topics, often jumping quickly in a stream-of-consciousness manner	Begins presentations with the big picture, goals, and objectives
		Often see people in groups where language is expressive and tone is enthusiastic	Uses logical, cause-and-effect reasoning
		Flowing, exaggerated, and often redundant	Avoids emotional issues, but can be passionate in theoretical debates
		Thinks out loud, and the pace is rapid	

FIGURE 14.2   Communication styles of the CAP2 personalities. *Continued*

Given the tension growing out of the 2001 merger of AOL and Time Warner, however, with turmoil in the executive ranks and a spiraling stock price, AOL Time Warner would be wise to consider its communications strategy carefully. If AOL-based executives place too much confidence in IM, they may further alienate the non-AOL components of the company, whose personality preferences are inclined toward face-to-face communications. In fact, the early failure to integrate e-mail communications—when Time Warner components refused to adopt America Online's service—indicated the seriousness of the AOL Time Warner culture clash. As the company reckons with the fallout from the collapse of its stock price, and Time Warner divisions reassert their prerogatives versus AOL upstarts, questions arising from internal communications media will indicate the success or failure of the cultural integration.

If AOL Time Warner's IM represents the innovative, fluid extreme of communications preferences, reliance on the written memorandum characterizes the medium of choice for traditional, "Solid as a Rock" organizations such as government agencies. Memoranda and other formal written communications conform to the "Solid as a Rock" preference for detailed, impersonal, task-oriented information. Because they create a permanent record, such documents also satisfy this kind of organization's respect for its heritage and considerations for the future. Archives of government documents—some of which eventually become public through declassification procedures—provide a guide to current decision making. Such materials also offer a focal point for face-to-face meetings, allowing Solid organizations to assess responsibilities and assign duties as efficiently as possible. Like all forms of communication, however, the formal memorandum sustains some bad personality habits associated with the "Solid as a Rock" profile. More complete, logical, detailed, and permanent than spoken or electronic communications, memoranda are also much easier to ignore, as the case of unheeded terrorism warnings at

AOL Time Warner: "Driven to Lead"

- Makes decisions using logic, analysis, and cause-and-effect reasoning
- Focused on the big picture, relationships, and connections between facts
- Energized by the outer world of people and activity
- Prefers a structured, organized, and planned environment

Federal Bureau of Investigation: "Solid as a Rock"

- Focused on information that is factual, real, and current
- Makes decisions using logic, analysis, and cause-and-effect reasoning
- Energized by the inner world of ideas and experiences
- Prefers a structured, organized, and planned environment

the FBI during 2001 makes clear. Informed about its preferential tendencies, the bureau might have encouraged its agents to reinforce their most important written messages with e-mail, telephone calls, and face-to-face communications.

You can smooth the operations of your own organization (and perhaps avoid the difficulties of some of the big players) by paying attention to the communications media you use most. Consider your personality preferences—especially the orientation of your organizational focus—when making choices about communications. Is your group energized by the inner world of ideas and experiences? Then you need to find a place for written communications in your various exchanges. And while Instant Messaging might be appropriate for a company with a flexible, spontaneous outlook, a competitor with a preference for structure might prefer something more permanent. It also helps to consult your CAP2 profile on communication style, which is described in detail for every type. This kind of insight into the content of your conversations may also be relevant to your communications media strategy.

Figure 14.2 illustrates common communication styles of each CAP2 personality, excerpted from the profiles in Chapters 4 through 7.

An organization's physical footprint is its chief material manifestation. As stewards of a living company, it's the leaders' responsibility to see to the organization's physical needs and desires. Appearances are important, because they set the tone and volume of a company's human interactions. When you cultivate harmonious surroundings, with facilities that make clarity and alignment possible, you provide a secure environment for your company's personality to express itself. What's more, alignment in the physical dimension can open channels of communication within the organization and in the larger community of partners and clients. Your company's physical plant is the human face of the organization, and CAP2 helps you show that face in its best light.

⑮ When Things Change

Change tends to catch up to most people when they least expect it. If you know yourself, the impact is less likely to knock you for a loop. For all their efforts and expense to forecast the future and plan accordingly, corporations often encounter change unexpectedly. Other times they can anticipate problems that all their foresight cannot help them avoid. Change can be constructive and even thrilling: Growth in revenues and the conquest of new markets is the stuff that for-profit companies dream of. But more often mergers, retirement, or loss of market share are a source of discomfort or even despair. Preoccupied by a sense of losing what is past, organizations that experience transitions can refuse to surrender to new realities and can compound their difficulties.

Understanding companies as people mitigates the sense of loss that comes with certain kinds of changes. If you take the analogy to heart, you see that actual changes in the environment or personnel of an organization have a limited impact on the workings of its true self. Indeed, certain kinds of changes might create new opportunities for the organization to thrive and grow. The concept of personality lends something enduring and essentially unchanging to your organization's preferences and values. When you know who you are, moreover, it's much easier to conceive of strategies for adaptation. Like a well-grounded individual, a company that understands its personality can prosper in the face of adversity, drawing confidence and strength from its self-esteem.

Leadership transitions occur periodically in the life of every organization, but they often create tremendous uncertainty and stress. In some cases, this anxiety attends primarily on the period before a longtime executive chooses to step aside (or gets the hook from frustrated directors). When there's a sense that the company is running on the wrong track, decision makers and front-line staff alike fear for the future. The same constituencies may also be alarmed by the impending retirement of a beloved CEO or the departure of a high-ranking subordinate to a more high-profile job. Such fears are well grounded. Thinking back to our examples from The Gap and Southwest Airlines, we can see how the departure of or loss of focus by talented leadership can create difficulties for organizations. The period after the appointment of new leadership also tends to be frustrating at times. If new leaders set out to make substantive changes, they may face charges of insensitivity or haste, while the failure to differentiate from the old guard leaves them open to another kind of complaint. In sum, the leadership transition represents one of the most significant challenges to organizational morale.

Companies that think of themselves as people find this kind of transition less intimidating. Leaders, remember the lesson of our previous discussion on leadership—it's not just about you. The focus on the organization as a character in its own right deemphasizes the importance of individual executives as captains of the company's fate. Conscious of the organization's needs and aspirations as an independent entity, employees at all levels understand that the company has priorities that transcend the moment. These employees are also equipped with the means to guide new leadership toward the goal of living in harmony with the company personality. In fact, the CAP2 profile provides a kind of blueprint of the organization for new employees at all ranks. On the whole, awareness of personality can create a more comfortable workplace during leadership transitions. At Elford, Inc., for example, confidence that the company continues to do the right thing has survived seven years and three CEO transitions.

MERGERS AND MATTERS OF MINE, YOURS, AND OURS

Mergers and acquisitions cut to the heart of the question of personality at work. If every company has its own personality, what happens when two or more corporations are combined into a single new organization? Mergers and acquisitions occur naturally in successful companies. When business booms, companies often look to reinvest profits in acquiring new personnel, skills, or clients through acquisitions. Other times, successful companies become takeover targets when competitors expand or when a client company decides to stop outsourcing key functions. Publicly traded companies are sometimes acquired when a drop in the stock price results in a favorable price-to-earnings ratio for prospective purchasers. Finally, the departure of key leadership sometimes results in the sale of small companies or divisions within a company. Whatever the motivation (and whether or not each party welcomes the merger), the conglomeration of corporate units almost always creates stress for an organization. In the adjustments that follow, company personality becomes a matter of real and sometimes urgent concern for management and employees.

Personality preferences are too deeply ingrained to be transformed by a mere financial transaction. Moreover, most mergers and acquisitions are planned and executed with little regard for compatibility in values, work style, and outlook. The process of acculturating to the new environment and getting to know new coworkers and procedures can be very contentious. Much like individuals confronting change, companies adjusting to mergers endure dislocating psychological shifts. The stages of a company's response to the change are analogous to the psychological processes of individuals. Even when prospects are rosy and each party is favorably disposed toward the merger, the initial encounter is primarily devoted to identifying differences in the new organization. All too often, these differences are perceived as a threat to established priorities. Defensive behavior, including complaints and noncompliance, sets in, in a pattern that may continue for years as a source of tension, waste, and lost productivity. Mergers and acquisitions that succeed eventually produce an accommodation among disparate factions, either by achieving a new consensus and identity or by dismissing problematic individuals and divisions. However, a leading longitudinal study of mergers and acquisitions reveals that the majority of the ventures end in failure, with the sale or dismantling of the acquired units within the first 15 years.[1] Personality conflicts at the organizational level entail tremendous costs for M&A companies and adverse consequences for the broader economy.

Understanding company personality can improve the chances of success after mergers and acquisitions. An organization's personality profile provides information about company goals, preferences, and work style that can facilitate a less tumultuous transition. Recognizing differences rooted in personality can help companies transcend rivalries and fears of persecution by establishing effective intergroup communications. The peculiar sensitivities or dreams of one group appear less problematic when showcased alongside similar proclivities on the other side. Understanding personality helps companies mark their common ground as well as territories that will remain off limits until a collective identity emerges. Awareness of the quirks of personality creates an atmosphere of tolerance and accommodation in the new corporate structure.

But how do you identify the personality of an organization made up of more than one corporate persona? Which personality prevails? When a large and powerful company acquires a much smaller group, the personality preferences of the purchasing group will often prevail. To ensure success in the merger, the larger component will be attuned to the new group's identity and goals. Personality analysis can help smooth the integration of formerly independent units into a functioning whole. In more equal matches, the outcome of the struggle to predominate is less certain. Market factors or the relative strength of the combined organizations will sometimes favor one group over another. Personality itself, especially in the case of assertive and tenacious organizations, can play a decisive role. Most often, however, the union of more than one corporate entity results in the creation of a new and distinct company personality. When they become part of a conglomeration, many companies find different sources of energy, other ways of gathering information and making decisions, and new standard operating procedures. In this sense, investing time in mutual self-discovery can do much more than merely smooth over the seams of a merger. Members of the new organization can uncover its inner strengths and competitive advantages.

Let's use a worst-case scenario to illustrate the constructive application of the concept of personality in a difficult merger. The union of America Online and Time Warner, Inc. in January 2001 produced the most spectacular—and so far the most disastrous—corporate merger in recent history. The two main components of the new company could hardly appear more different on the surface: AOL, the quintessential high-tech upstart, and Time Warner, with its roots in the flagship publications of the establishment elite. To complicate matters further, individual leadership in both of the major AOL Time Warner divisions was outspoken and aggressive, with a high public profile and access to the press. Even before the merger went into effect, big-name executives such as AOL's Steve Case and Robert Pittman, Time Warner's Gerald Levin, and the legendary Ted Turner of Time Warner's Turner Broadcasting Systems were jockeying for position by taking aim at one another's divisions. The rapid decline of AOL Time Warner's stock price—the currency of the AOL buyout—considerably sharpened the internal debate, especially as government agencies began to investigate America Online's accounting practices in the boom years. From the standpoint of the company's reputation and finances, the early years of the AOL Time Warner union have turned out to be a resounding failure. But the culture clash among the AOL Time Warner divisions has proven even more spectacular. In countless articles in the business press and the national news, company insiders have loudly outlined the terms of the rivalry among their divisions and speculated that the various teams could never work in harmony with one another.

The concept of companies as people suggests a more optimistic interpretation of the AOL Time Warner fiasco. While Companies Are People, Too can't help the great conglomerate with its legal and financial problems, we believe there's an answer to the conundrum of the culture clash in the CAP2 profiles of the various divisions. We've developed profiles for the better-known component companies of AOL Time Warner—a company built by the merger of two companies built by mergers. You might be surprised, but our research indicates a favorable outlook for combining cultures. And even where personality preferences clash, we see reason to believe that all sides can accommodate the reorientation of the overall profile. The key for AOL Time Warner—as for other companies struggling with mergers or interdivisional strife—is to be attuned to personality preferences and the interests of the collective soul.

Let's look at Time, Inc., Turner Broadcasting, and AOL—each in its own right among the most important companies in business and media history. All three seized on new technologies to broadcast a perspective-altering message to previously untapped audiences. For Henry Luce, who founded *Time* magazine and its media infrastructure in 1918, for "Captain Outrageous" Ted Turner, and for visionary-turned-CEO-villain Steve Case, broadcast media possessed almost mystical powers to transform civic culture. This fascination with technology and innovation and sense of transcendent mission reveal the influence of the intuitive information-gathering preferences at Time, Inc., TBS, and AOL. Focused on the big picture, relationships, and connections between facts, the three component companies share a dominant preference in one of the most dynamic categories of mental activity. And that's not all. They also share a common orientation in organizational focus, where the outer world of people and activity provides the primary stimulus. This extroverted tendency, which

AOL (Established 1982): "Driven to Lead"

- Energized by the outer world of people and activity
- Focused on the big picture, relationships, and connections between facts
- Makes decisions using logic, analysis, and cause-and-effect reasoning
- Prefers a structured, organized, planned environment

accounts for the long history of mergers and acquisitions by all parties (as well as a series of external partnerships with independent corporations such as AT&T that have created complications for the troubled giant), indicates the possibility of extensive common ground.

Opposing decision-making preferences, a vital category in the CAP2 profile, are the source of much of the difficulty in the AOL Time Warner merger. Here, the feeling sensibilities of Time Warner divisions have resisted the preference for logic and dispassionate analysis that AOL has tried to impose on the company as a whole. Human relations, especially within the *Time* empire, had long been the pride of the Time Warner workforce. Whether employees prized the victory culture of the Turner divisions or the fabled elite status and perquisites of *Time* personnel, the personal dimensions of work had always carried tremendous weight. AOL, in contrast, became famous for the arrogance and insensitivity of its all-star teams. In attempting to rationalize and coordinate the work of the divisions, AOL executives, who claimed operational leadership in the aftermath of the merger, took aim at the personal prerogatives that had accumulated in the Time Warner fiefdoms. In the name of communal interest and principle, AOL upstarts such as Robert Pittman tried to reclaim some Time Warner turf. The clumsy and unfeeling execution of their plans quickly became the subject of ridicule and censure in the media.

Time, Inc. (Established 1918): "Seeing the Big Picture in Human Terms"

- Energized by the outer world of people and activity
- Focused on the big picture, relationships, and cause-and-effect reasoning
- Makes decisions based on values and their impact on people
- Prefers a structured, organized, planned environment

Turner Broadcasting Systems (Established 1960):
"It's Fun to Do Good Work"

- Energized by the outer world of people and activity
- Focused on the big picture, relationships, and cause-and-effect reasoning
- Makes decisions based on values and their impact on people
- Prefers a flexible, spontaneous, changing environment

Readers of *Companies Are People, Too* may take a lesson from the AOL Time Warner experience: Before you join your fate to that of another organization, it is wise to consider likely points of conflict as well as the advantages of cooperation. We urge you to share the insights of Companies Are People, Too with your counterparts at the partnering firm, or to look into the possibility of a joint CAP2 workshop. Or perhaps you'll prefer to use the techniques described in the next chapter to create your own thumbnail sketch of the other company's preferences. Either way, once you've prepared yourself with CAP2 profiles for both companies, you can access tremendous insight into the merger scenario.

Speaking generally about personality type, there are no poison pill combinations—and no sure things, either, for that matter. A strong commitment to mutual respect and open channels of communication can be the threshold to success for companies at opposite ends of the personality spectrum. Likewise, the failure to communicate or to appreciate differences can burden the best of matches.

Our CAP2 merger worksheet gives an example of using personality preferences to facilitate an enduring union. The profile snapshot itself—which reveals preferences for organizational focus, information gathering, decision making, and work style—gives the first indications about compatibility. And the CAP2 profile categories can read as a checklist of likely areas of conflict or harmony. In Figure 15.1, we've identified the strengths and weaknesses that both types of organizations tend to exhibit and have listed them side by side for comparative purposes. We get even more specific in our survey of communications and work environment. Conflicts in these two fields are probably the biggest source of difficulty in most mergers. Our observations about behavior during conflict and signs of stress can help leaders interpret the reactions of either side to the demands of cooperation. For any serious venture in team building, we recommend meditation on vision,

Sample Situational Analysis Overview

Company One to Merge with Company Two

Company One is a New York–based marketing firm specializing in midsize to large business-to-business clients. It has a staff of 40.

Company Two is a Philadelphia-based strategic marketing firm specializing in marketing and creative consulting with Fortune 500 companies. It has a staff of 30.

Company One plans to merge with Company Two, whose current owner/CEO will retire.

Organizational Personality Types

Company One is an "It's Fun to Do Good Work" organization:
- Energized by the outer world of people and activity
- Focused on the big picture, relationships, and connections between facts
- Makes decisions based on values and their impact on people
- Prefers a flexible, spontaneous, changing environment

Company Two is a "Driven to Lead" organization:
- Energized by the outer world of people and activity
- Focused on the big picture, relationships, and connections between facts
- Makes decisions using logic, analysis, and cause-and-effect reasoning
- Prefers a structured, organized, planned environment

Characteristic Organizational Strengths and Weaknesses

Company One:
- Creativity
- Enthusiasm
- Idealism
- Problems with follow-through and structure
- Innovation
- Cutting-edge work
- Friendliness
- Sensitivity
- Good problem-solving skills
- Good ability to hire the right people
- Conflict avoidance
- Problems setting priorities
- Easily distracted

Company Two:
- Can be a visionary, pioneering services
- Tends to be a leader in the industry
- Analytical
- Makes quick decisions
- Good strategic planning
- Hardworking
- Direct
- Ambitious
- Good problem-solving skills
- Logical
- Tends to be aggressive
- Can be overly demanding or critical of others
- Low level of people skills, with possible high turnover

(continued)

FIGURE 15.1   Companies Are People, Too merger/acquisition profile.

Work Environment

Company One:
- High level of brainstorming and creativity
- Fun atmosphere with lots of laughter
- Prefers to have a variety of jobs
- Enjoys a challenge
- Less structure than usual
- Minimum of rules
- Offers freedom
- Little conflict
- Rewards enthusiasm and imaginative work
- Prefers to hire a diverse group of people.

Company Two:
- Efficient, well-organized operations
- Tight scheduling
- Emphasis on long-term strategic planning
- Creative problem solving
- Stimulation of intellectual curiosity
- Seeks powerful clients
- Competitive internal atmosphere
- Prefers to hire intelligent, ambitious, and creative people
- Objective performance standards

Values

Company One:
- Creativity
- Flexibility
- Joy
- Relationships
- Enthusiasm

Company Two:
- Logic
- Leadership
- Competence
- Knowledge
- Justice

Communication Style

Company One:
- Prefers face-to-face communication
- Can be dramatic and animated
- Talks about concepts
- Loves to explore ideas
- Prefers talking in person or on the telephone
- Enjoys talking about strategy and systems
- Tends to analyze out loud
- Tends to ask many questions

Company Two:
- Global idea generator
- Can be idealistic
- Lots of humor
- Moves quickly to closure on decisions
- Tends to be gregarious

Sources of Energy

Company One:
- Personal or group causes
- Affirmation
- Appreciation
- Brainstorming
- Organizing complexities

Company Two:
- Intellectual conversations
- Brainstorming
- Building models

Signs of Stress

Company One:
- Mild stress: no action
- Medium stress: emotional outbursts
- High stress: impulsive and defensive

Company Two:
- Mild stress: more outspoken and critical
- Medium stress: analysis paralysis
- High stress: aggressive with emotional outbursts

Behavior during Conflict

Company One:
- Tends to avoid conflict
- Becomes hostile if values are questioned
- Finds it difficult to forgive conflict
- Enjoys conflict

Company Two:
- Defends vigorously
- Difficult to persuade
- Can be stubborn
- Can seem arrogant

Likely Key Merger Issues

- Conflict avoidance style versus style that encourages argument
- Lack of structure versus strong structure
- Friendly organization versus impersonal organization
- Different preferences for clients and client treatment

Possible Areas for Improving the Organization

Company One can work on focusing more on real-world issues and improving structure. Company Two needs to become more open minded and less aggressive.

Approaches to Managing Change

Company One:
- Explain the importance of the change
- Take actions with enthusiasm
- Point out the possibilities
- Encourage lots of discussion
- Attach the change to a value
- Treat workers with respect

Company Two:
- Explain what will be gained
- Have a respected person serve as spokesperson for the changes
- Allow the organization to do as much planning as possible
- Give logical, clear reasons for actions
- Appeal to belief that the current situation can be improved
- Provide constructive feedback

mission, and values and a concrete plan for linking the organization's ideals to its behaviors.

Our two mostly hypothetical marketing firms relied on their different CAP2 profiles to smooth the integration of their new organization. The profiles are organized so that the most important categories of potential harmony and conflict are easily accessible. In the process of comparing the two personalities, each company can learn a lot about the best way to accommodate and communicate with their new partners. If your firm is contemplating an acquisition or a sale, the CAP2 profile can serve as a kind of watchlist for compatibility and mutual respect. The CAP2 Merger and Acquisition Profile facilitates open channels among companies that know themselves and are willing to share their core Vision, Mission, and Values with a partnering firm. Affirming that your company's M&A counterparts are people, too, is an important step toward building healthy and lasting relationships.

HARDWIRED FOR HARD TIMES

Adversity is as reliable as death and taxes: It comes around sooner or later for everyone, and no amount of preparation can permanently avert it. In the aftermath of the September 11 terrorist attacks, in the wake of a rupture of faith between the captains of industry and the investing public, and in the face of a prolonged economic downturn, we recognize that hard times affect the great as well as the small. For organizations as for people, the key to prosperity in the face of adversity is awareness, self-confidence, and a clear sense of purpose. Companies Are People, Too provides a tool for building your defenses against hard times by bolstering your self-awareness and your sense of the collective mission. Like a well-grounded individual, an organization knows how to remain true to its ideals in the face of adversity. When you respond with your strengths, you'll find the essence of the organization surviving and thriving despite material setbacks.

In another example from the rarified world of Fortune 500/Forbes 400 corporations, let's see how Johnson & Johnson, one of the most self-aware and idealistic companies in the United States, relied on the power of its personality and convictions to overcome a deadly assault on the integrity of its business. In 1982, Johnson & Johnson recalled 31 million bottles of Tylenol, the leading brand-name painkiller after a killer or killers took the lives of seven people by tampering with Tylenol capsules. In 1986, after

Johnson & Johnson had managed to restore public faith and save the brand, a second Tylenol poisoning claimed another life. These consecutive disasters might have shaken the foundations of a less secure company, and, in almost any other case, the tragedy would indicate a certain death for the onetime champion brand Tylenol name. But under the leadership of CEO Jim Burke, Johnson & Johnson responded with its strengths. Burke delivered a message to the Tylenol killers directly from the heart of his organization: "You are not going to defeat us."[2]

The company moved swiftly to uphold its commitment to public health, not only by recalling potentially contaminated items without regard for cost, but also by developing tamper-proof packaging and products. The public responded warmly, celebrating Johnson & Johnson's values and embracing the Tylenol brand with even greater enthusiasm.

You can channel this kind of confidence and strength on behalf of your organization in the face of a crisis. In anticipation of uncertain times, it's smart to have emergency procedures in place, including those that secure an organization's moral compass and its sense of community. What kind of company was Cantor Fitzgerald before the 2001 attack on its offices? It's likely that the public knows more today about the heart and soul of that company than its own principals could understand before. As the trading firm works to recover from its terrible wounds, its people would do well to think about the vital essence of Cantor Fitzgerald—its core personality, vision, mission, and values—which the terrorists failed to destroy. Leaders of organizations today will give serious thought to ensuring the physical security of their facilities; they should also think about safeguarding their intangible assets and processes against adversity. Understanding personality is a reassuring way to recognize the irresistible, immovable essence of the company that endures in the face of all hardship.

16 Sizing Up Your Competition, Partners, and Clients

Companies Are People, Too is primarily a tool for self-understanding, but the insights it provides can be adapted for understanding organizations other than your own. This is valuable information. Many business leaders would admit to being more curious about other companies than about the hidden dynamics in their own organizations. And who among us hasn't wondered what makes other companies behave the way they do? Curiosity notwithstanding, there are practical advantages to recognizing personality at work in similar or allied organizations. A little speculation about what makes the competition tick can help you recognize your company's competitive advantages and can alert you to differences worth emphasizing in marketing and sales.

Our method can also help you identify complementary strengths and potential conflicts in business-to-business relationships. You can recognize values shared with clients, vendors, and potential clients. Empowered by a new appreciation of its own strengths and weaknesses, your company can speak frankly and freely about the suitability of its products, services, and work style for particular clients, especially those for whom you have identified personality preferences. You may also identify differences that might create long-term problems or conflicts, thus avoiding them. In sum, CAP2 can help you attract and retain your ideal partners and clients while avoiding potential pitfalls in business relationships.

Like most goals in business, however, breakthrough insights about clients and competitors are difficult to achieve. You know from your own experiences in the early sections of this book that Companies Are People, Too is a comprehensive program of analysis that relies on insider information about your organization. But this book also provides plenty of examples of the power of speculation in identifying personality. Even though we haven't walked through the CAP2 diagnostic with employees of IBM or Nike, we still have a lot of confidence in our CAP2 profiles for these well-known companies, mostly because we've learned how to identify the way personality preferences manifest themselves in everyday business decisions and behavior. When you get enough information about the way an organization does business, you can make educated guesses about its inclinations in categories such as decision making, information gathering, or work style. The 16 CAP2 profiles in Chapter 5 can help you determine whether or not your estimates are on track. Your efforts to size up the competition and other organizations should produce a profile that sounds and feels right. Used discreetly and effectively, this information can serve as a guide to managing your company's relationship with the subject of your investigation.

In the following section, we'll share some of our secrets for identifying personality preferences in outside organizations. Perhaps you'll even want to take issue with some of our conclusions about your favorite companies! More likely, you will get a sense of how to use this technique to your own company's advantage.

CREATING A THUMBNAIL SKETCH

The basic task of identifying personality preferences in outside organizations is to create a thumbnail sketch of personality preferences. To do so, we need to look again at the four categories of personality preferences. Remember that every organization (and each individual) favors either one or the other of the two preferences in each category. The challenge is to correctly identify the preference that best suits your subject in most situations. Is your rival extraverted or introverted? Does your new vendor place more emphasis on saying what you want to hear than on telling the truth? How did a prospective client learn about and contact your company?

Looking at other companies, you may be surprised by how much small details can reveal about an organization. For example, reflect on the significance of the name Xerox, which is derived from xerography, the revolutionary dry copying process pioneered by the company in the 1950s. The name reveals the document company's extroverted organizational focus because of its conscious effort to evoke the name of Kodak, formerly Xerox's chief industrial rival. As a company that looked outside itself for models of success and geared its efforts toward what was missing in its industry, Xerox has consistently taken its energy from the outer world of people and activity. In other cases, the signals of personality preferences are broadcast loud and clear. Corporate partners of Home Depot Corporation, all of whom have endured searing heat, hunger, thirst, and hard bargaining at the company's annual vendor fairs (sometimes staged in open airport hangars or livestock sheds) would readily agree that Home Depot favors a thinking, get-down-to-business approach to decision making. A solid match in one of the four categories of preference can take you a long way toward identifying the overall complexion of an organization with a closer look.

Information about well-known public companies such as Xerox and Home Depot is readily available in media accounts and business school case studies. For some of your less famous friends and rivals, you will have to dig a little deeper. When working on a thumbnail sketch of company personality preferences, it's important to consult a range of sources about your subject. The following checklist should help you ensure that no stone is left unturned.

- *Read everything you can get your hands on about the company.* Possibilities include articles in local newspapers and business magazines or transcripts of radio or television interviews of key personnel. Publicly traded companies (and some others) also release annual reports that supply significant details about operations, and company newsletters provide the same kind of information in a more informal format. Web sites can be superb sources, especially when they include sections on company history, values, and divisional structures. Other promotional materials, especially brochures and advertising copy, may also shed light on personality preferences.
- *Talk to employees, customers, and corporate partners of your subject organization.* Without asking direct questions about personality preferences, you can learn a great deal from the kind of language they use. For example, consider the way exchanges about deadlines and delivery dates can reveal aspects of an organization's work style. If a vendor reports crisply that a service or product will be provided by a certain date, it sends a very different signal from a conversation that concludes without reference to the ultimate transaction. Conversely, you can gauge an outsider's reaction to a bald statement of your own company's organizational preferences. Try telling a representative of a structured, judging company

that you'll get around to that contract "when things start to come together," and you are likely to learn something about the nature of work style preferences at that firm.

- *Interview your counterparts in the other organization using specific questions about scheduling, processes, and priorities.* If you like, you can talk about work style preferences in very concrete terms—with or without revealing the overall concept of companies as people. Better yet, encourage your partners and clients to complete the diagnostic questionnaire in this book, or online. For the relationships that matter most, you may find that being open about your own company's process of self-discovery will add depth and strength to your collaboration.

- *Use your imagination.* Once you have a rough checklist of preferences in the four categories of personality preferences, consult the CAP2 profiles in this book to find the perfect match. If you've narrowed the field of possibilities to two or four types (since the either/or dialectic of personality preferences will ensure an even number of choices), you are likely to find that one description stands out as the most likely match for the company in question. Choose the one that feels right, or, if you just can't decide, try to calculate a strategy for dealing with each. Remember that there is no wrong way for a company to be itself, only differences that create or detract from harmony in its working relationships.

Once you've completed your thumbnail sketch of the companies that matter for your business, you can proceed to use that information to advance your relationship. Sizing up other companies—just like evaluating your own workplace—requires you to follow up on what you learn about personality preference. The process of discovery is only the beginning. In an equally important set of tasks, you need to articulate what this outside personality means for your business and determine how to adapt your behaviors to maximize the benefits of the relationship. When you understand your company's competition, business partners, and clients as people, you can personalize relationships to make them work for you.

COMPETITIVE ADVANTAGES

Almost every organization contends with competition. Businesses confront other companies that offer similar products and services, and even nonprofit institutions must secure financing and public support at the expense of other groups. While the world of work is hardly a zero-sum game—improvements and advances in technology pioneered by one firm can often bring benefits to a larger group—most of us define the interests of our companies in opposition to related institutions. To get ahead (and stay there) remains the ultimate objective.

When we think of companies as people, we perceive the nature of competition in new and compelling terms. While some organizations thrive on this kind of pressure—among "Going All Out for Greatness" firms, for example, competition is a kind of religion—others shrink from confrontation, self-promotion, and other aspects of the game. Once again, to know the character of your organization is to know how best to deal with the challenge. In this portion of the book, however, we are committed to using the Companies Are People, Too formula to assess and deal with companies other than your own. The CAP2 profile for your competition can be very revealing. It's not industrial espionage to look into a rival's character using the methods we describe, but we urge you to be judicious in the way you use the information that the profiles provide. When you think of companies as people, you can recognize the limits of what constitutes fair competition. Avoid hurtful personal attacks, but otherwise consider the material we provide about your rival as fair game.

The most relevant portion of the CAP2 profile for exploiting your competitive advantages can be found in Figure 16.1. A few of the items on each of the lists reveal quirks of personality in your competition that you can exploit. For example, if your rival is a "Quest for Meaningful Work" firm, you might note a number of weaknesses that limit the company's capacity to follow through on its promises. This type of organization has problems with scheduling, especially because its overwhelming desire for perfection can stall momentum toward completing a project. Its inherent enthusiasm is both a strength and a weakness, since that quality galvanizes commitment but sometimes leads the company to promise more than it can deliver. The creators of Atari computer games provide a vivid illustration of the promise and problems of the "Quest for Meaningful Work" persona. Caught up in the excitement of the work, Atari programmers signed on for larger and more lucrative contracts as the popularity of their game products mounted in the 1970s. In the end, however, the company's love of technical challenges and desire to push the limits of programming technology created difficulty delivering on all the promises. "Three months was not an unusual length of time to develop a game when I got there," remembers an Atari engineer from the 1970s. "Suddenly, it was taking a year, and a year and a half." Atari's competition, especially Nintendo (a division of an ancient and supremely businesslike Japanese conglomerate), seized on this weakness by creating a more disciplined and reliable mechanism for developing and marketing computer games.

Your company can capitalize on a rival's weaknesses by emphasizing its comparably desirable characteristics in marketing and advertising copy. Or you can simply provide a better service, like the people at Nintendo. Either way, your awareness of the soft underbelly of the competition gives you a clue to the kinds of frustrations that those companies' current customers and markets may be experiencing. If your company can offer what's missing, you can benefit from the others' limitations—but only so long as your own inherent flaws and preferences do not conflict with the strategy. In engaging in competition, it's particularly important to recognize the constraints of your own company's character.

BUILDING EFFECTIVE PARTNERSHIPS

Especially in these days of corporate scandal, it's important to recognize the character of organizations that you work with closely. The integrity and competence of vendors and corporate partners can have a direct impact on the performance of your own organization. Companies Are People, Too helps you build effective partnerships by helping you identify companies that share your values and goals. Our method can also improve your working relationship with allied firms by helping you develop a comprehensive communication strategy customized to their personality preferences. Once again, however, we remind you that the real key to effective partnerships is your company's awareness of and commitment to its own priorities. When you cultivate a strong sense of where your company is coming from, you are better equipped to map your route to success with other organizations.

Once you've created a thumbnail sketch of personality preferences at an allied firm, you should be able to see clearly the alignment of your counterpart's priorities with those of your company. Do you share preferences in two or more categories, or have you linked yourself with a company very different from your own? Either way, differences in personality preferences do not spell disaster for a working relationship. In fact, a diversity of styles may prove to be a

Solid as a Rock

Occasionally too rigid to respond to changing situations and opportunities

High standards may turn into unjustified self-righteousness

Frequently unable to appreciate the value and necessity of change

May not appreciate the benefits of process, teamwork, and collaboration

You Can Count on Us

Inherent skepticism toward unproved ideas may create lowered expectations, leading to diminished performance

Frequently unable to appreciate the value or necessity of change

May ignore the future for the present

Can decide too quickly, ignoring potentially critical data

Vision Driven by Values

Could champion a cause to the detriment of operations and performance

May jump to conclusions too quickly

Prone to be too rigid to respond to changing situations and opportunities

Could overly rely on intuition and fail to support decisions with critical analysis

Going All Out for Greatness

May be overly conceptual and lose grasp on reality

Frequently has difficulty juggling multiple priorities or when major initiatives are interrupted

Tendency to become complacent without complex challenges

Prone to be too rigid to respond to changing situations and opportunities

Action, Action—We Want Action!

So absorbed in action that it may lose sight of goals and the long term

Propensity to change direction and priorities may make it unstable at times

Can become perplexed or limit opportunities by avoiding solutions requiring innovation, new theories, or dealing with ambiguity

Tendency to misinterpret activity as progress

Working to Make a Difference

Desire for details and perfection may hinder action

Occasionally mistakes current optimism for long-term health

May apply a quick fix when a long-term solution is required

Can favor the means over the end, and may not be adequately bottom-line oriented

Quest for Meaningful Work

Gift of imagination may remove it from reality

Not uncommon for feelings to override good business sense

Focus can be fragmented by too many projects, causing deadlines to be missed

Desire for perfection may delay critical actions or decisions

In Pursuit of Intellectual Solutions

Can set standards and expectations so high that action is delayed or canceled

May not drop unproductive ideas soon enough

Difficulty translating concepts into action

So focused on the future that the present may be ignored

Thriving on Risky Business	We Aim to Please	It's Fun to Do Good Work	If We Can't Do It, No One Can
Propensity to change direction and priorities may make it unstable	Natural optimism and flair for risk may blind it to impossible situations	Not uncommon for feelings or instincts to overrule good business sense	Tendency to be weak at implementation
Juggles too many balls and may drop some	May use a quick fix when a long-term solution is needed	Tendency to drop current projects in favor of exploring new opportunities	Tendency to drop current projects in favor of exploring new opportunities
Can become perplexed or miss opportunities by avoiding solutions requiring innovation, new theories, or dealing with ambiguity	Juggles too many balls and may drop some	Occasionally lacks details to communicate and implement vision	Can get bored with routine activities and leave them unattended
Acting impulsively makes some risk taking more like gambling	Not uncommon for feelings to overrule good business sense	Could overly rely on intuition and fail to support it with proper critical analysis	May lack adequate systems and procedures to keep pace with its rapid rate of change

Playing by the Rules	Doing the Right Thing	Seeing the Big Picture in Human Terms	Driven to Lead
May miss great opportunities because of an aversion to risk and change	Occasionally assumes too many responsibilities, overburdening its resources	May act prematurely or without adequate business logic or hard data to support decisions	Tendency to decide too quickly, leaving too little time for reflection
Occasionally assumes too many responsibilities, overburdening its resources	Often too rigid to respond to changing situations and opportunities	May ignore a few high-priority tasks in the desire to complete many tasks	May be overly conceptual and lose grasp of reality
Can become perplexed or miss opportunities by avoiding solutions requiring innovation, new theories, or dealing with ambiguity	Can become perplexed or miss opportunities by avoiding innovation, new theories, or dealing with ambiguity	Could overly rely on intuition and fail to support decisions with critical analysis	So quick to move, may overlook important details
May lose sight of the larger picture	Not uncommon for feelings to overrule good business sense	Occasionally will implement change for the sake of change, without sufficient rationale	Prone to be too rigid to respond to changing situations and opportunities
Often too rigid to respond to changing situations			

FIGURE 16.1 Characteristic weaknesses of the CAP2 profiles.

significant asset. When skills and interests complement one another, personality differences can enhance your performance. To illustrate this, let's see what happens when a traditional and detail-oriented company with "Playing by the Rules" preferences joins forces with an innovative "Going All Out for Greatness" firm. So long as each party maintains a scrupulous commitment to respecting the work rhythms and styles in the partner firm, the results can be dynamic. Companies Are People, Too can help you identify complementary strengths and offset weaknesses identified in the CAP2 profiles. Our method is also ideal for alerting you to significant differences regarding scheduling, teamwork, and other work style preferences.

Using your company's CAP2 profile alongside your partner's, you can create a checklist of comparative preferences in the vital categories of your work together. Decide in advance what work categories are most important. For example, if your tasks require the development of new products or services, you would want to include that on the list. Likewise, the management of customer accounts could make up a substantial proportion of the job. Once your list is complete, consult the CAP2 profiles for notations in each category.

For our fictional example of our business-to-business checklist, we've imagined an idealistic foreign policy think tank joining forces with the FBI to fight terrorism. Our foreign policy experts—let's call them Islamic World Watch—have expertise about the membership and history of several activist Islamic humanitarian and political organizations. IWW employees, most of whom hold graduate degrees, are known for their trenchant analysis of international trends, and many are passionately committed to international and domestic American political causes. The organization specializes in establishing networks of confidential information sources, and can go to heroic lengths to keep cooperation alive and protect its reputation for discretion in a tense part of the world. Our IWW is modeled on the "It's Fun to Do Good Work" profile, a kind of organization that is especially well qualified to interpret the nature of relationships between individuals and larger international movements. As big-picture visionaries, IWW members are also painfully aware of the ethical and political implications of the war on terrorism. Nonetheless, they have agreed to cooperate with the FBI by providing surveillance on individuals implicated by IWW associates as dangerously suspect.

In aligning with the FBI, our foreign policy think tank has not only had to swallow some of its misgivings about betraying its sources; it has also joined forces with an organization at the oppo-site end of the spectrum of company personalities. While IWW's profile is "It's Fun to Do Good Work"—extroverted, intuitive, feeling, and perceiving—the Federal Bureau of Investigation mind-set is "Solid as a Rock"—introverted, sensing, thinking, and judging. We might expect a poor outcome from combining the most fluid and outgoing of all types with the organization that gave rise to the stereotype of the men in black. One group takes a fresh look at the wide world every morning, while the other is bound (some would say mired) in tradition. But, using information from the CAP2 profiles, we can create a checklist to guide these unlikely partners in their critical task.

First, we'll determine the work categories essential to their col-laboration. (See Figure 16.2.) We'll include client management (that is, dealing with Islamic activists), record keeping, and coop-eration with U.S. and international lawyers and judges. Because Islamic World Watch has credibility with a wide network of inter-national informers and has the trust of important Islamic institu-tions, it makes sense for that organization to manage client relationships. And as an "It's Fun to Do Good Work" company, IWW has a special gift for building enduring and beneficial rela-tionships both within and outside its own organization. However, the think tank's tendency to be disorganized and to act on impulse rather than data could be problematic. Fortunately, "Solid as a Rock" organizations like the FBI are masters of data management (the legendary files on the private lives of public figures during the Hoover era were the source of much of the director's political power). We'll put the FBI in charge of record keeping, but make sure that it doesn't have exclusive access to the materials. After all, a characteristic weakness of the Solid persona is overconfidence in its own high standards and a self-righteous refusal to cooperate with outsiders. As for cooperation with the soft side of law enforcement, we can count on the FBI to meticulously assist in the prosecution of accused parties. We'll have to hope that fun-lovers at IWW will bring their ability to solve complex problems to bear on protecting contacts they believe to be innocent. Among the weaknesses of their company's type, we should be wary of the tendency to chase the spotlight and disregard pending matters on behalf of something or someone new.

As you can see, our checklist shows a very promising prospect for the collaboration between the FBI and our fictional think tank, so long as values and work styles are taken into account. There's

Work category: client management	Who should lead: IWW	Personality indicator: "*It's Fun to Do Good Work*" Preferences: builds beneficial and enduring relationships; an enthusiastic and capable leader of causes; encourages growth and development of individuals; operates as a democracy; values integrity, harmony, and relationships
		"*Solid as a Rock*": Occasionally too rigid to respond to changing situations and opportunities; may ignore future for present; occasionally ignores or distrusts instincts; little room for chitchat
Work category: record keeping	Who should lead: FBI	Personality indicator: "*Solid as a Rock*" Preferences: probing, scrutinizing, critical; structured, analytical, observant, predictable; master of data and logical analysis; organized for success
		"*It's Fun to Do Good Work*": Tendency to drop current projects in favor of exploring new opportunities; occasionally will implement change for the sake of change; may miss critical deadlines or delay decisions until the last minute; unstructured, spontaneous, chaotic
Work category: cooperation with lawyers for the prosecution	Who should lead: FBI	Personality indicator: "*Solid as a Rock*" Preferences: procedures, standards, and guidelines exist to let employees know exactly what is expected of them; predictable high quality from developing, maintaining, and enforcing high standards; decisive, able to make quick decisions; delivers what it promises; clarifies complex issues using logical analysis
Work category: cooperation with lawyers and spokespersons for the defense	Who should lead: IWW	Personality indicator: "*It's Fun to Do Good Work*" Preferences: encourages and supports growth and development, often through mentoring and coaching; has good instincts about customer needs and what motivates them; can construct meaning and opportunity out of ambiguity and complexity

FIGURE 16.2   IWW and FBI sample merger.

plenty of room for contention in the relationship, however, so it behooves both sides to open channels for communication. Once again, the building blocks for communication across this gap are contained within the CAP2 profile, and we encourage you to be flexible about your company's own preferences when addressing those of your partners. It's important to say what you feel, but it's even more vital that your partner understand what you're saying. Do "It's Fun to Do Good Work" companies prefer face-to-face communications? Does the FBI require a written memorandum? Remember that there's little harm in saying something twice, and you can reinforce your messages by adapting to your partner's communication style.

ATTRACTING YOUR IDEAL CLIENTS

The relationships we value most in the work environment are those that put money directly into our pockets. Most organizations are willing to exert tremendous energy and often make tremendous sacrifices on behalf of good relationships with clients. However, despite their best efforts, many leaders of organizations find relationships with clients to be the most unpredictable and potentially frustrating aspect of their work. Too many business-to-client relationships prove to be short lived, resulting in wasted resources and lost opportunities. If businesses possessed a means of assessing their clients' needs and operations at the outset, they could avoid making commitments that seem likely to end in disappointment. While it's no crystal ball, the method used in Companies Are People, Too can help an organization identify at least some of the pitfalls that proceed from personality preferences.

As with business-to-business partnerships, relationships with clients and customers rely on open and effective communication, and we urge you to study the communication styles developed in the CAP2 profiles. Each list is one part a guide to understanding what a client organization is saying—identifying the loudmouths, the mealy-mouths, and close-mouths, all of whom bring a special character to written and verbal communications—and one part a guide to the best way to present yourself so that your company's intentions are understood. To repeat our advice from the previous section, anything worth saying is worth saying twice, and you do your company a disservice when you fail to accommodate the communication preferences of your clients. The thumbnail sketch of your best clients' preferences should help you devise effective

Solid as a Rock

- Need infrastructure, stability, and discipline
- Require reliable, long-term service with predictable quality
- Seek to associate with the company's conservative image and traditional values
- Value the peace of mind that comes from dealing with a rock-solid company that has its act together
- Need the development, maintenance, and/or logical analysis of huge databases
- Value the high quality that comes from hard work

You Can Count on Us

- Produce products or services that benefit people in some tangible way
- Value loyalty and seek a long-term relationship
- Require attention to detail in long-term projects
- Respect the high quality that comes from hard work
- Value a tradition of loyalty and reliability
- Enjoy being part of the corporate "family"
- Relish the peace of mind that comes from being in total control of the situation

Going All Out for Greatness

- Seek visionary solutions to complex, ambiguous, and long-term problems
- Prefer to work independently rather than collaboratively
- Appreciate a cool, logical, and detached approach
- Value knowledge and the learning process
- Value intellectual approach, competency, and zest for visioning possibilities
- Desire to clarify a complex market or industry change that is unprecedented and defies analysis
- Enjoy debating, challenging, and questioning ideas and theories

Action, Action— We Want Action!

- Desire a cool head to troubleshoot risky projects
- Appreciate a problem solver not afraid to bend or break the rules
- Need a quick fix based on logical analysis and prior experience
- Require a product or service that demands constant refinement
- Prefer an action-oriented and hands-on atmosphere requiring little formal communication

Working to Make a Difference

- Provide an important product or service to people
- Require attention to the smallest detail
- Appreciate flair and style
- Interface effectively with informal systems and structure
- Value long-term relationships
- Need to have a major impact in a short period of time, as when inspiration hits

Vision Driven by Values

- Need an ingenious problem solver that prefers to play behind the scenes
- Value an ethical and caring organization
- Desire to build and maintain long-term relationships
- Create or improve services or products that benefit people for the long term
- Produce a product or service the organization believes in
- Like a harmonious environment with little confrontation
- Willing and able to give the organization time to develop its ideas

Quest for Meaningful Work

- Value an ethical and caring organization
- Appreciate an organization that is honest and genuine
- Willing and able to allow the organization time to develop its ideas
- Share a common focus on developing people as the core of the organization
- Appreciate keeping commitments

In Pursuit of Intellectual Solutions

- Need to create a new system or design, or to understand and solve a complex problem
- Enjoy debating, challenging, and questioning ideas and theories
- Value knowledge and the learning process
- Appreciate a cool, logical, and detached approach
- Value intellectual approach, competency, and zest for visioning possibilities

Need to be shielded from problems through rapid, competent, and proactive response to developing problems

Require a variety of project work that leverages internal experience and databases

Enjoy rolling up sleeves (literally and figuratively) and getting the job done fast and accurately

Produce meaningful work that contributes to the well-being of people

Like a harmonious environment with little confrontation

Value being part of creative, brainstorming activity

If We Can't Do It, No One Can

Value intellectual approach, competency, and zest for visioning possibilities

Attracted to ability to do the impossible

Need a take-charge company to provide long-term vision and plans

Require breakthrough concepts

Desire an efficient solution using the resources at hand

Need a simple solution to a complex problem

Welcome a rational and objective perspective on sensitive issues

Thriving on Risky Business

Need to capitalize on an opportunity with a narrow window for action

Involved in high-stakes activities requiring a performance (of sorts), high-profile image, and coolness under fire

Need a troubleshooter that can operate without a lot of structure or formal communication

Value concrete and practical style of operating

Need quick solutions based on logical analysis

Need a crisis solved immediately

Appreciate a problem solver not afraid to bend or break the rules

Thrive in a fast-paced, high-risk environment

We Aim to Please

Want the best possible customer service

Produce a product or service that contributes to the benefit of all

Appreciate showmanship; sensitive to public image

Need immediate, though not long-term, solutions

Desire to capitalize on emerging trends with quick, focused effort

Appreciate and enjoy lots of personal and social interaction

Thrive on a demanding and quick pace

It's Fun to Do Good Work

Want the flexibility to capitalize on last-minute developments

Share values, especially those focused on people

Value enduring relationships

Require innovative, possibilities thinking grounded in meaningful customer needs

Require project work involving intense, challenging, and concentrated activity

Nonconfrontational

Like a friendly, relaxed atmosphere

Energized by personal contact and the collaborative exchange of ideas

Believe in and appreciate teamwork

(continued)

FIGURE 16.3 CAP2 profiles: ideal clients.

Playing by the Rules	Doing the Right Thing	Seeing the Big Picture in Human Terms	Driven to Lead
Need highly detailed work done	Want the best possible customer service	Want the certainty that projects will be completed on time	Appreciate a cool, logical, and detached approach
Insist on dependability and consistency	Produce products or services that contribute to the benefit of all	Share the company's values, especially those focused on people	Provide long-term vision and plans
Value a conservative and traditional company	Appreciate meaningful relationships built on ethical standards	Value enduring relationships	Desire to clarify a complex market or industry change that is unprecedented and defies analysis
Want to act immediately on developing opportunities that fit a predetermined plan	Require business results now	Require innovative, possibilities thinking grounded in meaningful customer needs	Need to move quickly and decisively to harness resources and people
Appreciate a logical, analytical, and practical assessment of complex or sensitive issues	Value reputation and integrity	Produce a product or service that contributes to the benefit of all	Require breakthrough concepts
Need problems solved immediately and with existing resources	Want to be associated with a blue-chip image	Energized by personal contact and the collaborative exchange of ideas	Enjoy debating, challenging, and questioning ideas and theories
	Enjoy being part of the "family" and collaborating as a team	Nonconfrontational	
	Need to identify and jump on emerging opportunities quickly	Like a friendly, relaxed atmosphere	

FIGURE 16.3 *Continued*

Your Ideal Customer

Use this space to list the names of your top three customers in terms of not only sales volume, but of those you do your best work for. Under each name, list the top three attributes you most appreciate. Look at the type table and see if you can profile these clients. This is the starting point for developing a profile of your ideal customer, matching it with your own profile, and working on being more of who you are every day, which will make you irresistibly attractive to your ideal customers!

Names:

_____

_____

_____

_____

Attributes:

_____

_____

_____

_____

What we most appreciate:

_____

_____

_____

_____

Personality type:

_____

_____

_____

_____

FIGURE 16.4   Ideal customer exercise.

means of making sure your message comes in loud and clear every time, and making sure you understand your instructions.

With communications and other vital categories of work in mind, Companies Are People, Too has also provided a specialized component of your company's profile with information about your ideal clients. (See Figure 16.3.) Here, it's not necessary to venture a guess about the personality preferences of your clients, because we've identified the kinds of companies that will be drawn to aspects of your own company's character. While some company personas are better suited to the strengths and work styles that we match with ideal clients, there should be a broad constituency in every industry for which your kind of services are appropriate. The key is to sell your company honestly and with the authority that comes from deep self-awareness. When clients see you deliver on your promises, their confidence in your relationship will grow.

Do you recognize your ideal clients in our CAP2 profiles? We hope our projections give you a better sense of who you're working with and what they expect of you (see Figure 6.4). As we've said throughout this chapter, honesty is the best policy in your relationships with clients, business partners, and competitors. So long as you know your company's strengths and personality preferences, you can deal with outsiders with confidence and authority.

Your company's own personality preferences should be the foundation of your relationships with other companies and key individuals. Using the insights developed for Companies Are People, Too, you can learn enough about the impact of preferences on work choices to predict where your own preferences may come into conflict with the desires of those you work with. We're not asking you to change the way you do things—in fact, we think the best way to build strong relationships is to collaborate in harmony with your preferences as well as those of the other company. Where conflict seems unavoidable, you can cut your losses by ending a relationship before problems ensue. With CAP2, you have a means of screening your business counterparts to determine which meet your standards for performance and integrity.

⑰ What If You Don't Like Who You Are?

Understanding personality is like looking in a mirror: Few of us like everything we see. As individuals, we can adapt our behavior and style and hope to reflect a better image. We can change our appearance, invest in physical and mental fitness, and even deemphasize personality preferences that we find unattractive. People sometimes make conscious decisions to change their lives; other times, they gradually evolve new interests, habits, and skills. But personality preferences and other earmarks of individuality remain remarkably consistent over time. Enmeshed in networks of family and friends, and consciously committed to lifestyle and work habits, people tend to remain pretty much themselves all their lives. A recognizable face appears in the mirror every time.

Organizations change according to a different kind of logic. Even though we think that companies are people, too, the authors of this book recognize some important differences. Most strikingly, corporations rarely have peer institutions that offer an analogy to the love and support provided by human families. That means they lack giving partners to compensate for shortcomings or to intervene on behalf of necessary changes. But it also means they have greater freedom to embrace change than an individual constrained by personal relationships, loyalty, and sentiment. Companies and institutions also benefit from the meeting of minds in the workplace. While the company has a single personality, individual employees and even whole divisions within the organization may bring a different perspective that favors change. Finally, leaders of organizations are equipped to promote change with disincentives and rewards that are far more effective than mere human willpower. These factors don't make it easy for corporations to change. No less than individuals, companies confront friction from a range of sources that resist momentum. However, an organization empowered by autonomy and institutionalized drive can transform itself entirely if a new corporate identity helps it to survive and thrive.

NEW RULES, NEW GAME

To initiate change, individuals and organizations first address basic operational priorities. Is there something they do that gets in the way of achieving their goals? Reincarnation at its most essential level requires restructuring. Whether it involves new leadership, a new divisional structure, new marketing partners, or new accounting procedures, dynamic companies modify their behaviors almost constantly and often without controversy. From the perspective of personality analysis, adaptations in company management sometimes produce substantive shifts in one or more categories of personality preference. An enhanced commitment to market research, for example, might push an intuitive company to rely more on its sensory perceptions of the customer base or the competition. While new habits may not be designed to create sweeping changes, a single switch between one of the polar opposites in a category such as information gathering can have consequences for the company persona as a whole. The dynamic interaction of the four preferences requires that the new orientation realign the predilections of the whole. Using its CAP2 personality profile, a company can gauge the way changes in one aspect of its behavior will affect communications, personnel considerations, relationships with clients, and other important matters. That knowledge equips us to anticipate the strengths and weaknesses of our new approach.

The transformations under way at Home Depot hardware stores demonstrate the implications of operational changes for personality in a very straightforward way. For more than 20 years after its establishment in 1978, Home Depot set the standard for aggressive expansion in the national retail outlet industry. From its origins in 3 Atlanta stores, the chain grew to include more than 1,000 big box outlets with \$53 billion in annual sales. Years of rapid growth had produced a classic case of big box blues by 2001, as stiffer competition, a declining stock price, and customer apathy began to take a toll on company morale. Among investors and do-it-yourself shoppers alike, loyalties began to shift to Lowe's, a North Carolina chain that has made serious inroads into Home

Depot's market base. To remain at the top of its class, Home Depot has initiated basic operational changes. Leadership of the company passed from founders Bernie Marcus and Arthur Blank to a new generation under Bob Nardelli, formerly a Jack Welch acolyte at GE. Nardelli instigated substantial changes, many of which chipped away at the celebrated autonomy of Home Depot's franchising merchants. While his policies have taken aim at basic operations such as hiring, promotion, and purchasing, the effect of Nardelli's reforms has produced a significant shift in Home Depot's personality profile.

The Home Depot way championed by Bernie Marcus and the other founders celebrated do-it-yourself as a business model as well as a consumer lifestyle. Home Depot embodied the "Action, Action—We Want Action!" personality profile: energized by the inner world of ideas and experiences; focused on factual, real, and current information; committed to logic and analysis in decision making; and (above all) flexible, spontaneous, and individualized. Franchising merchants enjoyed broad discretion in the management of their stores, so long as they met the basic requirements of the Action ideal. Store managers and employees aimed to be masters of their craft—professionals and experts committed to helping customers negotiate the difficulties of home improvement. Stores were to be visually appealing, with an emphasis on warehouse authenticity (to achieve this effect in the first Home Depot, Bernie Marcus himself laid down skid marks with an in-house forklift).[1] Rather than trying to be all things to all people, Home Depot managers were told to concentrate on being the best providers of do-it-yourself hardware and supplies and leave experiments to someone else. Fierce, argumentative competitiveness—Marcus described his store owners and employees as "piranhas" or workplace "misfits"—served to motivate the rank and file in the absence of overarching procedures and systems. An emphasis on constant self-improvement, epitomized by Marcus's repeated insistence that everything could always be better, indicated the strong influence of the perceiving tendency on the company's work style.

Under Bob Nardelli, Home Depot is working to embrace work style preferences that emphasize structure, discipline, and planning. As a GE man, convinced in the GE way that better systems mean better products and more profits, Nardelli embraces the judging tendency as the best model for business.[2] The most far-reaching of his moves toward structure takes aim at the vaunted independence of Home Depot merchandisers in purchasing their wares. A centralized buying system has replaced individual initiative in favor of scale, in an effort to secure lower wholesale prices and ensure uniformity in distribution. Partially in response to a recent well-publicized sex discrimination lawsuit, the company has instituted one of the country's first automated hiring and promotion systems, further chipping away at merchant autonomy (and leading to the departure of five store managers).[3] Relying on extensive quantitative data, as befits the CEO of a company with a preference for factual and current information, Nardelli has also called managers to account for what he calls "Key Performance Indicators" (KPI).[4] The emphasis on planning, assessment, and accountability created considerable turmoil, as evidenced by the departure of 24 of 39 senior officers of the company in Nardelli's first two years on the job. But higher profits and new corporate partnerships, led by a merchandising alliance with Disney, indicate only some of the benefits of Home Depot's reorganization.

Nardelli's operational shift has done more than merely institute new procedures and alienate old-timers. The move toward a more structured work environment has also subtly transformed Home Depot's personality. What had been an "Action, Action—We Want Action!" company has reemerged as a "Solid as a Rock" business. The "Solid as a Rock" big box shares important preferences with the Action profile; both manifestations of the company are committed to excellence and efficiency, logical decision making, and the careful monitoring of internal data. The "Solid as a Rock" company, however, is organized for success, more focused on its customers' needs, and somewhat more amenable to experimentation (as evidenced in the company's recent ventures into the professional building supply business). "Solid as a Rock" also makes room for celebrating and preserving traditional culture in the organization, a characteristic that promises to smooth ruffled feelings in the aftermath of the transition. Bernie Marcus, after all, has yet to leave the building. He continues to operate the Home Depot charitable foundation from an office one floor below

Home Depot, before: "Action, Action—We Want Action!"

- Energized by the inner world of ideas and experiences
- Focused on information that is factual, real, and current
- Makes decisions using logic, analysis, and cause-and-effect reasoning
- Prefers a flexible, spontaneous, changing environment

Home Depot, after: "Solid as a Rock"

- Energized by the inner world of ideas and experiences
- Focused on information that is factual, real, and current
- Makes decisions using logic, analysis, and cause-and-effect reasoning
- Prefers a structured, organized, and planned environment

Nardelli's. In fact, the shifting identity of the company represents the fulfillment of Marcus's original ambition to make Home Depot the model of the successful major merchandiser. Having seized the opportunity and crushed the competition during the first generation, in keeping with the Action profile, the mature Home Depot has evolved into the personification of the American corporate ideal as a "Solid as a Rock" institution. Its shift in a single category of personality preference has helped the company cultivate the culture of an industry leader.

SHOWING UP MORE LIKE YOURSELF EVERY DAY

If fast-growth companies such as Home Depot confront the need to enhance structure and planning in the work environment, other organizations wrestle with what happens when bureaucracy and complacency pervade the workplace. The case of Electronic Data Systems (EDS) illustrates the possibility (if also the complexity) of more sweeping changes in the corporate outlook and identity. The brainchild of H. Ross Perot, an IBM salesman who first conceived of outsourcing the maintenance of computers and records, EDS grew rapidly after its establishment in the early 1960s, earning millions and later billions from its management of computer records for government agencies, the military, and businesses of all sizes and types. Purchased and managed as a semiautonomous subsidiary by General Motors in the late 1980s, EDS gradually took on the characteristics of a corporate dinosaur. For all its emphasis on cutting-edge technology and information management, the company projected a stodgy, inflexible, unresponsive image that soon became a liability among potential clients and investors. The information technology boom of the 1990s revealed the severity of the EDS image problem, as start-up outsourcing firms ridiculed the company as a hapless giant and raided its customer base. By the turn of the century, facing the erosion of its client base and market capitalization, EDS had made a commitment to a comprehensive corporate makeover.

The old EDS style comprised a kind of hybrid between Perot's unique, country-fried brand of benevolent dictatorship and the clubby, hierarchical world of General Motors. In fact, EDS personality preferences matched the "You Can Count on Us" profile, the most insular and fraternizing of the company personalities. EDS employees embodied the Churchillian determination celebrated by the type. "Ross told us to hire people who have to win," remembered a veteran. "[Then] he said to go after the people who hate to lose."[5] Together, the ever expanding membership of the EDS team pioneered work procedures they trusted as ironclad. Ironclad guarantees of the company trust—demonstrated for the world in the rescue of EDS employees from revolutionary Iran in 1979—embraced all those who lived up to the conservative EDS ethos. Over time, however, the conformist atmosphere became the butt of industry jokes and the source of tension in the workplace, even as the company's lion's share of the data management industry remained formidable. Strains within management, coupled with the "You Can Count on Us" tendency toward inflexibility and turf building, resulted in a cultural crisis at EDS that became painfully visible to outside observers by the 1990s.

While seeking to preserve the atmosphere of confidence and trust created by the traditional emphasis on individuals at EDS, CEO Dick Brown, who took over in 1998, has sought to change almost everything else about the world's largest data management company. Under his leadership, the company has aspired to qualities consistent with the "We Aim to Please" personality profile, with more emphasis on the external environment and more opportunistic, flexible work style preferences. The new orientation embraces a firm commitment to EDS customers, including the ability to respond at high speed to their needs and opportunities. One of Brown's mechanisms for achieving the new style—the EDS Customer Service Dashboard—harnesses the company's long-standing commitment to sensory information gathering as well as its unrivaled experience in data management on behalf of customer service. The dashboard flashes green, yellow, or red in

EDS, before: "You Can Count on Us"

- Energized by the inner world of ideas and experiences
- Focused on information that is factual, real, and current
- Makes decisions based on values and their impact on people
- Prefers a structured, organized, and planned environment

EDS, after: "We Aim to Please"

- Energized by the outer world of people and activity
- Focused on information that is factual, real, and current
- Makes decisions based on values and their impact on people
- Prefers a flexible, spontaneous, changing environment

keeping with routine online surveys of EDS clients. By rationalizing the command structure of the organization, Brown has eliminated much of the hierarchy that made EDS procedures unwieldy and frustrating. "We Aim to Please"—in contrast to "You Can Count on Us"—specializes in public relations. Favorable reports of Dick Brown's restructuring (and one of the most successful Super Bowl commercials of the 1990s, in which EDS cowboys demonstrated their skill at herding cats) restored the confidence of clients, investors, and the blue suits as well as the nonconformists at EDS. As for the success of the makeover, the newly flexible, perceiving EDS is willing to go with the flow. "[T]he market will tell us if our aim is true," pronounced the top technology and information officer in the reorganized company. "The big challenge is to stay ahead and not miss any of the opportunities.[6]

⑱ Being Yourself on Purpose

Innovations at Home Depot and EDS represent the achievements of America's best corporate leadership, empowered by billions of dollars in revenue and a dominant market share. Readers of *Companies Are People, Too* probably confront their own workplace dilemmas with fewer resources. The model of problem solving developed in this chapter is designed to help you achieve the kinds of transformations that Bob Nardelli and Dick Brown orchestrated instinctively. Understanding personality provides the tools you need to make your company over in keeping with its needs and aspirations. Using CAP2, a company can assess the way its behaviors conform to its ideals and can anticipate the consequences of a new orientation in other aspects of the work environment. The example of Dixon Schwabl Advertising, a company that has embraced the CAP2 method, provides a working illustration of the purposeful transformation of a company's personality. Determined to remake the company to better suit their industry and their dreams, the DSA leaders reconsidered the firm's personality preferences in every category. The process gave birth to new sensibilities and confidence and greater harmony in the workplace.

Unlike Home Depot and EDS, Dixon Schwabl Advertising did not seek to transform its identity during a time of crisis. In 1998, when it completed its first CAP2 diagnostic, Dixon Schwabl was a leader in its East Coast market, with strong employee morale and steadily increasing revenues. The outcome of the profile exercise came as a surprise to the 10-year-old company, led by a husband-and-wife team. Dixon Schwabl had become known among New York State and East Coast clients as a "drive-through agency," capable of delivering quality advertising with rapid turnaround. The company personality—"Playing by the Rules"—reflected this commitment to reliability, customer service, and deadline fulfillment. But "Playing by the Rules" hardly matched the company's vision of itself and its niche in the regional advertising market. In discussions with an independent management consultant, the company learned that the emphasis on turnaround had been a source of great stress for the DSA creative department, which needed more latitude for exploration and expression but had hesitated to speak up. Identifying the company's personality gave the creative team a means to address this frustration without complaining about assignments. Dixon Schwabl began questioning if the focus on deadlines and turnaround satisfied a core value, or if the company had adopted the preference for structure and order without considering its connection to more fundamental goals. Soon, the discussion turned to which of the 16 personality types best matched the kind of agency Dixon Schwabl wanted to be.

The Dixon Schwabl leadership endorsed creativity, vibrancy, and fun as desirable characteristics for an advertising agency. But "Playing by the Rules" values placed a higher priority on customer service and reliability. Hoping to give a freer reign to the agency's underdeveloped imagination—and to accommodate the preferences of the company's large number of creative Catalyst and Explorer types—the DSA leaders embarked upon a wholesale makeover of the company's personality. The profile they adopted as their own—"It's Fun to Do Good Work"—is the most creative of the CAP2 personality types. The road to its rebirth as a Fun organization required Dixon Schwabl to reorient three of the four scales of personality preferences.

During its period of restructuring, Dixon Schwabl maintained its orientation toward the outer world of people and activity. Extroverted organizations, after all, are more likely than their introverted counterparts to develop the empathy and partisanship to represent the advertising needs of their clients. The decision to reverse its sensing information-gathering preferences and embrace its intuitive side reflected the agency's aspiration to become more visionary, innovative, and creative and less limited by tangible requirements. In practical terms, the shift elevated the priorities of the creative

Dixon-Schwabl Advertising, before: "Playing by the Rules"

- Energized by the outer world of people and activity
- Focused on information that is factual, real, and current
- Makes decisions using logic, analysis, and cause-and-effect reasoning
- Prefers a structured, organized, planned environment

> ### Dixon Schwabl Advertising, after: "It's Fun to Do Good Work"
> - Energized by the outer world of people and activity
> - Focused on the big picture, relationships, and connections between facts
> - Makes decisions based on values and their impact on people
> - Prefers a flexible, spontaneous, and changing environment

team (made up largely of intuitive, feeling, and perceiving types) to the forefront of the company agenda. For decision making, Dixon Schwabl elected to consider individuals and values first, and to value what was logical on a secondary level. As with many other companies that undergo personality analysis, the move from the thinking to the feeling perspective in this category accompanied an overarching commitment to understanding and accommodating individual perspectives. Communication figured prominently in the transition, as company president Lauren Dixon and others learned to adapt their personal communication style to suit the diverse personality preferences of the agency's employees. Above all, the personality makeover required that Dixon Schwabl drop its judging emphasis on deadline brinkmanship and focus instead on finding the rhythm and logic of the pitch. Remaking the office as a more unstructured place, the DSA team put its faith in its powers of improvisation.

In little more than a year, Dixon Schwabl Advertising completed the transition from its somewhat stodgy former self to the upbeat persona its people saw as most consistent with their dreams. The next workshop revealed that the company had succeeded in bringing its behaviors and preferences in line with the "It's Fun to Do Good Work" profile. Like other Fun organizations, the new, improved DSA emerged as a spontaneous, democratic, enthusiastic, and imaginative workplace. Its new willingness to sing its own praises (characteristic of the type) gave the agency the courage to seek clients that used to seem beyond its reach. With new offices that mirrored their fun-loving ethic, Dixon Schwabl staffers developed a new sense of camaraderie through events and exercises that emphasized their collective identity. The new personality took root, reappearing repeatedly in subsequent CAP2 workshops—thanks in part to the company's intense investment in the Up Close and Personal and keeper exercises. Dixon Schwabl's decision to be itself on purpose has also made an impact on the company's bottom line. Fired by new confidence and enthusiasm, the company has expanded its client roster and elevated its public profile. Annual revenues have climbed accordingly, from just over $18 million in 1997 to $65 million in 2001.

Is your company at ease with itself, or does a new identity seem more consistent with its needs and aspirations? Either way, you can expect to benefit when you decide to be yourself on purpose. Many business decisions are too important to be left to chance. Leadership is quick to intervene when inventory systems, client relationships, or outsourcing arrangements seem out of sync. Why stand aside and let the dynamics that drive your culture take their own course if they're not headed where your company needs to go? By understanding personality, you can keep what works and change the rest. But don't kid yourself: These kinds of changes happen only gradually and with great effort. In the end, we're convinced it's best to be yourself and make your peace with who you are. Making changes is not the only way to be yourself on purpose. When you think outside your company's preferences or rely on staff members who complement your weaknesses and strengths, you can achieve some of your goals at lesser cost.

When things do change, be sure to find a way of honoring the unchanging part of your company's identity. We like what Jim Collins and Jerry Porras have to say about change in *Built to Last:* To be truly successful, you need to embrace continuity and change simultaneously. Don't be so focused on what's missing from your personality profile that you overlook its inherent strengths. And when change is appropriate, take steps to ensure that your company's innovations remain consistent with its core mission, vision, and values. There's a very fine line between adaptations that are necessary for survival and changes that seek to embrace a trend or a whim. Companies that know about their preferences and priorities are best equipped to choose between changes that betray the core and those that help an organization fulfill its innermost ambitions. Using Companies Are People, Too, you can make the most of your company's inborn strengths.

CLARITY, ALIGNMENT, AND CONSISTENCY

We've talked about all kinds of ways that personality shapes the ultimate destiny and everyday routines of organizations. We want to leave you with a succinct statement about what CAP2 can do for you. For all the detail in our descriptions of the work of hiring and firing, mergers and acquisitions, goal setting, and culture building, we see the fundamental essence of CAP2 in three simple words: clarity, alignment, and consistency. We're talking about achievements that everyone can appreciate. Using insights from personality, your company can accomplish new feats, conquer old fears, and generate momentum and unity. It's what you get when you work to discover, articulate, and live the full dimensions of your personality.

Clarity

This book has aimed to help leaders of organizations get clear insights into the character of their work. Since all vision is, in part, a process of reflection, we've created concrete forms—the 16 CAP2 profiles—to objectify the spiritual and intellectual qualities of all kinds of organizations. And because vision is also a process of perception, we've tried to leave enough space for you to fill in the details that differentiate your group from every other. The result should be a recognizable figure, with characteristics so distinct that you remember and invoke it routinely in the course of your work. When your message gets this clear, it's easy to convey it to all your relevant audiences. Most important, everyone within the organization will see the way his or her own daily choices fit into the grand design.

Alignment

Alignment is the central task of top leadership in organizations or divisions within them. Companies Are People, Too provides management with easy-grip tools to help put component parts in working order. You can think of company personality preferences as a kind of program code or logarithm for the collective enterprise. If you want the program to run without glitches, you have to make sure you follow the proper sequence of events with every input. Alignment results from your ability to know the code well enough to adapt it to all the functions of your organization. The concept of the living company helps you understand these truths in everyday, familiar terms. When you stay true to the company's preferences instead of your own, you bring the workings of the whole organization into harmony with personality.

Consistency

Self-awareness is not enough, and we hope that *Companies Are People, Too* has helped you recognize the vital link between what companies believe and what they do. Personality is not merely a function of what we think as individuals or organizations; it's also very much a matter of how we act and interact with others in our business environment. When you link your everyday behaviors to your organization's core vision and values, you project the image of your best self to your employees, investors, customers, and business partners. If companies are people, then like people they can choose to live in harmony with their ideals and yet pursue the material requirements for survival. Achieving consistency means bringing that idealism into everything you do as an organization. It's the cornerstone and promise of the Companies Are People, Too approach.

Appendix:
Validating CAP2

Validation is the science of showing that a questionnaire like Companies Are People, Too really works. This appendix will cover the research conducted thus far to gather evidence of the validity of the questionnaire. This book is not a technical manual, but this section is designed to introduce readers to the methodology of validation and to comment on the early indications of validity for the Companies Are People, Too diagnostic.

There are various components of analysis necessary for research on validity. The initial components are item analysis, independence of the scales, and reliability. When acceptable results are obtained from these components, comparing the questionnaire to any available criteria and various related constructs further assesses validity.

Item analysis is the process of determining the predictive power of each of the questions on the instrument to make sure they work. Independence of the scales examines whether the different dimensions measured by the questionnaire are indeed separate and independent or if they overlap. The scales of a Jungian type indicator should not overlap, since the underlying ideas or definitions have no relationship to one another. Reliability looks at the consistency or repeatability of the measurement process.

Criteria are standards that you can compare to your instrument to determine if you have gotten it right. In psychology it is difficult to get true criteria, so often the only one used is the person's (and in our case the organization's) confirmation of the accuracy of the results. More often, we use comparisons with related constructs or parallel ideas that are more readily available. Appropriate relationships with these various constructs build support for the validity of the questionnaire.

The CAP2 research began with the development of the questions. A great deal of effort was invested in building a pool of questions that tapped into how personality would express itself in a group or organizational situation. The authors spent 18 months looking for and evaluating research about personality and organizational behavior. They initially developed a set of 224 questions, from which they culled 70 questions for the initial version of CAP2. There were 10 questions for each preference in the focusing energy functions, and 20 questions for each preference in the remaining three functions. This was increased to 74 questions in 1997, to have an odd number of questions on each dimension to eliminate tied scores.

This version of the questionnaire was used until May 1999. In the spring of 1999, the first analysis of the research on the effectiveness of the instrument was conducted using a database of 483 responses from approximately 15 organizations. In the summer of 2000, this study was repeated using a sample of 860 people from 26 organizations completing the 74-item version.

This first analysis examined only reliability. It was calculated using a method called coefficient alpha. Acceptable reliability numbers should exceed 0.60, good reliability exceeds 0.70, very good exceeds 0.80, and superb exceeds 0.90. Figure A.1 shows the values obtained on two subsets of the 483-response sample and the 860-response sample.

The results for the EI scale were consistently poor, so 10 new questions were developed for that dimension in 1999 to try to improve its reliability.

The sample of 860 was also used to conduct an item analysis. The item analysis is a Bayesian procedure. In simple terms, it calculates the odds that the question is predictive of a preference for its respective dimension. Ninety-three percent of the questions were discovered to have greater than a 60 percent probability for predicting to the dimension for which they were designed. The most obvious failing questions were dropped and replaced with new questions. Some borderline questions were retained to see if they would indeed work when reexamined with a bigger research sample.

Version	Number of Subjects	EI	SN	TF	JP
70 items	286	0.53	0.80	0.87	0.77
74 items	197	0.43	0.72	0.75	0.50
74 items	860	0.52	0.73	0.81	0.68

FIGURE A.1   Reliability of all indices as of May 1999.

One difficulty faced at this point in the research is the distribution of the sample. In type research it is important to have a sample with an equal number of each of the 16 types. We have not yet been able to collect such a sample. When conducting research with individuals, this can be a challenging constraint, but when conducting research with organizations it is very daunting. Twenty-five people of each of the 16 types is a sample of 400 people. Since the types are not found in equal numbers in any country, it usually takes collecting a sample of 800 to 1,000 to get the 400 of each type.

None of the samples to date contain all of the 16 types. Thus the findings on the item analysis, while important, will be incomplete until such a sample can be collected. Furthermore, results from the analysis of the independence of the scales, while calculated, are completely uninterpretable because they are skewed by these lopsided type distributions.

One of the benefits of getting this sample will be using the mathematical predictive power in each question to score the CAP2 questionnaire with even more precision. Using individual item weights for each question will increase its reliability and validity.

In the spring of 2001 and the summer of 2002, analyses were conducted on samples with the new items included. The samples still are not composed of an equal number of the 16 types, so reliability was the main analysis. The results in Figure A.2 show the much improved reliability of the EI index.

The last analysis is criteria validity. This is the only kind of validity study attempted to date. The approach used is the self-reported agreement with the results of CAP2 by the organization. To date, 100 percent of the organizations taking the instrument have verified the results to be accurate. Clearly, this is a very high rate of agreement. As more data is collected, it is unlikely that this perfect rate will continue. In fact, some of the agreement may be erroneous, and the subjects may have failed to see a lack of fit. Further research in which organizations are kept blind to their results and run through a verification process will allow us to see how large this kind of error might be. Despite these concerns, it is

Version	Number of Subjects	EI	SN	TF	JP
84 items (2001)	1,041	0.84	0.73	0.81	0.69
84 items (2002)	339	0.71	0.78	0.80	0.65

FIGURE A.2   Reliability of the indexes as of 2001 and 2002.

still a very high rate of agreement and provides very encouraging support for the validity of CAP2.

The results of these analyses show good support for the reliability and validity of the Companies Are People, Too assessment. With ongoing research, we will strive to continuously improve its measurement power.

—Gerald Macdaid

Notes

Preface

1. James C. Collins and Jerry I. Porras, *Built to Last: Successful Habits of Visionary Companies*. New York: HarperBusiness, 1994.
2. Arie de Geus, *The Living Company: Habits for Survival in a Turbulent Business Environment*. Boston: Harvard Business School Press, 1997.
3. James C. Collins, *Good to Great: Why Some Companies Make the Leap . . . and Others Don't*. New York: HarperCollins, 2001.

Chapter 1

1. de Geus, p. 6–7.
2. Collins and Porras, p. 68–71.

Chapter 3

1. MBTI is a registered trademark of Consulting Psychologists Press.

Chapter 5

1. William Bridges, *The Character of Organizations: Using Jungian Type in Organizational Development*. Palo Alto, CA: Davies-Black, 1992, p. 46.
2. David Pilla, "Meeting Life Today," *Best's Review*, vol. 102, September 2001, p. 104.
3. Carrie Coolidge, "Snoopy's New Tricks," *Forbes*, April 15, 2002, p. 100.
4. Pilla, p. 104.
5. Coolidge, p. 100.
6. Collins and Porras, p. 141.
7. David Callahan, *Kindred Spirits: Harvard Business School's Extraordinary Class of 1949 and How They Transformed American Business*. New York: John Wiley & Sons, 2002, p. 90.

8. Graham Button, "The Man Who Walked Out on Ross Perot," *Forbes,* vol. 152, November 22, 1993, p. 68.
9. Bridges, p. 57.
10. Ibid., p. 53.
11. "KFC Taps Vendor for 'Networked Kitchen' Project," *Nation's Restaurant News,* vol. 36, November 25, 2002, p. 47.
12. "KFC to Trial Fingerprint ID System," *Caterer and Hotelkeeper,* July 25, 2002, p. 8.
13. Joanne Wojcik, "KFC Plucks Comp Savings from Human Resource Solutions," *Business Insurance,* vol. 31, November 10, 1997, p. 94.
14. Richard R. Rogers, "CEO Tip," *Sales and Marketing Management,* vol. 154, March 2002, p. 60.
15. Bridges, p. 41.
16. Bridges, p. 38.
17. "DOT Analysts Dub Chain of Airplane Events 'Southwest Effect,' " *Travel Weekly,* vol. 52, May 20, 1993, p. 9.

Chapter 8

1. Malcolm Gladwell, "The Talent Myth," *The New Yorker,* July 22, 2002, p. 28.
2. Faith Popcorn with Adam Hanft, *Dictionary of the Future.* New York: Hyperion, 2001.
3. Some of the most important works on personality type have been published in association with Consulting Psychologists Press, which owns the rights to the Myers-Briggs Type Indicator. See Isabel Briggs Myers, *Introduction to Type.* Palo Alto, CA: Consulting Psychologists Press, 1998; Isabel B. Myers and Peter B. Myers, *Gifts Differing.* Palo Alto, CA: Davies-Black, 1995; and Roger R. Pearman and Sarah C. Albritton, *I'm Not Crazy, I'm Just Not You.* Palo Alto, CA: Davies-Black, 1997.
4. Jim Collins, *Good to Great: Why Some Companies Make the Leap . . . and Others Don't.* New York: HarperCollins, 2001, 13.

Chapter 9

1. Peter F. Drucker, "The Best Book on Management Ever," *Fortune,* vol. 121, April 23, 1990, p. 149.
2. Ibid.

Chapter 10

1. Nina Munk, "Gap Gets It," *Fortune,* vol. 138, August 3, 1998, p. 68.
2. Katrina Brooker, "Can Anyone Replace Herb?" *Fortune,* vol. 141, April 17, 2000, p. 186.

Chapter 11

1. Mike Hofman, "A Brand Is Born," *Inc.*, December 1, 2001.
2. Julie Clark, "Do You Like Piña Coladas?" *Display and Design Ideas*, vol. 13, November 2001, p. 25.

Chapter 12

1. James Collins, "Leadership: Building Companies to Last," *Inc.*, May 15, 1995.
2. Ibid.
3. Collins and Porras, p. 47–54.
4. Ibid., p. 222.
5. Collins and Porras, p. 71.

Chapter 14

1. Julie Bick, "Inside the Smartest Little Company in America," *Inc.*, January 1, 2002, p. 59.
2. Genevieve Soter Capowski, "Designing a Corporate Identity," *Management Review*, vol. 82, June 1993, p. 37.

Chapter 15

1. Michael Porter, "From Competitive Advantage to Corporate Strategy," *Harvard Business Review*, May-June 1987, p. 43–59.
2. Callahan, p. 214.
3. Ibid., p. 215.

Chapter 17

1. "Can Home Depot Get Its House In Order?" *Business Week*, vol. 3709, November 27, 2000, p. 70.
2. Patricia Sellers, "Exit the Builder, Enter the Repairman," *Fortune*, vol. 143, March 19, 2001, p. 86.
3. Cora Daniels, "To Hire a Lumber Expert, Click Here," *Fortune*, vol. 141, April 3, 2000, p. 267.
4. Patricia Sellers, "Something to Prove," *Fortune*, vol. 145, June 24, 2002, p. 88.
5. Bill Breen, "How EDS Got Its Groove Back," *Fast Company*, October 2001, p. 112.
6. "It's Time to Open the Corporate Portal Door," *Info World*, vol. 23, April 9, 2001, p. 34.

Index